THE ḤAMADSHA

THE ḤAMADSHA

A Study in Moroccan Ethnopsychiatry

VINCENT CRAPANZANO

UNIVERSITY OF CALIFORNIA PRESS
BERKELEY, LOS ANGELES, LONDON

UNIVERSITY OF CALIFORNIA PRESS
BERKELEY AND LOS ANGELES, CALIFORNIA
UNIVERSITY OF CALIFORNIA PRESS, LTD.
LONDON, ENGLAND

FIRST PAPERBACK PRINTING 1981
ISBN 0–520–04510–6
LIBRARY OF CONGRESS CATALOG CARD NUMBER: 72–75529
PRINTED IN THE UNITED STATES OF AMERICA

1 2 3 4 5 6 7 8 9

Contents

Preface

This study is based primarily upon field work with the Ḥamadsha of Meknes and the Jebel Zerhoun in 1967 and 1968. My research was supported by a grant from the National Institute of Mental Health (MH 13776–01), a Quain Grant from the Institute of Intercultural Research, and an award from The Committee on Research in the Sciences and Humanities of Princeton University.

For preliminary advice I should like to thank Professor Ernest Gellner of the London School of Economics; Professor Clifford Geertz, then of the University of Chicago; Professors Abdelqadar Khatibi and Abdelouahed Radi of the University of Rabat; Drs. Lawrence Rosen, Stuart Schaar, and John Waterbury; Mr. Erich Alport of Oxford; Mr. Ahmed El Yacoubi of New York and Tangier; and a nameless Sicilian waiter at a Perpignan cafe, who first told me that the Ḥamadsha were still in existence. To Mr. David Hart of Almería I am especially grateful not only for his preliminary suggestions but for his continual encouragement and advice throughout my term of field work. To Dr. Benykhalef, Secretary General of the Moroccan Ministry of Health; Dr. J. J. Maupomé, médicin-chef of the Hôpital el Ghazi in Salé; Dr. George Brown; and Mr. William Stott, then of the American Embassy in Rabat, I am indebted for facilitating my research.

Although I assume full responsibility for the contents and theoretical premises of this study, I should like to thank Professors Conrad Arensberg, Margaret Mead, Robert F. Murphy, and Abraham Rosman of Columbia University; Dr. Theodora Abel of the Postgraduate Center for Mental Health in New York; Dr. Nicholas S. Hopkins and Dr. Dale F. Eickelman of New York University; and Mr. Roy Mottahedeh, then of Harvard, for their many suggestions. Professors Mead, Murphy, Rosman, and Hopkins have read and commented on the text. To Dr. George Devereux of the Ecole Pratique des Hautes Etudes, I am particularly grateful. Not only have his keen psychological insights been of great value to me, but his many comparisons with the ancient Greek world have added perspective and depth to my thinking about the Ḥamadsha.

It is of course impossible to thank all my Moroccan friends who not only offered me their hospitality but devoted themselves to my study with patience and understanding. I am especially grateful to the mizwar of Sidi Ahmed Dghughi and the muqaddims of the Ḥamadsha lodges and teams of Meknes; to Ahmed bel Louafi of Beni Ouarad; Hamadi ben Salah and Hadda and Labid ben Mohammed of Meknes; and Moulay Abdeslem ben Moulay Mahajub, who treated me as both son and student.

Finally I should like to thank my wife, Jane Kramer, and my field assistant, who has asked to remain anonymous. Without them this study could never have been made, and to them I dedicate it.

A Note on The Rendering of Arabic Words and Phrases

Arabic words and phrases in this study have been rendered in the simplest manner yet recognizable to the Arabic speaker. Diacritical marks have been avoided wherever possible. Only the *ʿain*, the *ḥa*, and the internal glottal stop (by an umlaut) have been used. Place and tribal names and the names of my informants have been written in the French fashion currently in use in Morocco. Other words have been written in a manner more in keeping with English phonetics or as they appear in the Merriam-Webster *Third New International Dictionary*. With the exception of a few plurals such as "jnun," "foqra," and "ghiyyata," which occur frequently in the text, all other plurals of Arabic words are indicated by adding an "s" to the singular form. Italics are generally used only on the first occurrence of a foreign word in each of its contexts. A glossary appears at the end of the study.

The reader will be able to approximate Moroccan Arabic pronunciation by pronouncing consonants as in English and vowels as in Italian. The *g* is always hard as in "go" or "geese." The *j* is pronounced like the "s" in "pleasure." The *q* is like an English "k" but much further back in the throat. The *gh* is pronounced like the uvular "r" in French. The *kh* is like the German "ch" in "Bach." The *sh* is like the "sh" in "ship." ᶜ and *ḥ* have no English or European equivalents. The ᶜ is pronounced a little like "a" in father; *ḥ*, like an "h" in a loud stage whisper. The glottal stop indicates a break between vowels as in "uh oh."

In the pronunciation of place names the reader has only to remember that an initial *ou* is pronounced like a "w" and a *ch* like an "sh." The final *e* is not pronounced.

And they cried aloud, and cut
themselves after their manner
with knives and lancets, till
the blood gushed out upon them.
(1 Kings 18, xxviii)

A Ḥamadsha Performance

The square in front of the tomb of Sheikh al-Kamal in Meknes was just beginning to fill up with townsmen, families from the nearby shantytowns, and a few Berber and Arab tribesmen when we arrived at 2:45 on a Friday afternoon in January. We were immediately surrounded by children—whom we had to fend off, sometimes violently, as they gaped and grabbed with curiosity at us. In one corner of the square a line of beggar women, huddled together, were blankly watching a woman prance around to the wailing of four or five singers, hawking blessings for a few francs. Near them, a tiny, wizened old man, dressed in a white tunic, was neatly laying out a plastic tablecloth. He sat down on it, held up his staff between his legs, and wept. He was generally ignored. A circle of children had formed around another man who bandied a stick and shouted at them, and occasionally pulled open his shirt and puffed out his lungs through a round hole in his chest. Here and there crowds were starting to press around candy and orange vendors, con men and tricksters, story-tellers and preachers, dancers and fortune-tellers. In the corner closest to the tomb of their saint, Sheikh al-Kamal, the founder of the famed brotherhood of the ʿIsawiyya and the patron of Meknes, a group of adepts began their dance. As we moved through the crowd to watch them, we were suddenly attracted by the sound of the oboe known as the *ghita* and were told that the Ḥamadsha, whom we had come to see, were about to start their performance.

We were greeted warmly by Ali, a denizen of the nearby shantytown whom we had met earlier in the day when he chased children from our car with a big stick. He shook our hands over and over again while the rest of the Ḥamadsha prepared their instruments. There were nine in all: three *guwwala* who played a large pottery drum shaped like an hourglass; one *tabbal* who played a snare drum; two *ghiyyata* who played the oboe; two money collectors, Ali and another man who reminded me of a New England church usher; and a dance leader, or *muqaddim.* The drummers were tightening their drums over a paper and cardboard fire as the ghiyyata tuned their instruments. Ali began to recite a prayer, or *fatḥa,* and to ask for money from the spectators who had gathered in a circle around the Ḥamadsha. He had a showman's sense of gesture and timing.

Suddenly the ghiyyata began to play. It was now 3:11 p.m. The crowd of men, women, and children pressed inward and were violently pushed back by Ali and the "usher" until a semi-circle was formed, with the musicians at one end, against the wall of the square, and a group of ten or eleven men standing shoulder to shoulder opposite them. The men raised themselves up on their toes and pounded down hard on their heels to the rhythm of the drums. At the same time, they raised and lowered their shoulders in a sort of ongoing shrug and hissed out air, occasionally chanting "Allah! Allah! Allah the eternal! Allah the adorable!" The muqaddim, a yellow-faced man dressed in a bright green acetate robe, danced directly in front of them, encouraging those who had fallen out of rhythm. Sometimes he would jump in the air, spin around, and land hard on his heels. At other times he would leap into the air and, as he landed, bring his outstretched fists in against his chest as though he were lancing himself. And at still other times he would pound his chest with his fists in a sort of breaststroke motion.

Almost immediately after the line of male dancers had formed, two women, one in a pale blue jallaba and the other in a black one, pushed their way through the crowd and began to dance directly in front of the ghiyyata. They did not move their feet as the men did, but instead bobbed up and down from the waist, their heads nearly hitting the ground, or swayed their bodies back and forth in much the motion that Arab women use to wash their floors. Their hair had come loose and was flying out in all directions. They reminded me of ancient maenads. Two other women joined them; all the women seemed to fall into trance much more quickly, and easily, than the men.

By 3:30 there were four women dancing and the line of men had grown to 21. There must have been between 200 and 300 spectators standing in the circle and perched on the walls of the square. Ali and the "usher" made the rounds, collecting—almost extracting—a few francs from each of the spectators. The drumming remained constant, or so it seemed to me; it was the ghita which was producing the variations in sound. The drumming, by this time, had begun to have a dulling effect on me, and the music of the ghita an irritating one. I noticed that many of the spectators, especially those nearest the ghiyyata, were in a light trance or at least dazed. Their eyes seemed glazed, fixed on the musicians or the dancers. The smell of all the hot, close, sweating bodies was stifling.

The performance went on, without much variation, until a few minutes after 4. Occasionally one of the male dancers would leave the line and dance in the center space, alone or with the muqaddim. Usually such dancers were in an entranced frenzy and were not able to follow the rhythm of the dance very well. One of the female dancers was led by a fat man, who participated only peripherally in the dance and seemed to be a sort of helper to the performers, over to the line of male dancers and made to dance with them. This seemed to relax her, to "bring her down."

At 4:15 there was a hush in the crowd as an extremely tall man in white robes, with a gold scarf around his neck, entered the dance area. A woman poked me and told me that he was a seer and a true Ḥamdushi. A man signaled that he was a homosexual who played the passive role. His costume was, in fact, effeminate, his breasts well-developed, his hair long and curly, and his neck so swollen that I suspected some sort of glandular disorder. In a few minutes he was deep in a "chattering" trance: his mouth was opening and closing at a rate well out of the range of voluntary behavior. His head was thrust far back, his eyes were popping. He wandered, disoriented, around the center of the circle. Then the ghiyyata changed their tune slightly, and he was immediately "drawn" to them. He danced before them, his back to the audience, in a way which was closer to the women's dance than to the men's. He seemed more closed in upon himself than the other dancers, more separated from the audience and the other performers. Suddenly he began to beat his head with what appeared to be his fists but were in fact two pocket knives, one in each hand. The woman next to me whispered, " ʿAïsha, ʿAïsha Qandisha." Faster and faster he slashed at his head (the music too seemed faster), until his long curls were matted down with blood and his back and face were streaked with it.

Many of the men and women looked on dispassionately, but the children in the audience grew restive and excited. More than one mother raised her baby high in her arms to see the slashing. The muqaddim began to dash frenetically around the perimeter of the circle. His eyes bulging, he asked for a knife, but the "helper" refused and, pulling the muqaddim toward him, took the leader's head under his arm and scratched it. When the muqaddim finally regained his senses, the helper kissed him on the cheek and released him. By this time the head-slasher had stopped and was seated in a corner near some women, a very pained expression on his face. The musicians continued to play the same tune and in a minute or two he was up again, dancing and slashing with even more abandon than before. Then suddenly, unexpectedly, he sat down again among the women. One of them began to bind his scalp with a pale blue scarf, another kissed his bloody hands and licked the blood that had stained her veil. A baby was lifted over the crowd and handed to the slasher, who kissed him. A third woman smeared a little blood on the baby's stomach. The slasher no longer looked pained; his expression now was radiant.

It was now 4:35. The musicians had changed their tune, and the dance seemed calmer to me. Twenty men were still pounding and hissing in their line. Several women had danced through the head-slashing scene, quite oblivious to it; one of them, a woman in black, had been bobbing up and down since the beginning of the performance, an hour and a half before. The rest of the dance seemed very unreal to me. I felt very distant, very removed from what was going on in front of me.

At 4:55 the ghiyyata blew two or three long, wailing blasts, and the performance was over. A few of the performers shook hands while the crowd dispersed. Several women came up to the slasher to ask his blessing. The ʿIsawa, the followers of Sheikh al-Kamal, were still dancing in their corner, but they had drawn a much smaller crowd than the Ḥamadsha. We were told that the Miliana, the followers of an Algerian saint who specialize in playing with and eating fire, had also performed, as well as a branch of the ʿIsawiyya that charm snakes.

Friday, January 12, 1968
Sheikh al-Kamal, Meknes
Morocco

Introduction

The Ḥamadsha are members of a loosely and diversely organized religious brotherhood, or confraternity, which traces its spiritual heritage back to two Moroccan saints of the late seventeenth and early eighteenth centuries, Sidi ʿAli ben Ḥamdush and Sidi Ahmed Dghughi. Despite a certain notoriety due to their head-slashing and other practices of self-mutilation, the Ḥamadsha have received comparatively little attention in the literature, ethnographic or other, on Morocco and North Africa.[1] This has probably resulted less from any secretiveness or lack of cooperation on their part than from their political insignificance and from the fact that they have been overshadowed by larger, more spectacular brotherhoods like the ʿIsawiyya.

The Ḥamadsha have been classified by French scholars as an extreme example of the *confrérie populaire*, a sort of degenerate form of the Sufi brotherhoods of the Muslim high tradition, corrupted by the base imagination of *le peuple*, by survivals from the ancient religions of the circum-Mediterranean culture area, and by pagan influences from sub-Saharan Africa. They are considered, then, to be part of the cult of saints, or *maraboutism*, which has been generally regarded as the hallmark of Maghrebian Islam. The French word "maraboutisme" is derived from the Arabic *murabit*, which describes a man attached to God—the root itself means "attach" or "fasten"—and has been used for any of the warrior-saints who brought Islam to Morocco. "Maraboutisme" has become in French a catch-all expression for all sorts of activities associated with the worship of saints. It may, for our purposes, serve to define two basic institutions: the cult of saints and the religious brotherhoods.

The saints of Morocco—they are referred to as *siyyid*, *salih*, or *wali*

[1] The most complete study is a 19-page article by Herber, published in 1923.

—may be descendents of the Prophet, founders and sheikhs of religious brotherhoods like the Ḥamdushiyya,[2] political heroes of the past, scholars reputed for their piety and religious learning, holy fools, or "simply vivid individuals who had tried to make something happen" (Geertz 1968:8). Associated with the tribal structure of Morocco, they run a gamut of importance from the purely local saint about whom all but his name is forgotten, and who is perhaps visited by half a dozen women each year, to a saint like Moulay Idriss, to whom all Moroccans, Berbers and Arabs alike, pay homage (Dermenghem 1954:11–25). Some, like Moulay Abdeslem ben Meshish, Sidi Harazam, or Sidi Said Ahansal, were historical figures of considerable fame; while others, as Westermarck (1926 (I):49) put it, seem to have been invented to explain the holiness of a place.

The object of the cult of saints is the saint's tomb—usually a squat, white cubical building with domed roof (*qubba*). These dot the Moroccan countryside and are cared for by the saint's descendants—celibacy is not a prerequisite for sainthood in the Islamic world—or by a caretaker (*muqaddim*) who lives on part of the alms received from pilgrims. The tombs are visited and venerated by men, women, and children anxious to obtain from their saint some favor such as a male child, a cure for a bout of rheumatism or a case of devil-possession, a favorable verdict at court, political asylum, or simply good fortune. A particular behavioral set designed to enable the pilgrim to obtain the saint's blessing or holiness (*baraka*) is associated with each tomb. Its components may vary from the offering of a candle to the sacrifice of a bull or even a camel; from kissing the four sides of the tombstone to chanting long litanies; from rolling a holy stone over aching parts of the body to receiving massages from descendants of the saint. Sacred springs and grottos, trees, stones, and animals believed to contain baraka, and spots to which the *jnun*, or devils, are said to gravitate, are often found near the tombs. These too have their behavioral dictates which are linked to the veneration of the saint (Basset 1920).

The brotherhoods are associated with the cult of saints, for their members follow the path (*tariqa*) of a spiritual leader, or *sheikh*, who is usually considered to be a saint. There is considerable variation in the organization, function, degree of theological sophistication, and ultimate aim of the brotherhoods. The members of the more sophis-

[2] The Ḥamadsha brotherhood is referred to as *at-tariqa al-Ḥamdushiyya*, or simply as *l-Ḥamdushiyya*. A male adept of the brotherhood is a *Ḥamdushi;* a female adept, a *Ḥamdushiyya*. The plural for both male and female adepts is *Ḥamadsha*, which I also employ as an adjective.

ticated are recruited, as might be expected, from the wealthiest, best-educated strata of Islamic society; the members of others, like the Ḥamadsha, come from the illiterate masses. All of the orders involve certain ritualized acts: the mechanical recitation of supernumerary prayers, reminiscent of the Sinaitic and Athonic prayers of Jesus or the chants of mantra yoga; listening to music; dancing. The popular orders tend to be extreme: wild dances inducing ecstatic, frenetic trances; drinking boiling water; eating spiny cactus and other defilements; charming poisonous snakes; and innumerable acts of self-mutilation. All of them attempt to produce some sort of extraordinary psychic state which may be interpreted as union with God or possession by a demon.

Unlike the members of the more sophisticated orders, who consider their founding saint as a spiritual master who has provided them with a path to God, the members of the popular orders often consider their saint as an object of devotion in his own right and the source of power for their miraculous feats. Some of the orders have an extensive network of lodges located not only in Morocco but as far East as Mecca and deep into sub-Saharan Africa; others are limited to a few members who meet when and where they can. Some have close ties with the descendants of their founding saint, to whom they must give their complete allegiance and all of the alms they collect each year; others have almost no contact with the families of the saint. Some have a very elaborate hierarchy of initiates; others no hierarchy whatsoever. Some meet in well-constructed lodges, others in the open or in private houses. All of them are firmly convinced that they are faithful members of the Orthodox Muslim community. Some of these confraternities still flourish today, others are moribund, and still others defunct.

The Ḥamadsha are, in fact, members of two distinct brotherhoods which are closely related to each other and often confused. The *ʿAllaliyyin* are the followers of Sidi ʿAli ben Ḥamdush, and the *Dghughiyyin* follow Sidi ʿAli's servant, or slave, Sidi Ahmed Dghughi.[3] Both saints are buried and venerated some 16 miles by road northwest of the city of Meknes on the south face of the Zerhoun massif—Sidi ʿAli, whose tomb is one of the largest in Morocco, in the comparatively wealthy village of Beni Rachid, and Sidi Ahmed about a mile farther up the mountain, in the much poorer village of Beni Ouarad. The inhabitants of Beni Ouarad are much darker than those of Beni Rachid. Roughly

[3] I shall use the term *Ḥamadsha* to refer to both orders and to practices common to both. *ʿAllaliyyin* and *Dghughiyyin* will refer to the specific orders and their specific practices.

a sixth of the population of each village claims agnatic descent from their respective saints. They are collectively referred to as the *wulad siyyid*, the children of the saint. As the "children" of both saints claim descent not only from their saintly ancestors but from the Prophet as well, they may also be called *shurfa*, the Moroccan Arabic plural for *sharif*, a descendent of the Prophet Muhammad through his daughter Fatima and his son-in-law ʿAli. Since the children of each saint are all able to trace their descent back to a single ancestor, they constitute, in anthropological terminology, a maximal lineage. Each of the two maximal lineages, which are in turn divided into a number of smaller patrilineages, is governed by a headman, or *mizwar*. A descendant of Sidi ʿAli or Sidi Ahmed has the option of becoming a member of his ancestor's brotherhood, but rarely takes this option.

The members of the Ḥamadsha brotherhoods—they are most commonly called *foqra*—are divided into teams. A team (*taïfa*) may have a specific meeting place, or lodge, called a *zawiya*. Although the word "zawiya" refers, strictly speaking, only to the meeting place of a particular taïfa, I will follow common Moroccan usage and use it to refer to members of a particular lodge as well. The taïfa must also be distinguished from the *tariqa*, which is either a brotherhood or the "path" or "way"—that is, the teachings—of a particular saint.

Although the Ḥamadsha may be related historically to the mystical tradition of Islam, they do not usually conceive of the goal of their practices as union or communion with God, but rather as the cure of the devil-struck and the devil-possessed. They are essentially curers, and it is in this spirit that I propose to examine them. This is not to say that the Ḥamadsha would consider such an investigation appropriate or even desirable. They have received their power (*baraka*) to cure from Allah by way of His servant, their saint and intermediary to Him, and they are content with their lot. The ways of Allah are not to be questioned. To ask whether they conceive of their cures as essentially religious in nature, however "religious" may be defined, is to ask a question which has no meaning for them. All activities are religious insofar as they are contingent upon the will of Allah, and this very contingency is brought home to them with particular poignancy by the fact that the cures they effect are extraordinary, outside the tone and content of everyday life.

The Ḥamadsha are not just curers but successful curers at that, in terms of the standards their society sets and, in some instances, in terms of the standards set by modern medicine. They are able to effect, often dramatically, the remission of symptoms—paralysis, mutism, sudden blindness, severe depressions, nervous palpitations, paraesthesias, and possession—which led the patient or his family initially to seek their help. The symptoms they treat are frequently expressions of the common anxiety reaction found in many primitive societies (Wittkower 1971) or expressions of more severe hysterical, depressive, and even schizophrenic reactions. The Ḥamadsha are, in their own fashion, superb diagnosticians and generally avoid treating those illnesses which are regarded by Western medicine as organically caused. They seldom treat epilepsy.

The Ḥamadsha complex is to be regarded here, then, as a system of therapy. Therapy is considered to be a structured set of procedures for the rehabilitation of an incapacitated individual—an individual who is, from a sociological perspective, unable to meet role expectations and effectively perform valued tasks (Parsons 1964). Therapeutic procedures effect changes in the ailing individual's social situation as well as in his physical and psychological condition. He is moved through the roles of sick person and patient back, in the case of successful treatment, to his original role. If the treatment is not completely successful, he may be regarded as "a chronic case," or as handicapped. The ideal is of course full restoration to his "old self."

Certain therapies, however, of which the Ḥamadsha is but one of many examples, may often be incapable of, or do not even aim at, restoring the distressed individual to his previous condition. Rather, they introduce him to a new social role and concomitant tasks. The individual may become a member of a cult like that of the Ḥamadsha. He is provided thereby not only with a new social identity but also with a new set of values and a new cognitive orientation—that is, with a new outlook. This new "outlook" may furnish him with a set of symbols by which—in the case of psychogenic disorders, at any rate—he can articulate and give expression to those particular psychic tensions which were at least in part responsible for his illness. This symbolic set is closely related to the cult's explanation of illness and theory of therapy.

Aside from techniques designed to alter the physical and psychological condition of the patient and his social situation, a therapy must provide the distressed individual, the curer or curers, and other members of the society with an explanation of the illness and a theory of cure.[4] In the case of cure by incorporation into a cult, such explanations may be considered the ideology, or belief system, of the cult. Berger and Luckmann (1967:113) have written:

[4] In what follows I am indebted to Berger and Luckmann's *The Social Construction of Reality* (1967).

Since therapy must concern itself with deviation from the "official" definitions of reality, it must develop a conceptual machinery to account for such deviations and to maintain the realities challenged. This requires a body of knowledge that includes a theory of deviance, a diagnostic apparatus, and a conceptual system for the "cure of souls."

To the extent to which such explanations are commonly known, or at least known to the ailing individual, they tend to formulate the illness and furnish, thereby, a ground for therapeutic procedures. This is particularly true of psychogenic disorders.

In therapies like that of the Ḥamadsha the elements of explanation consist, as we shall see, of symbols which represent both social and psychic realities for the ailing individual (and other members of his milieu). These elements—images, in Godfrey Lienhardt's term—serve not only to articulate but to interpret the individual's experience immediately, and must be at once congruent with both psychological needs and socio-cultural realities. They are not individual projections. They are givens in the world into which the individual is born and, as such, serve from the start to mold his reality and to realize themselves in his psychic life. They provide a schema for the interpretation of his experiences and make them congruent with the realities of his world and that of other members of his culture. Their locus, which may be sought within the recesses of the soul or without—in the world, say, of saints and demons—may reflect the characteristic stance of an individual within a particular cultural tradition to others within his world (Crapanzano 1971). Such explanations—they may be called symbolic-interpretive—are characteristic of many so-called primitive therapies and cannot be divorced from the curing practices themselves. Therapy, in such cases, involves the manipulation of symbols not only to give expression to conflicts within the individual, but also to resolve them (Lévi-Strauss 1963a).

It is suggested here that the Ḥamadsha effect their cures by incorporating their patients into a cult which provides them with both a new role—one which is probably more in keeping with their individual needs—and an interpretation of their illness and its cure. This interpretation permits during the curing ceremonies the symbolic expression of incapacitating conflicts and the consequent discharge of tensions which may impede social behavior. This discharge of tensions is not merely an emotional outburst, which may be of little therapeutic import, but a highly structured process which involves the symbolic resolution of such tension-producing conflicts. The process of resolution serves not only to "resocialize the deviant into the objective reality of the symbolic universe of the society," as Berger and Luckmann (1967:114) maintain, but to reestablish or reinforce his motivation.

It must be emphasized that the practices and, to a lesser extent perhaps, the beliefs of the Ḥamadsha and the members of other similar brotherhoods are not characteristic of "Moroccans" in general. The Ḥamadsha complex is a fringe phenomenon, peripheral but by no means unrelated to the mainstream of the Moroccan socio-cultural tradition. Many Moroccans, especially Berbers and the educated Arabs, look askance at the practices of the Ḥamadsha; they consider them to be uncouth, unorthodox, disgusting even, and are often embarrassed when reference is made to them by foreigners. Still, it has been my impression that even among the better-educated—though perhaps not among the best-educated—disapproval is tempered by a certain awe which results, if for no other reason, from the dramatic quality of the Ḥamadsha performance and the "spectacular" nature of the Ḥamadsha cure. These performances, and these cures, are after all the will of God.

The Ḥamadsha, who are almost exclusively Arabs, consider themselves to be members of the Orthodox (Sunni) Muslim community and follow—or, perhaps more accurately, believe they follow—the laws and traditions of that community which find their inspiration, if not their very source, in the Koran and in the Prophetic tradition (*ḥadith*). Indeed, they find the very ground not only of their religious belief and worldview but of their social organization in the Koran—or, again more accurately, in what they impute to the Koran. The Ḥamadsha are in this respect not dissimilar to the millions of illiterate or quasi-literate Muslims of North Africa and the rest of the Middle East. As heterodox as their beliefs and practices may be, they do recognize the fundamental importance of the "five pillars" of Islam—profession of faith, prayer, almsgiving, fasting, and the pilgrimage to Mecca—and attempt to lead their lives accordingly.

Like Arabs throughout the world, the Ḥamadsha are patrilineal and patrilocal; that is, they trace their ancestry through the male line and live, if not under the same roof as their fathers, then in the same village or neighborhood. People in the newly created shantytowns, however, often live tens if not hundreds of miles from their fathers' homes; but even they still hold patrilocality as an ideal which they have had to abrogate by force of circumstance. Although the nuclear family tends to be the basic residential unit in the shantytowns—and to a lesser extent in the city and country—the extended family is perhaps the basic social unit. Extensions beyond the extended family do not play an important role in the shantytowns and among the Ḥamadsha of the old quarter of Meknes; they do of course play an important role for the descendants of the Ḥamadsha saints. Genealogies of the former are shallow, seldom exceeding five generations; those of the latter are very extended, theoretically all the way back to the Prophet himself by way of his daughter. Parallel-cousin marriage, considered the ideal marriage among Arabs, is rare in all the Ḥamadsha settings.

The father, or grandfather, as head of household, is all-powerful. He has strong and direct jural control over his wife or wives, and his sons (and daughters) must remain subservient to him until the very day of his death. No hostility whatever can be expressed toward him in his presence—or, for that matter, in his absence. Sons who are already middle-aged, for example, will not smoke in front of their father. His rule is absolute, and to foreign observers often appears arbitrary and harsh. There is considerable rivalry between brothers—often directed against the dominant one, who is usually but not necessarily the eldest —and this rivalry receives its fullest expression in disputes over inheritance. (According to the Koran, all sons inherit equally; daughters inherit a half of what their brothers receive.) Sons were traditionally economically dependent upon and responsible to their fathers, who provided them with the bride-price necessary for marriage. Although this economic dependence is breaking down with wage-work in the cities and in Europe, economic responsibility is not. Sons still send home to their fathers much of what they earn.

Women are considered inferior to men. Fathers—and mothers too —desire sons and not daughters, in spite of the fact that they receive a bride price upon their daughters' marriages. Women are considered weak, defenseless, treacherous, and untrustworthy. They must be constantly watched, locked up even, by their husbands or male kin, and must always remain submissive to the aggressive dominance of their menfolk. (Sons at a very early age will begin to demand such a submissive attitude from their mothers.) Women are considered sexually insatiable by Moroccan men, at least by those of the Ḥamadsha's milieu. The virginity of an unmarried girl—a symbol of her family's honor— must be preserved at all costs. Wives must be prevented from amorous adventures. Fear of adultery is rampant. Lone women are always fair game. Although women are veiled and sequestered whenever possible, housing conditions in the *bidonvilles*—shantytowns which have grown up on the outskirts of most Moroccan cities, in the years following the arrival of the French—give at least the illusion that they have more freedom than do the women of either the old quarter or the Zerhoun. Polygamy is rare in all the Ḥamadsha settings. Often it is desired by a wife who wants help in household matters. Usually there is rivalry between co-wives for their husband's favor. Older sons are often resentful of their fathers' second wives, or their stepmothers, who plot, they claim—not without justification—for their own children to inherit at the sons' expense.

Men must demonstrate no overt emotional dependence upon women; they must show no signs of femininity. They must strive continually to live up to the ideal of male behavior: domination; extreme virility; great sensitivity to matters of honor, independence, and authority; not to mention, of course, adherence to the canons of Islam. These ideals are embodied, realistically or not, in their image of their fathers. Indeed, the Arab male of the Ḥamadsha's milieu is caught in a dilemma between the dependence, the submission, the obsequiousness, even the passivity that he must show for years, often for more than half his lifetime, toward his father, and the independence, the domination, the authority, the aggressiveness that he must demonstrate to his sons and womenfolk. From the conceptual point of view, he must be at once both male and female. It is this dilemma that receives symbolic expression, as we shall see, both in the hagiographic legends and in the Ḥamadsha cures themselves.

A few words on the nature and organization of this study are in order here. It is an attempt, on the one hand, to present the not-altogether-taken-for-granted world of the Ḥamadsha and, on the other hand, to uncover and make explicit the structures and symbols of that world. Its final aim is to offer an explanation, albeit hypothetical and incomplete, of how the Ḥamadsha effect their cures. Substantively, the study is necessarily biased. My interest in the Ḥamadsha as essentially curers not only influenced my own perception of them and the questions I asked them but also the manner in which I have chosen to present the collected material. Naturally I have tried whenever and wherever possible to compensate for this bias, but it would be foolish to claim that I have overcome it. The Boasian ethnography must always remain in the realm of the ideal. I was fortunate enough, however, to have had a view of the Ḥamadsha which was not altogether alien to their own view of themselves. Certainly in the shantytowns, and to a lesser extent in the old quarter of Meknes, the Ḥamadsha considered themselves to be primarily curers and were proudest of all of this activity. Their devotees were most taken with their extraordinary cures; and I am certain that I too was captured by their enthusiasm.

Fieldwork itself was conducted in the standard anthropological fashion, with perhaps more than an average amount of material collected by free-association, imaging, and fantasizing techniques. My field assistant, a Berber, not a member of the Ḥamadsha brotherhood and not a permanent resident of Meknes or its environs, was present at many of my interviews. He was very gifted, endowed with a fine ethnographic curiosity and imagination and with that rare unobtrusive quality that makes for a superb ethnographer. He did not serve as an informant.

This study is divided into three main parts. Part One is concerned with the Ḥamadsha's past, both in historical and legendary terms. Chapter One treats the Sufi tradition from which the Ḥamadsha are in part derived and with which at least the most knowledgeable Ḥamadsha recognize an affinity. It is a background chapter for the nonspecialist, and makes no new contribution to the study of the Islamic mystical tradition. Chapter Two relates what little of the history of the Ḥamadsha is known. Chapter Three is concerned with the hagiographic legends of the order, legends which are accepted by the Ḥamadsha and other Moroccans of their background as historically true. Indeed, it is the historical facticity of the legendary events that "charters" the Ḥamadsha worldview and ritual activity. The legends are regarded here as givens in their world and provide the Ḥamadsha with a set of symbols, or perhaps more accurately with a justification for a set of symbols, by which they organize and give expression to at least part of their life situations, the most notable being of course their ritual activities. The analysis of the legends is carried out from a combined structural and psychoanalytic perspective which reveals, it is hoped, not only underlying themes, perhaps indicative of tensions within Moroccan society and personality, but also the possible symbolic significance of certain elements that recur in the Ḥamadsha's therapeutic theory and receive symbolic enactment in their rituals.

Part Two is concerned with the component institutions of the Ḥamadsha complex and their intricate interrelationships. Descriptions of the order in the saintly villages of Beni Rachid and Beni Ouarad, as well as of the teams in their urban and shantytown settings, are given in Chapters Four, Five, and Six. The diverse personnel of the complex are described sociologically, and their relationship to one another and to the saints they worship is examined in detail in Chapter Seven. The logic of *baraka,* or blessing, already found to be of singular importance in the legendary material, is related to the social and economic organization of the order. A digression, not properly speaking part of the phenomenological orientation of this study, describes how the Ḥamadsha serve to integrate newcomers to the city by providing them with an enlarged social field and more complex interpersonal relations.

Part Three is devoted to Ḥamadsha therapy. Chapter Eight, on the theory of therapy, attempts to present—in a manner comparable to the presentation of Western therapeutic practices—the Ḥamadsha's own explanation of their cures. It is again concerned with the givens of their world. Particular attention is paid to the way in which members of the order, and other Moroccans, relate to the *jnun,* or demons, and how the jnun themselves are related to the saints. Baraka is found to be the curative element par excellence, but is in itself insufficient to effect a cure. Chapters Nine and Ten are devoted to a description of the curing rituals—the pilgrimage and the trance dance—both from the perspective of an outside observer and from that of the actors themselves. "Elements" which occur in both the legends and the theory of therapy are given symbolic enactment in the rituals themselves.

The final chapter of the book, Chapter Eleven, attempts a synthesis of the diverse components of the Ḥamadsha complex. It is predicated on the fact that every therapeutic system functions at all levels of human existence: the physiological, the psychological, and the sociological. Apart from whatever effects the Ḥamadsha's rituals have on the physiological condition of their patients and themselves, they provide them with a symbolic set, historically justified and socially and ritually reinforced, which is integrated with their social organization and expressive perhaps of tensions inherent in at least that segment of Moroccan society from which the Ḥamadsha are recruited. This symbolic set, it is suggested, serves to articulate and give expression equally to the Ḥamadsha's experience of their physical and social, if not their physiological, environment. It enables them to act out, albeit symbolically, the scars of their past, and may indeed be of therapeutic import. How exactly the structured symbolic set functions for the individual is relegated to a sequel to this work.

PART ONE

1

Historical Origins: Sufism

Islamic mysticism is known as Sufism, a word derived from the Arabic for wool, *suf*, and originally applied to certain ascetics who wore clothes of coarse wool as a sign of penitence and worldly renunciation. The aim of Sufism, like that of other mysticisms, has been to realize a union with the Ultimate Reality or Godhead (*fana fi-l-ḥaqq*). This union has both a negative and a positive aspect: it involves, on the one hand, an escape from the bondage of the phenomenal self and an absorption or annihilation into the Divine (*fana*), and on the other hand a continuance of *real* existence in the Divine (*baqa*) (Nicholson 1963: 18). The Sufi's quest has been to bridge the distance between himself and his God, and Sufism itself has generally been considered by Islamic scholars as a reaction to the "cold" and formalistic tenets of Orthodox Islam, which lays great emphasis on the absolute gulf between man and God (Evans-Pritchard 1949: 1–2; Gibb 1961: 135).

Historically, the origins of Sufism have been related to such diverse movements as Christianity, Neo-Platonism, Gnosticism, Zoroastrianism, and Buddhism. Within the Islamic tradition itself, it has been considered an outgrowth of the ascetic pietism of the first centuries of Islam which—by stressing both the fear of God and man's responsibility to the moral ideal, and not simply to the mechanical observance of the law—encouraged introspection of the moral motive and promoted an awareness of the inner life (Rahman 1966: 154; Massignon 1934). The first Sufis were most often quietists who pursued their quest for God in isolation and usually through ascetic discipline. With the development of Islamic law and theology, however, a split developed between those members of the Muslim religious intelligentsia, the *ʿulama* or canonists, whose emphasis was necessarily impersonal, and those—the

Sufis, properly speaking—who looked for a more personal basis for their piety (Rahman 1966:155–156). The canonists were displeased with the Sufis' emphasis on the searching of conscience, since the Koranic law had only legislated for an external tribunal and had no weapon against religious hypocrisy. They accused the Sufis of heterodoxy because the Sufis held that intention was more important than act, practical example (*sunna*) superior to the law (*fard*), and obedience better than observance (Massignon 1934:682).

From the ninth century on, a number of Sufi thinkers attempted to integrate Sufism with Orthodoxy—a movement culminated in the twelfth century by al-Ghazzali—and, as they won converts from the more orthodox position, the simple piety and gospel of love of the earliest Sufis were transformed into an elaborate mystical doctrine of a spiritual journey toward God (Rahman 1966:162). The way or path to God, like the *scala sancta* of St. John Climacus, consisted of a number of stages such as repentance, abstinence, poverty, and trust in God, through which the mystic had to pass in order to achieve his goal. These stages (singular form, *maqama*), which constituted the ethical discipline of the Sufi and had to be mastered by his own effort, must be distinguished from those states (*aḥwal;* singular form, *ḥal*)—meditation, nearness to God, intimacy, certainty, and the like—which formed a psychological chain and over which the mystic had no control. They descend from God. Once the mystic has passed through all the stages and has experienced as many of the states as God has been willing to allow him, he is raised to a higher plane of consciousness called Gnosis (*maʿrifa*) and Truth (*ḥaqiqa*), in which he realizes that knowledge, knower, and known are one (Nicholson 1963:28–29).

The fact that by following the Sufi path a man could realize a coalescence with the Divine led to the elaboration of the doctrine of sainthood—a doctrine which was to permit the introduction of Gnostic and Neo-Platonic ideas like the notion of the Perfect Man of late antiquity (Van Grunebaum 1954:23) and of pagan beliefs and practices like ancestor worship. The Arabic word *wali*, or saint, derived from a root which means "nearness," is used to refer to an individual, living or dead, whose holiness has brought him near to God and who has received, as a special favor from God, miraculous gifts (singular form, *karama*). Less emphasis has been placed on the exemplary quality of the saint's life than on his ability to perform miracles—a sign of God's favor. The saints were said to form an invisible hierarchy upon which the order of the world rested and to be headed by a *Qutb*, or Axis, the greatest Sufi of the age, around whom the universe rotated. Careful attention was paid, however, to the difference between saints and prophets and between saintly miracles (singular form, *karama*) and prophetic miracles (*muʿjizat*); and so long as these distinctions were kept, the Orthodox had no qualms about incorporating the doctrine of sainthood, which was not expressly forbidden by the Koran. From the tenth century on there developed a derivative notion which was not within the spirit of Orthodoxy: the absolute and unquestioning submission to a *sheikh*, or spiritual master, who often founded his own particular path, or *tariqa*.

The development of these "paths" has been traced, on the one hand, to a class of preachers and story-tellers (singular form, *qassas*) who enlarged upon Koranic stories, and on the other hand to informal gatherings (*ḥalaqa*) for religious discussion and recitation of religious formulæ (*dikr*). These particular preachers succeeded in introducing new ideas, especially of Shiʾite origin, which were vigorously condemned by the more orthodox Muslims. By the middle of the ninth century many of the important ideas of Sufism had been developed and were being publicly taught in Baghdad and other centers of Islam, with great popular success. From the simple Koranic recitations of the eighth century, there developed a complex congregational ritual which was designed to send the participants into religious ecstasy (*wajd*). Some of these exercises consisted, first and by way of preparation, of communal recitations of religious writings (*ḥizb*) and then of prolonged repetition of shorter phrases (*dikr*), until the words no longer made an impression on the senses of the participant and nothing but the form of the Divine Name was left. Others involved playing and listening to musical instruments (*samaʿ*); dancing (*raqs* or *ḥadra*); tearing clothes(*tamziq*); acts of self-mutilation like those of the Ḥamadsha; and the contemplation of a young man, an ephebus, believed somehow to represent or embody the Divine (Ritter 1955:491–501). The more extreme practices were considered heretical by the canonists, and the legality of music and dance has long been debated both within and without the Sufi movement (Molé 1963).

During the twelfth and thirteenth centuries the first organized *tariqas*—or dervish brotherhoods, as they are sometimes called—began to appear. Famous teachers gathered around them in lodges disciples who, once initiated into their teacher's way, started branches in other lands. The founder of a brotherhood was usually venerated as a saint, and his place of burial, like that of other saints, became a site of pilgrimage. Not only was he provided with a genealogy of spiritual authority, a *silsila*, which led back to the Caliph ʿAli, but often also with a socio-biological one which traced his ancestry back to the Prophet and thereby gave him the right to be called a *sharif*. Although his sons—there were no rules of celibacy in most of the brotherhoods—often inherited his position as leader, this was not universally the case. The adepts themselves, who owed absolute allegiance to their master, were divided into two principal groups: the disciples, usually literate, who were involved in the religious activities of the lodge and in the collection of revenues; and the lay members, usually illiterate, who were nominally attached to the order and participated on certain stated occasions in the ceremonial (Gibb 1961:152).

Some of the brotherhoods not only spread throughout the Islamic world but served also to introduce their particular brand of Islam into non-Islamic lands (Gibb and Bowen 1957:75; Abun-Nasr 1965). Although the hierarchical organization and the ties between main and subordinate lodges were often loose, the brotherhoods—particularly during times of stress such as the French invasions of North and West Africa in the nineteenth century (Abun-Nasr 1965:1)—did bring together, at least temporarily, structurally disparate social groups. This unifying function must not be exaggerated, however, for the orders did not have the organization to knit their branches together permanently (Gibb and Bowen 1957:78). Appealing largely to artisans and members of the lower classes (Gibb and Bowen 1957:182), they tended not to ally themselves with the ruling classes, and often served as a bulwark against political despotism (Rahman 1966:182). Thus the continual hostility between the Sufis and the canonists, supporters of the central government, must be seen not only along theological lines but also within its political context.

Sufism, which followed its own particular course in Morocco and helped to diffuse Islam through the country, was intimately linked with the tribal structure and political development of the area. Mahdi ibn Tumart, the founder of the great Almohad dynasty of the twelfth century and successor to the Almoravids who had played an important role in the spread of Islam in Morocco, was deeply influenced by Sufism. The most influential of the earliest of the Moroccan Sufis was perhaps Abu Medyan of Tlemcen, who died toward the end of the twelfth century. Not only had he traveled to the East, where he became a disciple of Moulay Abdelqader al-Jilani (1077–1127 A.D.), the founder of the first organized brotherhood, the Qadiriyya, but he had also studied the works of al-Ghazzali at Fez under ʿAli ben Hirzihim (Sidi Harazam) (Michaux-Bellaire 1921:143; Rinn 1884:211 et seq.).

Although Abu Medyan's teachings emphasized quite simply the absolute concentration on God and the abnegation of the world—"Say 'God' and abandon all that is material or pertains thereto, if thou desirest to attain the true end" (Gibb 1961:158)—he served, at least symbolically, to synthesize the teachings of the three most influential mystics in Moroccan Sufism: al-Jilani, al-Ghazzali, and their spiritual ancestor al-Junayd.

The Sufi movement, already powerful in the twelfth century, developed during the fourteenth and fifteenth centuries its own particular Moroccan cast, which has come to be called "maraboutism." A marabout, identifiable with the Sufi saint, is a man bound to God, and in Morocco as elsewhere in the Islamic world such a man is believed to be possessed of a miraculous force or power called *baraka,* or blessing —which, as we shall see, is not only transmissible to his progeny but has in certain special circumstances a contagious quality. Clifford Geertz (1968:44) has attempted to capture its meaning in impressionistic and somewhat romantic terms. He writes:

Literally, "baraka" means blessing, in the sense of divine favor. But spreading out from that nuclear meaning, specifying and delimiting it, it encloses a whole range of linked ideas: material prosperity, physical well-being, bodily satisfaction, completion, luck, plenitude, and, the aspect most stressed by Western writers anxious to force it into a pigeonhole with mana, magical power. In broadest terms, "baraka" is not, as it has so often been represented, a paraphysical force, a kind of spiritual electricity—a view which, though not entirely without basis, simplifies it beyond recognition. Like the notion of the exemplary center, it is a conception of the mode in which the divine reaches into the world. Implicit, uncriticized, and far from systematic, it too is a "doctrine."

More exactly, it is a mode of construing—emotionally, morally, intellectually—human experience, a cultural gloss on life. And though this is a vast and intricate problem, what this construction, this gloss, comes down to, so at least it seems to me, is the proposition (again, of course, wholly tacit) that the sacred appears most directly in the world as an endowment —a talent and a capacity, a special ability—of particular individuals. Rather than electricity, the best (but still not very good) analogue for "baraka" is personal presence, force of character, moral vividness. Marabouts have "baraka" in the way that men have strength, courage, dignity, skill, beauty, or intelligence. Like these, though it is not the same as these, more even of all of them put together, it is a gift which some men have in greater degree than others, and which a few, marabouts, have in superlative degree. The problem is to decide who (not only, as we shall see, among the living, but also among the dead) has it, how much, and how to benefit from it.

And one might add, rather more concretely: how it manifests or is believed to manifest itself. Although baraka is indeed in certain instances a quality, not always as positive and beneficial by either Moroccan or Western standards as Geertz' definition might lead us to believe, it has at times, in the popular imagination at any rate, a more independent existence—and, in either case, a logic of its own which, as we shall see, must be situationally understood.

The religious brotherhoods, whose members played an important role in the diffusion of baraka, first appeared in Morocco in the thirteenth century and have more or less retained the form of the traditional Sufi confraternities. The Portuguese invasions in the fifteenth and sixteenth centuries served as a spur to their development and diffusion among the urban and rural masses; and from the collapse of the Merinid dynasty in the fifteenth century to the establishment of the present, or Alawite, dynasty in the seventeenth, the brotherhoods played a dominant role in Moroccan political history (LeTourneau 1958; Terrasse 1930). The anarchical conditions immediately preceding the reign of Moulay Ismaïl and following his death may have provided an atmosphere conducive to the development of such popular brotherhoods as the Ḥamadsha.

Most of the principal extant orders of Morocco, including the Ḥamadsha—the Jilaliyya and the Tijanniyya are the outstanding exceptions—are said to be derived from al-Jazuli (d. 1465 A.D.?), a disciple of al-Shadhili (d. 1258 A.D.), himself a disciple of a disciple of Abu Medyan. The teachings of al-Shadhili—he himself left no writing and founded no order—seem to have been orthodox and to have emphasized devotion to God. He discouraged monasticism and encouraged his followers to pursue their worldly professions. The five principal points of his teaching were the fear of God in secret and in open; adherence to Prophetic custom (*sunna*) in word and deed; contempt for mankind in prosperity and adversity; resignation to the will of God in matters great and small; and recourse to God in joy and sorrow (Margoliouth 1934:247).

The fame of al-Jazuli, which overshadows his master's in Morocco, is perhaps less the result of the man than the epoch. Jazuli, who at the time of his death was the head of a large network of lodges in the south of Morocco, was buried in the Valley of the Sous. It is claimed that his disciple al-Sayyaf carried his master's corpse on his campaigns for twenty years and illuminated it each night with a candle the size of a man. Seventy-seven years later, at the height of a period of religious fervor and political consolidation, his body was exhumed and transported to Marrakech by one of the Saadian sultans as a rallying point for anti-Portuguese sentiment (Michaux-Bellaire 1921:148; 1927:58 et seq.).

The ʿIsawiyya, the oldest extant order which traces its origin to al-Jazuli, was founded by Mʾhamed ben ʿIsa al-Mukhtari, the Perfect Sheikh (Sheikh al-Kamal), around 1500 A.D., and has probably influenced the practices, if not the doctrine, of the Ḥamadsha. The Ḥamadsha themselves trace Sidi ʿAli's spiritual ancestry to al-Jazuli by way of Buʿabid Sharqi, the patron of horsemen (d. circa 1600 A.D.), whose tomb is located in the town of Boujad near Beni Mellel (Schoen 1937). The author of the *Salwat al-Anfas*, quoting from the *Saluk at-Tariq al-Qariyya*, reports that Sidi ʿAli had received instruction from Sidi Muhammad al-Ḥafyan, who was in turn instructed by Buʿabid Sharqi. Buʿabid Sharqi had received instruction both from his father, Sidi Abu al-Qasim al-Zari al-Jabiri al-Ratsami, the pupil of al-Tebba, and from Sidi Abdallah ben Fasi, himself a pupil of al-Tebba through his teacher al-Ghezwani (Paquignon 1911:534). Sidi ʿAli himself is said to have taken a disciple, Sidi Ahmed Dghughi. Around these two men there developed two quasi-distinct orders, the history of which is, as we shall see, almost totally unknown.

2

The Saints and the Orders: Their History

Little is known historically of the lives of either Sidi ʿAli ben Ḥamdush or Sidi Ahmed Dghughi. Neither the saints nor any of their descendants or followers have left any writings, and although the "children of Sidi ʿAli" have in their possession a hand-written history of their ancestor, recently prepared by a scholar from Fez, it appears to be little more than a genealogical justification for their claim to be descendants not only of Sidi ʿAli but of Morocco's national saint Moulay Idriss and the Prophet himself. They are thus able to carry with impunity the title of *sharif*.

Sidi ʿAli is, according to the document,[1] descended from Moulay Abdeslem ben Meshish,[2] the teacher of al-Shadhili himself. Sidi ʿAli spent ten years in a corner of the Qarwiyyin University of Fez (near the entrance which faces the Bab Semmarin), praying all night and fasting all day. He kept to himself, never moving or speaking to anyone. He repeated the *shahada*, or profession of faith, 18,000 times a day. (Such supernumerary exercises occur in the lives of most Islamic saints.) Then he moved to the village of Beni Rachid, on the south face of the Jebel Zerhoun (Mount Zerhoun), where he was visited by countless pilgrims from all over Morocco. They were careful to keep a respectful distance and never to sit down near him or talk to him.

[1] The content of the document was translated and paraphrased for me by the son of one of the lineage heads of the *wulad* ("children of") Sidi ʿAli.

[2] To be consistent I spell "mulay" with an "ou"—*moulay*—in both personal titles and place names. Thus Moulay Idriss the saint and Moulay Idriss the village are spelled the same way.

He did, however, like to hear men talk of the Prophet; he would nod his head up and down, and afterward rise and perform the *ḥadra,* or ecstatic dance. Then when he no longer knew what he was doing, he would recite "Allah! Allah! Allah the eternal! Allah the adorable!" His head would spin, and he would begin to perform miracles. His following increased. He never turned from his path until his death in either 1131 or 1135 H.J. (1718/19 or 1722/23 A.D.). All the inhabitants of Meknes, Moulay Idriss, and the other villages of the Zerhoun came to Beni Rachid for his burial. During the period of mourning, his tomb was visited every day by mourners who founded lodges dedicated to him all over Morocco and even in Algeria and Tunisia. He is said to have been primarily influenced by Buᶜabid Sharqi and to have influenced, among others, Sidi Ahmed Dghughi.

The author of the *Salwat al-Anfas* has written of Sidi ᶜAli in the following words:

> Of their number is Abu l-Ḥasan ᶜAli ben Ḥamdush, buried on the mountain of the Zerhoun near Meknes. He is to be classed (May God have mercy upon him) among the sheikhs of the mystical tradition in which the ecstatic trance [*ḥal*] is powerful. He liked mystical reunions [*samaᶜ*], ceremonies having the same object [*ḥadra*], and panegyrics to the Prophet. He had a taste for instrumental music. . . .
>
> At certain times, becoming like a lion, he hit people with whatever fell into his hands, be it a stick, stones, some sort of vase, or other objects; no one could approach him then. He accomplished a number of feats, celebrated miracles. His followers and his companions have reported his ecstasies and his mystical seances; his very numerous companions spread throughout many lands; each year with pious ardor they gathered around him. He had zawiyas in all countries; and he fashioned a number of virtuous and beneficent men, all of whom were illuminated [*madjazib*] or at least had the reputation of being so. (Paquignon 1911:533–534)

Of Sidi Ahmed's life even less is known. Although it has been claimed that he came from the Beni Dghugh of the Dukkala tribe (Schoen 1937:93), the present leader, or *mizwar*, of Sidi Ahmed assures me that his ancestor in fact came from the Beni Hsen tribe and left family and property there. I have also been told that he came from Mdari in the Sahara.[3] Sidi Ahmed is said to have had three wives—one from the Beni Hsen, a second from Fez, and a third from the village of Beni Ammar on the Jebel Zerhoun—and to have left children by each of these

[3] I have not been able to locate Mdari.

women. According to the descendents of Sidi ʿAli, Sidi Ahmed was chosen by their ancestor from among the pilgrims to Beni Rachid to be his servant or even his slave; according to the descendants of Sidi Ahmed, their ancestor was chosen to be Sidi ʿAli's pupil and friend. When Sidi ʿAli died, Sidi Ahmed is reported to have slashed his head in despair. He died a few years after Sidi ʿAli and is buried in the village of Beni Ouarad, a mile up the mountain from Beni Rachid. His "children" are also in possession of a document which traces their ancestry back to the Prophet. Rumor has it that they paid for this genealogy with the few houses that Sidi Ahmed left them in Fez.

Not only is little known historically about either the descendants or the followers of Sidi ʿAli and Sidi Ahmed, but there is a curious absence of legendary material about them—which contrasts, as we shall see, with the rich legendary biography of the saints themselves.

Sidi ʿAli is said to have died celibate and childless—a fact which "his children" are anxious to disguise and which accounts in part for their contracting the scholar from Fez to do up their genealogy. Although the scholar is said to have found a marriage certificate for Sidi ʿAli in the library of the shurfa of Ouazzane, it is commonly accepted, even among Sidi ʿAli's "children" themselves, that Sidi ʿAli died childless and that those who claim him as their ancestor are in fact descended from one of his brothers.[4] Some of Sidi Ahmed's children are settled in Beni Ouarad. Those who remained among the Beni Hsen have lost all but nominal contact with those who settled in Beni Ouarad.

I have been able to learn nothing of the origin and spread of the Ḥamadsha. The legends suggest only that Sidi ʿAli founded zawiyas on his way from Buʿabid Sharqi in Marrakech to Beni Rachid,[5] and that pilgrims and mourners who visited Sidi ʿAli's tomb established lodges throughout Morocco. No mention whatsoever is made in the legends of the origin and spread of the brotherhoods dedicated to Sidi Ahmed Dghughi. Montet (1902:12–13) lists the following brotherhoods which, he claims, are related to the Ḥamadsha: *Sidiqiyyin*, the followers of Sidi Muhammad es-Sadiq who came from the South and whose followers hit their heads against each other during their ceremonies; *Riaḥin,* the followers of Sidi l-ʿAmar Riaḥi of Meknes, whose followers stick knives and forks in their stomachs without blood flowing; and the *Miliana*, who follow Moulay Miliana. Quedenfeldt (1886:689) adds the *ʿAlamin,* the followers of Sidi Qadur al-ʿAlami of Meknes; the *Sejinin,*

[4] To be sure, Sidi ʿAli's children prefer to keep their doubts about their saintly ancestry secret.

[5] See Chapter Three.

the followers of Sidi Hamid es-Sejinin, also of Meknes; and the *Qasmin*, the followers of Sidi Qasim bu ʿAsria. Neither author lists his criteria for affiliation, and none of the Ḥamadsha I talked to recognized any affiliation with these orders, many of which are by now defunct. The Miliana do not themselves acknowledge any ties with either Sidi ʿAli or Sidi Ahmed, and the ʿAlamin, "a bourgeois order," would be loath to admit any such ties.

It seems reasonable to assume that the two saints of the Zerhoun consolidated practices of an ancient origin under a single banner and integrated them into the particular brand of Islam characteristic of the Maghreb. A legend recorded by Michaux-Bellaire and George Salmon (1906:336) is suggestive of how a local cult was integrated with the larger cult to Sidi ʿAli. Sidi ʿAli Sanhaji, a disciple of Sidi ʿAli ben Ḥamdush who is buried in the valley of Lekhous near the city of Larache, was said to be the sheikh of Sidi Abderrahman al-Majdub, the putative ancestor of the Wulad Majdub—all of whom were, in 1906, Ḥamadsha.

Sidi ʿAli Sanhaji was a bandit who had already killed 99 people. At this time another man was chasing after a young girl who refused him. He swore that he would have her dead or alive. The girl died and was buried. Sidi ʿAli Sanhaji was waiting around near the girl's tomb, to perform some misdeed. He saw the man approach the girl's tomb in the night and immediately hid himself and watched the man open the tomb, take out the virgin, tear off her shroud, and try to possess her. By a miracle which Sidi ʿAli could not account for, the virgin placed her arm between the rapist and herself. The rapist cut off her arm. The virgin resisted with the other arm, but this too was cut off. She closed her legs, but the rapist cut these off too. ʿAli became indignant and called upon God, saying that he could not find a better occasion to kill his hundredth victim, who would be his last and with which he would buy back the 99 others. He heard a voice which cried out three times: "Acquit yourself, O Father of Acquittals." (It is from this that Sidi ʿAli Sanhaji has come to be known as the Father of Acquittals.) ʿAli then killed his hundredth victim, buried the virgin again, after having joined together her limbs which had been cut off, and replaced her shroud. Having covered her with earth, he planted an olive branch at the head of the tomb and said: "God Almighty, if tomorrow I find the branch green, I shall know that you have accepted my vow and pardoned me."

The following morning, ʿAli found his stick transformed into an olive tree covered with leaves. He fell to the ground and paid homage to God. He got up enlightened and wandered among the tribes, preaching the divine word. He stopped at Sehulijin, where the inhabitants built him a zawiya which still exists. He died and was buried there. They built him a qubba (mausoleum) which fell a short time later, and when a second qubba was built and collapsed, Sidi ʿAli Sanhaji appeared to the muqaddim and ordained that he should be without a qubba. (Michaux-Bellaire and Salmon 1906:336)

The muqaddim of the zawiya at Sehulijin was also the muqaddim of the Ḥamadsha, and the zawiya itself was one of the meeting places of the Ḥamadsha who were going to attend the annual pilgrimage to Sidi ʿAli at Beni Rachid. A second Ḥamadsha zawiya in the area had been the home of one of Sidi ʿAli's descendants who had settled there for a short time. In fact, many of the Ḥamadsha lodges are reputed to have been the home or burial place of one or more of Sidi ʿAli's or Sidi Ahmed's children, and are therefore the receptacles of some of the saint's baraka.

It is impossible to determine how widespread membership in the Ḥamadsha brotherhood was before the French arrival in Morocco in 1912. Reports of early French observers indicate teams in Fez (Aubin 1904:319; LeTourneau 1949:366), Rabat (Mercier 1906:122), Salé (Mercier 1906:135), Tangier (Salmon 1904:105), Casablanca ("Casablanca et les Chaouia" 1915:63), Moulay Idriss (Canal 1902:136), and in the Gharb (Michaux-Bellaire and Salmon 1906:334 et seq.). Captain Garcia Figueras (n.d.) maintains that, along with the ʿIsawa, the Ḥamadsha were the most important brotherhood in the western part of the Spanish zone.

The presence in rural areas of the Ḥamadsha, as well as other popular brotherhoods, should be emphasized, since it is sometimes assumed that such orders are restricted to urban and shantytown settings. The fact that all the members of the Wulad Majdub, mentioned in the legend of Sidi ʿAli Sanhaji, were Ḥamadsha suggests that membership in tribal areas often followed tribal lines and may at times have been restricted to saintly lineages. I have heard that the Wulad Khalifa of the Gharb, who like the Wulad Majdub claim descent from a saint, today consider themselves to be Ḥamadsha, whereas at the time of Michaux-Bellaire's investigations in 1913 they appear to have been primarily members of another popular brotherhood, the Jilaliyya (pp. 282 et seq.). They were famous then, as they are today, for their complete abandonment in acts of self-mutilation during their ecstasies. Michaux-Bellaire, generally a keen observer, also noted that many of the Ḥamadsha were black (p. 236). There is no mention of the Ḥamadsha among the Berbers. The early reports also indicate that the Ḥamadsha of the cities were then, as now, recruited primarily from the lowest strata of urban society (Salmon 1904:101; LeTourneau 1949:366; Aubin 1904:

318–319). The town of Moulay Idriss appears to have been an exception; there the Ḥamadsha came until recently from all strata of society (ben Talha 1965:22). In Fez they appear to have been street porters, blacksmiths, oven attendants, shoemakers, and tanners, and to have been associated with their respective guilds (LeTourneau 1949:366).

Ḥamadsha practices as they are described in these early reports closely resemble what takes place today in Meknes. There appear, however, to have been public processions in the cities, during which the Ḥamadsha would work themselves into frenzies and slash at their heads with single- and double-bladed axes, clubs, iron balls, and other objects. These processions, which usually took place before the annual pilgrimage, or *musem*, to the Zerhoun, were often combined with the processions of the ʿIsawiyya, whose musem took place on the Prophet's birthday, a week before the Ḥamadsha musem. I have been told that in Marrakech at the time of the ʿIsawa musem, the Ḥamadsha followed the ʿIsawa, and then a week later during the musem of the Ḥamadsha the ʿIsawa followed. In Salé the Ḥamadsha would parade through the streets on the day preceding the musem on the Zerhoun, collecting money and candles which were sold at the end of the day. The proceeds were given to the descendants of Sidi ʿAli. At sunset, the educated Ḥamadsha—there were about a hundred of these—would go to the zawiya to recite litanies. The uneducated would return home. The following day the Ḥamadsha from Rabat, across the river, would arrive in Salé at the time of afternoon prayers and would perform the ḥadra there until evening prayers, when they were served a meal with which the ceremony would end (Mercier 1906:135–136). These processions may have reinforced ties between brotherhoods or teams which were located in neighboring cities or quarters and between which there was undoubtedly an element of competition[6] (ben Talha 1965:22).

There are no figures for membership in the Ḥamadsha brotherhoods at the beginning of the Protectorate. Mercier (1906:122) cites figures for Rabat (200 adepts) and Salé (350 adepts, which he breaks into 100 *foqra* and 250 *khuddam*)[7] (1906:135), but these figures should not be

[6] See Part Two.

[7] It is not altogether clear how Mercier distinguishes these two groups. He may be referring to the distinction between *foqra* (adepts) and *muḥibbin* (devotees) (see Chapter Five). Or perhaps the Ḥamadsha of the time distinguished between a core group of at least semi-literate adepts and a peripheral group of illiterate members who were not familiar with the litanies and other esoteric matters. Such distinctions are not uncommon in the Algerian brotherhoods (Depont and Coppolani 1897).

taken too seriously—for, as we will see, membership is impossible to determine without defining *exactly* what we mean by it. Mercier's figures suggest, nevertheless, that there were many more Ḥamadsha in Rabat-Salé in 1906 than there are today.

The same criticism is applicable to George Draque's report in 1938 (p. 122). The Ḥamadsha appear then to have been the ninth largest brotherhood in Morocco, numbering about 3400. This figure is broken down for region:

Oujda	none
Taza	none
Fez	822
Meknes	1161
Port Lyauty (Kenitra)	552
Rabat	221
Casablanca	134
Mazagan (Mohammedia)	136
Safi	192
Central Atlas	27
Marrakech	120
Tafilelt	24
Confins Algéro-Marocains	10

These figures, which presumably refer to both the ʿAllaliyyin and the Dghughiyyin, are undoubtedly low; they do give, however, some idea of the distribution of the Ḥamadsha in Morocco, and support the opinion of other observers and of the Ḥamadsha themselves.

Although I have made no attempt to number the Ḥamadsha in Morocco today, I was provided with lists of about 40 teams from the leaders of both brotherhoods.[8] This number should not be taken too seriously either. The leaders were reluctant to admit that some of the teams were defunct and that Dghughiyyin and ʿAllaliyyin were combined in others, such as in the Marrakech lodges. Moreover, they did not list "renegade" teams which did not show them great allegiance, like

[8] According to the list provided for the ʿAllaliyyin, there were teams in Asila, Casablanca, Ceuta, Demnat, El Jadida, Essaouira, Fez, Ksar el Kebir, Larache, Marrakech, Meknes, Moulay Bouchaib, Rabat, Safi, Salé, Tamazd (Ait Baha), Tangier, Taroudant, and Tetuan. Marrakech was said to have 2 teams and Fez 3. The list for the Dghughiyyin included Casablanca, Fez, Ksar el Kebir, Marrakech, Meknes, Moulay Idriss, Moulay Yacoub, Ouazzane, Rabat, Salé, Tangier, and Tetuan. Marrakech, Moulay Idriss, and Moulay Yacoub each had 2 teams, and Fez 3.

the seven teams operative in the shantytowns of Meknes and others in the Gharb, or Western Plains.

On the basis of the figures I obtained for Meknes and from casual observations of the Ḥamadsha in other parts of Morocco, I am able to state that membership in the Ḥamadsha brotherhoods is today smaller than it was at the turn of the century, especially in the cities of Fez, Rabat, Salé, and Tangier, and that the Ḥamadsha are most active in Meknes, the Gharb—especially in the area of Sidi Slimane, Dar- bel-Amri, and Sidi Yahya du Rharb—and on the Jebel Zerhoun. The ʿAllaliyyin are more numerous than the Dghughiyyin. The Ḥamadsha appear to be less active in the old quarters of the cities than in the shantytowns. This pattern generally holds true for other "popular" orders such as the ʿIsawiyya, the Jilala, and the Miliana. One must be careful, however, not to assume that membership is increasing in the shantytowns. I have found that the majority of Ḥamadsha in the Meknes bidonvilles, for example, were Ḥamadsha before they came to the city or were at least familiar with their practices, and that there are comparatively few recruits among the second-generation inhabitants of the shantytowns. Since the oldest of these slums is only about 40 years old, no definite patterns can yet be discerned.

3

The Legends

Although the lives of both Sidi ʿAli and Sidi Ahmed are poor in historical fact, they are, like the lives of most Moroccan saints of any importance, rich in legend. The legends themselves are rooted in a historical reality which has been greatly elaborated and distorted by the addition of popular themes. These themes, or *traits flottants*, as the Bollandist Hippolyte Delehaye has called them, appear to be limited in number and to recur again and again in the lives of not only the Moroccan saints but of saints throughout the Islamic world (Voinot 1948; Goldziher 1880). Like the Christian saints and martyrs, the Islamic saints appear to have lost their individual character in their legendary form. Referring to Christian saints, Delehaye (1955:23) writes:

> Ainsi dépouillés de leur individualité, isolés en quelque sorte du temps et de l'espace, enlevés à leur cadre naturel, les personnages historiques prennent dans l'esprit du peuple une forme irréelle et sans consistence. Au portrait vivant et nettement caracterisé que nous a légué l'histoire se substitue un être idéal qui n'est que la personnification d'une abstraction; au lieu de l'individu, le multitude ne connaît que le type.

If, as Delehaye (1955:2) maintains, one of the hallmarks of the Christian hagiographic legend is the goal of edification, we must be careful not to attribute the same goal to the Moroccan legends. The saint, as we have noted, is not considered a *wali* by virtue of his exemplary life but by virtue of the miracles he has performed. His life, in legendary form, is in fact often little more than a list of such miracles, which are considered to be proof of his saintliness. *Burhan* is often used by the uneducated Moroccan as a synonym for miracle (*karama*), but it usually means "manifest evidence," "decisive and irrefutable proof," or "clear demonstration." It also carries with it the Koranic connotation of "shining light" or "brilliant manifestation" (Gardet 1960:1326). The legends create wonder and awe in the individual and affirm the position of the saint, whose role is of central importance in the lives of his devotees. The saint, an inexhaustible font of baraka, serves not only to effect cures, to eliminate barrenness, and to control the jnun and other spirits, but also as a reference point by which much of reality, especially in its spatial and temporal dimensions, is organized. The annual pilgrimages—and individual ones as well—mark the flow of time; directions are often given by reference to saints' tombs (cf. Eliade 1965: 21–98).

The legendary versions of a single saint's life vary from region to region, from individual to individual, from circumstance to circumstance. There are, to be sure, certain constant themes which recur again and again; the very consistency of these themes often appears to be less a product of the historical matrix upon which the legend is built than upon a theme's reflection of social and psychological tensions. It is important, however, not to overemphasize a social and psychological analysis of the content and structure of the legends themselves at the expense of their rhetorical and demonstrative functions. Their reflection, both in structure and content, of the Moroccan (and the individual's) social and psychological background only strengthens their persuasiveness.

The legends are told over and over again in marketplaces, among friends and members of religious orders, and at the saints' tombs and lodges. Most often, to demonstrate or emphasize a particular point, only episodes of the lives are told. Throughout my field notes there are fragments from the lives of Sidi ʿAli and Sidi Ahmed which were introduced into a conversation to convince me of one or another truth: the greatness of one of the saints, the superiority of Sidi ʿAli over Sidi Ahmed, Sidi ʿAli's dependency on Sidi Ahmed, the curative power of one of the saints, or his special control over the jnun. These examples often reflected tensions that were at play within the society at large or within the individual himself and which were corroborated in the course of the interview. They appear to have served a symbolic-interpretative function for the narrator.

The Legendary Cycle

I have chosen to present here the most complete legendary life of the two saints that I obtained. It was told to me by the then recently-appointed muqaddim of the zawiya of Sidi ʿAli in Meknes, Sidi Mohammed Touijer, who had developed a very strong sense of responsibility toward my work and was anxious to make a good impression. It is therefore more ordered and complete than any other legend that I have collected. Told, as it is, from the point of view of a follower of Sidi ʿAli, it tends to play up the importance of Sidi ʿAli with respect to Sidi Ahmed—a reflection of the social and economic competition between the descendants and followers of the two saints. I have included in notes which follow the legend both Muqaddim Touijer's and my own explication of obscure parts of the legend, as well as important variations I have recorded at other times.

Sidi ʿAli was caid to Moulay Ismaïl. Moulay Ismaïl was a ferocious man who cut off the heads of liars. One day he ordered Sidi ʿAli to fetch Buʿabid Sharqi. Sidi ʿAli went to Sharqi with his troops. Sharqi asked Sidi ʿAli if he had come to get him. Sidi ʿAli answered that he had. Sharqi then gave Sidi ʿAli a hand-mill and told him to turn it. Sidi ʿAli turned the mill, and when he stopped, the mill continued to turn on its own. Sidi ʿAli threw some grain into the mill. A black woman came up to him and exclaimed that the mill was grinding the grain by itself. Sidi ʿAli told the woman to shut up and cursed her blind. The woman immediately became blind. When Sharqi saw that the woman was in fact blind, he threw Sidi ʿAli out and immediately fell ill and vomited into a pail. Then he ordered the blind woman to get rid of his vomit. Feeling her way along the wall, she took the pail to the door, whereupon Sidi ʿAli, who had been hiding there, grabbed the pail and drank all of the vomit. This is how he got the remainder of his baraka from Buʿabid Sharqi.

Then Sidi ʿAli began a long trip and arrived at the ʿAyn Kabir [*the Great Spring*] *and sat down.*

Someone came up to Sidi ʿAli. His name was Sidi Ahmed Dghughi. Sidi ʿAli told him to heat some water so that he could wash for his prayers. Sidi Ahmed asked if Allah would give him baraka if he did this. Sidi ʿAli assured him that He would.

At this time the son of Moulay Ismaïl, ʿAbdelḥaqq, was in the habit of shooting arrows into passersby. Before killing them, he would invite them in to drink some buttermilk. Then he would shoot them. Sidi ʿAli told Sidi Ahmed to go to the palace to do something about this. Sidi Ahmed answered that he could not because the palace was so far away. Sidi ʿAli told him to close his eyes. When he opened them, he found himself in front of Moulay Ismaïl's palace. ʿAbdelḥaqq called him in and offered him some buttermilk. Sidi Ahmed drank a whole pail of buttermilk, then a second, and then a third. Nothing happened. His stomach did not explode. It was not even swollen. A fourth pail still remained. Sidi Ahmed offered it to ʿAbdelḥaqq, who drank it. Then Sidi Ahmed shot him with an arrow.

The soldiers ran to Moulay Ismaïl and told him what Sidi Ahmed had done. Moulay Ismaïl ordered the soldiers to get both Sidi ʿAli and Sidi Ahmed. Both men refused to come. When Moulay Ismaïl heard this, he ordered his soldiers to bring them by force, to drag them all the way if necessary. The soldiers returned to Sidi ʿAli, who asked them if the sultan wanted him to come alone or with his friends. The soldiers returned to Moulay Ismaïl to ask whether or not he wanted Sidi ʿAli alone or with his friends. Moulay Ismaïl answered, "Tell him to come with his monkeys and dogs." The soldiers returned and told Sidi ʿAli to bring his "monkeys and dogs." As Sidi ʿAli started to get up, the mountain bent over and rocks began to slide down. The soldiers told Sidi ʿAli not to move. They would have to ask the king what was to be done. Moulay Ismaïl answered, "If he has so much baraka, let him take my oil to Mecca." The road to Mecca was blocked at the time, and Moulay Ismaïl could not send oil there.

The soldiers returned to Sidi ʿAli and told him what the sultan had said. The saint instructed them to bring him the oil, which they brought in skin bags and poured down the throat of the reclining saint. Then, as they were on their way back to the palace to fetch more oil, a messenger arrived from Mecca to tell Moulay Ismaïl that the oil had already arrived safely.

Lalla ʿAuda, one of Moulay Ismaïl's wives, heard about Sidi ʿAli's miracles and wanted to visit him because he had so much baraka. She had not had any children and hoped that the saint would be able to help her. Moulay Ismaïl sent her with some slaves and told them that he would have both her head and theirs if they were not all back by sunset. When Lalla ʿAuda arrived, she found Sidi ʿAli asleep. She woke him and explained that she was in a hurry. Sidi ʿAli told her not to worry. She had plenty of time, he said. Lalla ʿAuda remained at the saint's until there were only fifteen minutes to sunset. Then Sidi ʿAli pulled Moulay Ismaïl's hand all the way from Meknes to massage her belly so that she would have children. When one of the slaves saw Sidi ʿAli massaging his master's wife's belly, he started to protest, but Sidi ʿAli told him to shut up or he would have him shot. Then Sidi ʿAli dismissed Lalla ʿAuda, telling her to say when she arrived in Meknes, "O, Sun, set and may Allah be thanked."

When she arrived in Meknes, she found the whole city in an uproar.

Everyone was wondering why the sun had not set. Moulay Ismaïl himself was staring at the sun! Lalla 'Auda asked him what was wrong and then told him what Sidi 'Ali had said. He ordered her to repeat the words, and then the sun set. Moulay Ismaïl then turned to his slave and asked him what he had done when Sidi 'Ali had massaged Lalla 'Auda's belly. The slave answered that he had tried to stop him. Moulay Ismaïl cried out, "You fool. It was my hand." He ordered his soldiers to load their guns and shoot the slave. This they did.

Sidi 'Ali turned to his side and found Sidi Ahmed there. He told him to go to the Sudan to get the ḥal. *Sidi Ahmed answered that it was far away. It was at least a six-months' journey. Sidi 'Ali told him to close his eyes, and when he opened them he found himself in front of the palace of the king of the Sudan. Sidi Ahmed entered the palace, where, praise be to God, the soldiers were all asleep. There he found an* 'awwad [*a short reed flute*], *a* daff [*a square flat drum*], *and 'Aïsha Qandisha* [*a she-demon, or* jinniyya, *to whom the Ḥamadsha are devoted*]. *Sidi Ahmed took them with him. Then the soldiers and the king awoke. The king asked them where his 'awwad, his daff, and 'Aïsha Qandisha had gone. The soldiers said they did not know and assured him that no one had entered while he was asleep. The king told them that it must have been Sidi Ahmed who did it, and ordered them to follow the saint to the 'Ayn Kabir.*

When Sidi Ahmed found out that the king knew it was he, he sent a message by pigeon to Sidi 'Ali to pray for him so that he would not be taken prisoner. Because of the baraka of Sidi 'Ali, the soldiers were all turned into frogs. When the king died, his body was taken to the 'Ayn er-Rjal at Moulay Idriss and buried. After his burial, whenever the inhabitants of Moulay Idriss prepared couscous or tajin [*stew*], *frogs jumped from their plates. They brought a sacrifice to Moulay Idriss, who woke and told them that they had brought the sacrifice to the wrong person, that they should go to Sidi 'Ali ben Ḥamdush. The townspeople then went to Sidi 'Ali and told him that frogs were jumping all over the place. Sidi 'Ali asked them who had sent them, and when he learned that it was Moulay Idriss, he instructed them to return to their village. There they would find a man dressed in a* darbala [*a tattered and patched cloak*], *sleeping. They were to ask him his advice, and he would tell them what to do. They found the man, woke him, and asked him if it was he who had let out all the frogs. The man asked them who had sent them, and when they told him that it was Sidi 'Ali, he told them that they should work the ḥal of Sidi 'Ali. The people agreed to do this and have made sacrifices to Sidi 'Ali ever since.*

One day Sidi Ahmed went to fetch water for Sidi ʿAli. When he returned, he found the saint dead. He began to hit his head with his hands, crying "Allah! The saint is dead!" Since that time there has been the gwal [*drum*] *and the head-slashing.*

Explication of the Legends

I will now consider the various sections of the legend in some detail.

Sidi ʿAli was caid to Moulay Ismaïl. Moulay Ismaïl was a ferocious man who cut off the heads of liars. One day he ordered Sidi ʿAli to fetch Buʿabid Sharqi. Sidi ʿAli went to Sharqi with his troops. Sharqi asked Sidi ʿAli if he had come to get him. Sidi ʿAli answered that he had. Sharqi then gave Sidi ʿAli a hand-mill and told him to turn it. Sidi ʿAli turned the mill, and when he stopped, the mill continued to turn on its own. Sidi ʿAli threw some grain into the mill. A black woman came up to him and exclaimed that the mill was grinding the grain by itself. Sidi ʿAli told the woman to shut up and cursed her blind. When Sharqi saw that the woman was in fact blind, he threw Sidi ʿAli out and immediately fell ill and vomited into a pail. Then he ordered the blind woman to get rid of the vomit. Feeling her way along the wall, she took the pail to the door, whereupon Sidi ʿAli, who had been hiding there, grabbed the pail and drank all of the vomit. This is how he got the remainder of his baraka from Buʿabid Sharqi.

The legend begins typically in the middle of Sidi ʿAli's life, at the time when he is about to obtain the "remainder" of his baraka. We are not told where Sidi ʿAli came from or how he became Moulay Ismaïl's caid. When questioned about this, the muqaddim explained that Sidi ʿAli was a descendant of Moulay Idriss (d. 791 A.D.) who is popularly considered to have brought Islam to Morocco; he founded the first Moroccan dynasty. (Moulay Idriss is also buried on the Jebel Zerhoun, midway between Fez and Meknes, and just above the Roman ruins of Volubilis.) The muqaddim then corrected himself and explained that Sidi ʿAli was, in fact, born in Mecca and came West with Moulay Idriss and Moulay Idriss' freedman Moulay Rachid, both of whom stopped at the village of Moulay Idriss while Sidi ʿAli went on to Beni Rachid. He could not explain how Sidi ʿAli became Moulay Ismaïl's caid.

Although the lives of Sidi ʿAli and the sultan Moulay Ismaïl (d. 1727), the founder of the city of Meknes, did overlap, it should be noted that Moulay Ismaïl is a stock character in many of the hagiographic legends. He is reputed for his extreme and arbitrary cruelty, which is usually expressed in terms of promiscuous beheadings. Often —and later in the muqaddim's account itself—he is seen as a protagonist to the saint—an expression, perhaps, of an incipient schism between the secular and the sacred order of things, or simply Moulay Ismaïl's emphasis on the strong-man aspect of his role as sultan, rather than on the holy-man aspect (cf. Geertz 1968:53). It may also be proof of Sidi ʿAli's power over as virile a figure as the sultan (who beheads his antagonists). That Sidi ʿAli is seen as an emissary of Moulay Ismaïl is unusual. The muqaddim may have wished to emphasize the saint's importance and therefore identified him with Moulay Ismaïl, whose strength he admired. Perhaps he wanted to begin his tale as the heroic tales of kings and warriors recounted by professional storytellers in marketplaces and cafes begin.

Interpretation of the episode is difficult. Unlike other versions of the passage of baraka from Buʿabid Sharqi to Sidi ʿAli, which conceive of it as a friendly gift, the muqaddim has emphasized the competitive element. But in his interpretation he suggests—and thereby contradicts himself—a more friendly aspect. Originally he described the episode as a competition between the two saints. First Buʿabid Sharqi performs a miracle (*burhan*): he makes the mill turn on its own. (The muqaddim later added that it was only after Sharqi had touched Sidi ʿAli's arm that the mill turned on its own.) Then Sidi ʿAli also performs a burhan: he blinds the black woman. The muqaddim saw no wrong in this. When I asked him why Sidi ʿAli blinded the woman, he answered: "Well, for example, there is an old man sitting down. A little boy comes up to him and asks what he is doing. The old man tells the boy to scram. Then the old man curses the child." Sidi ʿAli was presumably irritated at the black woman for bothering him, for pointing out the strength of Sharqi's baraka, and he cursed her. Still, even when pressed, the muqaddim could not conceive of the two saints being jealous of each other.

Sidi ʿAli did not stay at Sharqi's in order to deceive the saint. He remained, the muqaddim explained by adding a new scene to his version, because his warriors had left with the horses. They thought their caid was dead. Sharqi himself knew that Sidi ʿAli was at the door waiting, and would drink the vomit. He had seen that Sidi ʿAli had a lot of baraka and wanted to give him his own baraka before he died.

The conception of the passage of baraka—the master-disciple relationship—by the oral incorporation of vomit, polluted water, bathwater and other foul materials occurs frequently in the legends of various Moroccan saints. In another version of the same story, Sidi ʿAli comes to work for Bu'abid Sharqi as a water-carrier and not only drinks the water that drips from Sharqi's water-sack—Sharqi himself is a water-carrier who takes no money for the water he carries—but drinks the water with which the saint has washed himself before his prayers. Sometimes, however, the baraka is passed to the saint in the form of bread—bread being a recurrent symbol for baraka in both legend and ritual. Sidi 'Ali works in disguise for Sharqi because "Sharqi had destroyed Sidi 'Ali's papers" as a water-carrier; and he makes the mills of eighty of Sharqi's women turn on their own. A Negro woman tells Sharqi; Sidi 'Ali blinds the woman; and Sharqi, recognizing Sidi 'Ali as a saint, gives him two loaves of bread and tells him that he will obtain the rest at Moulay Idriss. At Moulay Idriss, Sidi 'Ali encounters forty saints guarding the bread for him.

Then Sidi 'Ali began a long trip and arrived at the 'Ayn Kabir and sat down.

The muqaddim was ignorant of Sidi 'Ali's adventures as the saint traveled from Sharqi's to the 'Ayn Kabir. He simply stated that the saint wandered from village to village, gathering followers and founding lodges. The 'Ayn Kabir, or Big Spring, is a spring that flows from the cliffs just below Sidi 'Ali's tomb in Beni Rachid and is believed to contain much baraka. It is visited by pilgrims to Sidi 'Ali's tomb who either drink the water, take a little home, or bathe in its waters. The muqaddim explained that the water was not filled with baraka until the saint had bathed in it.

Although the muqaddim himself knew nothing of what happened to Sidi 'Ali on his trip to the 'Ayn Kabir, a number of episodes concerning this period were told to me by other informants. They are all concerned with Sidi 'Ali's acquisition of baraka or with his recognition as a saint.

According to one version, Sidi 'Ali drank all of the water in Sharqi's water-bag. The saint had been in the habit of giving a little of the water—a little of his baraka—to forty people each year, but Sidi 'Ali took it all for himself. Sharqi ordered his men to chase Sidi 'Ali all the way to Tadla, if need be, and assured them that they would die if Sidi 'Ali ever returned to Marrakech, where Sharqi was living at the time. Sidi 'Ali fled to Fez to stay with Sidi l-Husayn, who was dying and surrounded by forty saints. Sidi 'Ali stood at the door and drank Sidi l-Husayn's vomit. When the saint heard about this from his serving women, he cried praise to Allah and died in peace as the other saints filed out of his room.

Sidi ʿAli then went to the Qarwiyyin University at Fez—or so this particular version continues—and sat down in a corner praying and spitting. He did not move for many years. The scholars of the university grew suspicious. One of them, a member of the well-known ben Suda family of Fez, decided to chase him out; but somehow, every time he approached the saint, he would forget his purpose. One night ben Suda dreamed that the sultan, the royal guard, and the army were in the university courtyard. The sultan was holding out a loaf of bread to the scholars and his warriors; but each time one of them tried to take the bread, he was curiously stung. Finally, when all had tried, only Sidi ʿAli remained. He stood up, took the bread, and left the university for Beni Rachid. When ben Suda awoke, he rushed to the university and discovered Sidi ʿAli's corner empty. Then he knew that Sidi ʿAli was indeed a saint.[1]

Sidi ʿAli also spent time with Sidi Qasim, it is said, in the town of Sidi Kacem in the Gharb, where he worked as a gardener for four or five years and never touched any of his master's fruits. He fasted continually. One day Sidi Qasim was entertaining guests and asked the gardener to bring him some good pomegranates. Sidi ʿAli, who never touched the fruit, could not tell a good pomegranate from a bad one and simply brought in the biggest pomegranate he could find. The fruit was spoiled. Sidi Qasim then called his gardener and asked him why he had chosen a bad pomegranate. When the saint explained that he could not distinguish because he had never tasted one, Sidi Qasim realized that Sidi ʿAli was in fact a saint.

Someone came up to Sidi ʿAli. His name was Sidi Ahmed Dghughi. Sidi ʿAli told him to heat some water so that he could wash for his prayers. Sidi Ahmed asked if God would give him baraka if he did this. Sidi ʿAli assured him that He would.

The muqaddim expanded this episode in his explanation. When Sidi ʿAli arived at the ʿAyn Kabir, he was visited by people from all over Morocco. Once a particularly large group of pilgrims arrived. Sidi ʿAli saw Sidi Ahmed in their midst and called him out to work for him. He saw that he was devout; his heart told him that Sidi Ahmed should work for him.

The descendents of Sidi Ahmed Dghughi are always careful to point out that Sidi Ahmed was not Sidi ʿAli's servant or slave but a friend

[1] My informants were not so much awed by the fact that Sidi ʿAli was able to take the bread as by his ability to remain immobile for years.

and an equal. Sidi ʿAli is often seen as dependent on Sidi Ahmed in the legends told by them. Once, for example, when members of Sidi Qasim's family were jealous of Sidi ʿAli, they tried to poison him with a couscous made with snakes.[2] (Snake meat is considered poisonous in Morocco.) Sidi Ahmed warned his master. As it turned out, Sidi ʿAli ate the couscous anyway, and the skins of his enemies began to peel off. Most of the legends about Sidi Ahmed are concerned with the missions he performed for Sidi ʿAli, although his descendants have recounted several which do not involve Sidi ʿAli. Two of these are about Sidi Ahmed's conflicts with the canonists of Fez (the Sufi versus the *ʿulama*).

While Sidi Ahmed was in Fez, the scholars asked him to give a discourse on prayer and other religious matters. Sidi Ahmed said, "All that is necessary is a silo of wheat and a silo of barley." The scholars did not understand. Sidi Ahmed then invited them into his house, which he locked and in which there was no food. For three or four days the men talked of prayer and other religious matters. Finally they began to ask for food, but Sidi Ahmed simply replied: "Continue your discussion." Finally they became so hungry that they could not even say their prayers. Then they realized the wisdom of Sidi Ahmed's words. The proverb, "Without bread there is neither prayer nor devotion," comes from this.

The scholars of Fez did not believe that Sidi Ahmed was a saint. "You say," they said, "that you can make a camel of a man. Show us how this is possible." Sidi Ahmed asked them to bring prickly pears which were still covered with spines. One of his followers who was in ecstasy (ḥal) *devoured the pears, spines, skin, and all, and cried out that he was still hungry and wanted bread. The scholars said that the bread was still in the oven. Sidi Ahmed asked them to lead him and the "camel" to the oven. The "camel" ate all of the bread as the scholars waited for the two men to come out of the oven-house, and then they escaped by a back door of the oven, which opened miraculously. When the scholars discovered this, they pursued the two men all the way to Mehdiya near Kenitra to present their apologies.*

This episode refers to certain followers of Sidi Ahmed (and Sidi ʿAli) who act like camels and eat the spines or skins of prickly pears when in trance. The reader should also be reminded that bread is a symbol of baraka.

[2] In other versions the poisoners are Sidi ʿAli's brothers.

The third episode concerns Sidi Ahmed and Moulay Ismaïl, and again reflects the conflict between saint and sultan that was noted earlier.

A lot of people considered Sidi Ahmed a magician because he would become like a camel and eat spiny cactus when he was in ḥal. The people told this to Moulay Ismaïl, who went to see him and challenged him to a battle. Many of Sidi Ahmed's followers were afraid of Moulay Ismaïl and did not follow him. The two "armies" met at a bog between Fez and Meknes, where the two leaders decided to fight it out alone. As they touched hands before the duel, the earth suddenly opened up, forming a huge chasm around Moulay Ismaïl, who then realized that Sidi Ahmed was a saint and surrendered to him.

I have heard this story told of Sidi l-Hasan l-Yussi of Sefrou too.

At this time the son of Moulay Ismaïl, ʿAbdelḥaqq, was in the habit of shooting arrows into passersby. Before killing them, he would invite them in to drink some buttermilk. Then he would shoot them. Sidi ʿAli told Sidi Ahmed to go to the palace to do something about this. Sidi Ahmed answered that he could not because the palace was so far away. Sidi ʿAli told him to close his eyes. When he opened them, he found himself in front of Moulay Ismaïl's palace. ʿAbdelḥaqq called him in and offered him some buttermilk. Sidi Ahmed drank a whole pail of buttermilk, then a second, and then a third. Nothing happened. His stomach did not explode. It was not even swollen. A fourth pail still remained. Sidi Ahmed offered it to ʿAbdelḥaqq who drank it. Then Sidi Ahmed shot him with an arrow.

The soldiers ran to Moulay Ismaïl and told him what Sidi Ahmed had done. Moulay Ismaïl ordered the soldiers to get both Sidi ʿAli and Sidi Ahmed. Both men refused to come. When Moulay Ismaïl heard this, he ordered his soldiers to bring them by force, to drag them all the way if necessary. The soldiers returned to Sidi ʿAli, who asked them if the sultan wanted him to come alone or with his friends. The soldiers returned to Moulay Ismaïl to ask whether or not he wanted Sidi ʿAli alone or with his friends. Moulay Ismaïl answered, "Tell him to come with his monkeys and dogs." The soldiers returned and told Sidi ʿAli to bring his "monkeys and dogs." As Sidi ʿAli started to get up, the mountain bent over and rocks began to slide down. The soldiers told Sidi ʿAli not to move. They would have to ask the king what was to be done. Moulay Ismaïl answered, "If he has so much baraka, let him take my oil to Mecca." The road to Mecca was blocked at the time, and Moulay Ismaïl could not send oil there. The soldiers returned to Sidi ʿAli and told him what the sultan had said. The saint instructed them to bring the oil, which they brought in skin bags and poured down the throat of the reclining saint. Then, as they were on their way back to the palace to fetch more oil, a messenger arrived from Mecca to tell Moulay Ismaïl that the oil had already arrived safely.

The muqaddim explained that since ʿAbdelḥaqq was the son of Moulay Ismaïl, there was no one who could control him. He found this quite understandable. ʿAbdelḥaqq gave his victims buttermilk because it pleased him to see their stomachs swell and then to see the milk come squirting out of their pierced stomachs. (Buttermilk is said to contain baraka, and offering it is considered a sign of hospitality. It is popularly believed to make the stomach swell and even explode if one drinks too much of it.) ʿAbdelḥaqq did not shoot Sidi Ahmed because, thanks to Sidi ʿAli, his stomach did not swell. The sultan's son had to accept Sidi Ahmed's challenge because he was surrounded by viziers and courtiers. It would have been shameful (*ḥshuma*) to refuse. Besides, ʿAbdelḥaqq thought that he himself had so much baraka that his stomach would not swell either. Sidi Ahmed killed ʿAbdelḥaqq because —the muqaddim quoted the proverb—"People who kill others for no reason will be killed by an emissary of God." The courtiers did not take Sidi Ahmed prisoner because he had so much baraka.

The sultan called for both Sidi ʿAli and Sidi Ahmed, the muqaddim continued, because they were responsible for the death of his son. He was angry and insulted Sidi ʿAli's friends by calling them "monkeys and dogs." He wanted to see what miracles (*burhans*) Sidi ʿAli could perform, and gave him the impossible task of getting oil to Mecca. When Sidi ʿAli drank the oil, it was not he but "others" who took the oil to Mecca. The muqaddim seemed uncertain as to whether the "others" were angels (*malaïka*) or jnun. Finally he decided on angels.[3] The messenger who informed Moulay Ismaïl of the arrival of the oil was also an "invisible."

This tale of Sidi ʿAli's drinking Moulay Ismaïl's oil in order to "send" it to Mecca is popular in the area of Meknes. In another version, Moulay Ismaïl calls for Sidi Ahmed; Sidi ʿAli takes his place because he is not married and Sidi Ahmed is. When Sidi ʿAli arrives at the palace, the sultan tells him that he must produce fifteen jugs of oil to be sent to Mecca by the end of the week or he will lose his head. Sidi ʿAli returns at the end of the week and drinks the sultan's and his family's bath water and vomits it out into the waiting jugs as oil.

[3] This confusion is not as great as the English glosses for "malaïka" and "jnun" suggest. The jnun are not necessarily evil and harmful. Many of my informants confused angels and jnun in their tales and associations (cf. Chelhod 1964:67–92).

Lalla ʿAuda, one of Moulay Ismaïl's wives, heard about Sidi ʿAli's miracles and wanted to visit him because he had so much baraka. She had not had any children and hoped that the saint would be able to help her. Moulay Ismaïl sent her with some slaves and told them that he would have both her head and theirs if they were not all back by sunset. When Lalla ʿAuda arrived, she found Sidi ʿAli asleep. She woke him and explained that she was in a hurry. Sidi ʿAli told her not to worry. She had plenty of time, he said. Lalla ʿAuda remained at the saint's until there were only fifteen minutes to sunset. Then Sidi ʿAli pulled Moulay Ismaïl's hand all the way from Meknes to massage her belly so that she would have children. When one of the slaves saw Sidi ʿAli massaging his master's wife's belly, he started to protest, but Sidi ʿAli told him to shut up or he would have him shot. Then Sidi ʿAli dismissed Lalla ʿAuda, telling her to say when she arrived in Meknes, "O, Sun, set and may Allah be thanked." [4]

When she arrived in Meknes, she found the whole city in an uproar. Everyone was wondering why the sun had not set. Moulay Ismaïl himself was staring at the sun! Lalla ʿAuda asked him what was wrong and then told him what Sidi ʿAli had said. He ordered her to repeat the words, and then the sun set. Moulay Ismaïl then turned to his slave and asked him what he had done when Sidi ʿAli had massaged Lalla ʿAuda's belly. The slave answered that he had tried to stop him. Moulay Ismaïl cried out, "You fool. It was my hand." He ordered his soldiers to load their guns and shoot the slave. This they did.

This episode is one of the most popular in the life of Sidi ʿAli and accounts for his title "Guide of the Sun" (*gawwad sh-shamsh*) or "Caid of the Sun" (*qaïd sh-shamsh*). I have been told that if one looked at Sidi ʿAli's knees, one could see the sun shining both by day and by night.

The muqaddim corrected himself in his explanation. Lalla ʿAuda went to Sidi ʿAli with only one slave whose name was Brahim. Lalla ʿAuda wanted a son so that she could remain Moulay Ismaïl's favorite wife. (*ʿAuda* means mare in Moroccan Arabic.) Sidi ʿAli could not touch the woman's belly with his own hand, because then Moulay Ismaïl would never be able to touch her himself. She would have become taboo (*ḥaram*). The descendants of the saint still massage the bellies of barren women, the muqaddim explained, and they receive gifts every day from women who have then had children. Moulay Ismaïl had Brahim killed, even though the slave did not know that Sidi ʿAli was in fact massaging Lalla ʿAuda's belly with his master's hand, because he had questioned the saint. The muqaddim seemed surprised

[4] According to the version of this legend cited by Herber, Lalla ʿAuda was to say: "Continue your journey, O Sun, by the power of Allah" (1923:224).

when I asked him if the fact that the slave did not know it was Moulay Ismaïl's hand made any difference. He assured me it did not.

Other versions of the episode suggest that Moulay Ismaïl was very discontented with Lalla ʿAuda because she had not borne him a son and threatened to have her head if she did not conceive the following day. That night, she dreamed of Sidi ʿAli, and she visited him the following day. Sidi ʿAli did not massage her belly but gave her a scarf which she was to wear against her belly, under her clothes.

Sidi ʿAli turned to his side and found Sidi Ahmed there. He told him to go to the Sudan to get the *ḥal.* Sidi Ahmed answered that it was far away. It was at least a six-month's journey. Sidi ʿAli told him to close his eyes, and when he opened them he found himself in front of the palace of the king of the Sudan. Sidi Ahmed entered the palace, where, praise be to God, the soldiers were all asleep. There he found an *ʿawwad,* a *daff,* and ʿAïsha Qandisha. Sidi Ahmed took them with him. Then the soldiers and the king awoke. The king asked them where his ʿawwad, his daff, and ʿAïsha Qandisha had gone. The soldiers said they did not know and assured him that no one had entered while he was asleep. The king told them that it must have been Sidi Ahmed who did it and ordered them to follow the saint to the ʿAyn Kabir.

When Sidi Ahmed found out that the king knew it was he, he sent a message by pigeon to Sidi ʿAli to pray for him so that he would not be taken prisoner. Because of the baraka of Sidi ʿAli, the soldiers were all turned into frogs. When the king died, his body was taken to the ʿAyn er-Rjal at Moulay Idriss and buried. After his burial, whenever the inhabitants of Moulay Idriss prepared couscous or *tajin* [stew], frogs jumped from their plates. They brought a sacrifice to Moulay Idriss, who woke and told them that they had brought the sacrifice to the wrong person, that they should go to Sidi ʿAli ben Ḥamdush. The townspeople then went to Sidi ʿAli and told him that frogs were jumping all over the place. Sidi ʿAli asked them who had sent them, and when he learned that it was Moulay Idriss, he instructed them to return to their village. There they would find a man dressed in a *darbala,* sleeping. They were to ask him his advice, and he would tell them what to do. They found the man, woke him, and asked him if it was he who had let out all the frogs. The man asked them who had sent them, and when they told him it was Sidi ʿAli, he told them that they should work the ḥal of Sidi ʿAli. The people agreed to do this and have made sacrifices to Sidi ʿAli ever since.

Sidi Ahmed's trip to the Sudan is considered to be the most important episode in the legendary cycle, for it explains both the origin of the *ḥal,* or ecstatic trance, into which the Ḥamadsha work themselves, and the arrival of ʿAïsha Qandisha.

ʿAïsha Qandisha is a she-demon, sometimes called a *jinniyya*, or female jinn, sometimes an *ʿafrita*, or giant jinn-like creature, and sometimes she is considered to be quite different from either of these. She is said to appear sometimes as a beautiful woman and sometimes as an old hag, but always with the feet of a camel or some other hoofed animal. Despite a widespread belief in ʿAïsha Qandisha among the northern Moroccan Arabs, the Ḥamadsha, as we shall see, are her special devotees. They hold her responsible for their trance. Although her Sudanese origin is almost universally accepted, it has been claimed that she was in fact a woman and Sidi ʿAli's slave and that when she was buried she suddenly disappeared and was heard laughing. "I am here," she called out. "I am dead. I've been carried away by my *mamluk* (jinn)." Some hold her to be the daughter of Sidi Shamharush, the king of the jnun; and on at least one occasion I was told that her mother was human and her father Ighud, the shepherd of the wind (*riḥ*), who carried her mother off to the forest. This is said to explain why she has both a human name, ʿAïsha, and a devil's name, Qandisha[5] (Haimer 1968:52).

The muqaddim's version of the episode is the most complete I have heard; the frog section is unique to him. (The jnun are often said to take the form of frogs.) Sometimes Sidi Ahmed is said to have gone to the Sudan by way of Mecca. The Sudan refers to the area immediately south of the Sahara and is considered by many Moroccans to be the home of the ḥal. I have been told that Sidi Ahmed found ʿAïsha Qandisha in a place called Sakqia al-Hamra, probably in the northern part of the Spanish Sahara. In another version, it is the jnun, alerted by the whinny of Sidi Ahmed's horse, who pursue him. He blinds them by throwing tar (*qatran*) in their eyes, and then sand. This explains why pilgrims to Sidi Ahmed's tomb take back a little earth (*tuba*) with them as protection from the jnun. The instruments referred to by the muqaddim are not used by the Ḥamadsha today, but the muqaddim claimed they were once played.[6] Often Sidi Ahmed is said to have obtained ʿAïsha not from the king of the Sudan but by pulling open a cord which held a bundle of wood together[7] and to have returned to Sidi ʿAli followed by thousands of devotees including the most famous saints of the land. In most versions Sidi ʿAli has died. He then makes

[5] See Chapter Eight for a more detailed account of ʿAïsha Qandisha. See Jones (1951:279–286) for similar myths.

[6] See Garcia-Barriuso (1941:105) for a description of the daff (*deff*).

[7] The Ḥamadsha occasionally beat themselves with bundles of sticks (an example of which may be seen in the Musée de l'Homme in Paris), along with their other instruments of self-mutilation.

a pact with ʿAïsha: she must never come near him. The man in the darbala is claimed to have been Sidi ʿAli in disguise. He could not very well himself have told the townspeople of Moulay Idriss to devote themselves to his ḥal.

> One day Sidi Ahmed went to fetch water for Sidi ʿAli. When he returned, he found the saint dead. He began to hit his head with his hands, crying "Allah! The saint is dead!" Since that time there has been the gwal and the head-slashing.

This version of the legend explains at least why the followers of Sidi Ahmed slash their heads—self-mutilation during mourning is not uncommon in Morocco. It has been claimed that only Sidi Ahmed's followers abandon themselves to such practices (Aubin 1904:431), but in fact the followers of both saints do, and other legends suggest that Sidi ʿAli himself also did so. Cat (1898:401) reports that the Ḥamadsha slash their heads in commemoration of Sidi ʿAli's putting his head back together after it had been split open by a shell. Sidi ʿAli is also said to have pounded his chest while he said his beads (*tasbiḥ*). The beads were attached to a tree and every time a bead was passed the saint would beat his chest (Herber 1923:225). I have heard neither of these legends.

The general belief is that Sidi Ahmed, finding his master dead, first washed and buried him and then climbed to the top of the Jebel Zerhoun, where he became so upset that he slashed his head with an ax as he called out the names of all the saints. The people tried to calm him. "You are lucky to be alive," they said. "You are lucky to have children. These children will carry on your blood and your baraka. You must not be angry or sad. You will always have children. They will always replace you."

They told him that before Sidi ʿAli died, he said "For you Thursday, for me Friday," by which he meant that Sidi Ahmed had inherited his baraka and would be visited first, on Thursdays, at the annual pilgrimage, or *musem.* It has been said that the first musem took place when Moulay Ismaïl came to Sidi ʿAli's tomb on the last day of the mourning period (forty days after the saint's death). Sidi Ahmed lived for several years—he would slash his head whenever he was falling asleep as he prayed—and when he died, some say among the Beni Hsen, he was put on a mule, as he requested, and carried as far as the mule would go. The mule collapsed at Beni Ouarad, a mile from his master's tomb, and it was here that he was buried and that some of his descendants settled.

Although I was personally unable to learn of the origin of the instruments with which the Ḥamadsha slash their heads, Herber gives the following two legends, which account for the use of the single- and double-bladed axes the Ḥamadsha traditionally employed and still use during their annual pilgrimage. The first of these concerns Sidi Raḥal, a saint who is buried southeast of Marrakech in the town named after him and who is the founder of the Raḥaliyyin brotherhood, whose members are reputed for drinking boiling water when in an entranced state, and another saint, Sidi Ahmed l-Arusi.

Sidi Raḥal was living on a mountain near Marrakech; he was a hermaphrodite and had with him two chaste women who served him. The sultan, having heard his saintliness praised, wanted to see him. He sent two of his people to fetch him: one was Sidi ʿAli ben Ḥamdush, the other Sidi Ahmed l-Arusi. But these two were moved by his piety to the point that they attached themselves to him and did not want to return to Marrakech. The sultan sent his soldiers for them, and they were condemned to death. As they arrived at the place of execution, Sidi Raḥal appeared in the skies, holding an axe which filled the spectators with dread. He gave it to Sidi ʿAli ben Ḥamdush and told him that, thanks to it, he should have no fear of anyone at all. Then he took Ahmed l-Arusi by the belt and carried him off in flight. The belt tore, l-Arusi fell into the [Valley of the] Sous, where he ended his life in retirement. Sidi Raḥal returned to his hermitage; Sidi ʿAli retired to the Zerhoun, where he bequeathed his axe to his followers and died. (Herber 1923:225, fn. 1)

The origin of this legend is not given. The following one was told to the author by an interpreter in Rabat.

Sidi ʿAli ben Ḥamdush retired to the mountain, several kilometers from Meknes, in order to lead a solitary life and to pray to God. Several of his companions followed him. They lived on alms and nourished themselves principally on the roasted heads of sheep, the bones of which soon formed a big pile in front of the cave in which Sidi ʿAli and his companions lived. Every day, at sunrise and after prayers, Sidi ʿAli's disciples gathered around him and began their dances which they did not stop except during the hours of prayer and at meals.

One day, not seeing the arrival of their leader, the brothers were taken with fear; none dared to go to learn the news of which they had a foreboding; they took counsel and chose Sidi ʿAli's favorite disciple, who sat to his right during the recitation to God. All trembling and soaking with sweat, the elected one went to the cave of their venerated leader; he reappeared soon, his mouth wide open, his eyes out of their sockets, and threw himself on the sheep bones. He took a jawbone and hit his head saying: "Allah! Allah! There is no God but Allah!" His companions, understanding the truth, hit themselves in imitation of their new leader. Hence, the origin of the ax which "is almost in the shape of a jawbone." (Herber 1923:225, fn. 1)

Interpretation of the Legends

All of these legends may be analyzed on many different levels and from many different theoretical perspectives. Some of the legends, for example, appear to be explanations for certain ritual practices, such as taking home a little earth from the tomb of Sidi Ahmed or slashing one's head with an axe "shaped like a jawbone." Others appear to reflect primarily economic tensions, as between the descendants and followers of Sidi ʿAli and Sidi Ahmed; politico-religious tensions, as between Moulay Ismaïl and the saints; differences in theological perspective, as between the canonists of Fez and the saints of the Zerhoun; or notions of the relative importance, the hierarchization, of saints—Sidi Ahmed, Sidi ʿAli, and Moulay Idriss. I will be concerned, however, only with those elements of the legends which are germane to an understanding of the Ḥamadsha therapeutic system.[8] On the one hand, I will focus on the image of the saint as expressed in his existential stance vis-à-vis certain significant elements within his life; and on the other hand, on the passage of *baraka*—the curative force—from saint to saint.

Despite the fact that there is no fixed order of events in the legends in general, a thematic analysis of Muqaddim Touijer's version of the life of Sidi ʿAli reveals a definite development, at the most literal level of analysis, from the earliest episode, which is concerned with Sidi ʿAli's acquisition of baraka, to the final one, which deals with the passage of his baraka to Sidi Ahmed. Sidi Ahmed is recognized as a saint and is responsible for the head-slashing of the Ḥamadsha. The intervening episodes are concerned with Sidi ʿAli's recognition as a saint by various other saints, canonists, and political figures such as Moulay Ismaïl, and with his acquisition of disciples, such as Sidi Ahmed, and devotees, such as the people of Moulay Idriss.

[8] At this stage of investigation, my choice of "significant elements" may appear arbitrary, but later the reasons for my selection should become apparent.

Each of the episodes appears, literally, to be concerned with the relationship between the saints and some other significant figure. In each of them the saint overcomes—or at least obtains the recognition of—the other figure, his antagonist. The relationships are of power and control. The figures are saints—Buʿabid Sharqi, Sidi l-Husayn, Sidi Qasim, Sidi Raḥal, and Moulay Idriss; intellectual leaders—the canonists of Fez; political leaders—Moulay Idriss, Moulay Ismaïl, ʿAbdelḥaqq, and the king of the Sudan; military leaders—again Moulay Ismaïl; foreigners—the king of the Sudan and his soldiers; women—the blind servant woman, Lalla ʿAuda, and even ʿAïsha Qandisha; servants—Sidi Ahmed Dghughi; members of the "spirit realm"—ʿAïsha Qandisha, and the angels and jnun who help the saint send oil to Mecca; and the general populace—the people of Moulay Idriss. Sidi ʿAli also has control over nature. He is able to defy the laws of nature by sending Sidi Ahmed instantaneously to Meknes and even to the Sudan, by stopping the course of the sun, and by changing soldiers into frogs. Significantly, none of the legends indicate Sidi ʿAli's relationship with God. He is, of course, considered, like all saints, to be an intermediary between man and God.

It is suggested that each of these figures represents or is symbolic of a significant aspect of the Moroccan's experiential world, with which he must enter into some relation. These relationships seem to be conceived primarily in terms of dominance and submission. Dominance is, of course, the ideal, and the saint is seen to be in a dominant position at the end of each of the episodes. In this respect he overcomes all of an individual's major social confrontations but two—the economic and the sexual—which are not mentioned. The saint lives on alms. By choosing the world of prayer and meditation, he has placed himself above the concerns of a daily life which he, nevertheless, can master.

The *Leitmotif* of the legends is the passage of baraka. Baraka is the essential quality and emanation of the saint. It is rooted in both the physiological and social life of the Moroccan. Baraka passes from Buʿabid Sharqi and several other saints to Sidi ʿAli, and then from Sidi ʿAli to Sidi Ahmed. The passage is disjunctive and does not involve women. Usually baraka is passed either from father to son (and daughter) or from a highly endowed individual or place to a visitor or supplicant. In the case of agnatic passage, I have been told that baraka is carried in the semen itself. Women cannot pass on baraka. According to the Moroccan Arabs, women do not contribute at all to the hereditary background of the child; they are only a receptacle which receives the male seed. This seed is molded into the infant by angels who descend into the womb in early pregnancy.[9]

Baraka that is passed from father to child is and remains contagious. Baraka that is passed from an endowed person or place to a supplicant can no longer be transferred. The fact that both Sidi ʿAli and Sidi Ahmed were able to obtain it in its contagious and enduring form from saints from whom they were not descended is exceptional. Their means of obtaining it were equally unusual. In both cases the acquisition of baraka involved the feminization of the saint.

Sidi ʿAli, who has an endowment of baraka in his own right, obtains the remainder from Sharqi (and other saints). His innate endowment, despite the muqaddim's subsequent retraction, enables him to acquire it by deception; he blinds the slave woman and tricks the saint (who is, nevertheless, aware of what Sidi ʿAli is doing). Whether it is Sidi ʿAli's own baraka or the baraka he acquired when Sharqi touched his arm that is responsible for his ability to turn the mills automatically, it is noteworthy that hand-mills are normally turned by women. Sidi ʿAli demonstrates, thereby, his expertise in woman's work. He blinds the slave woman for revealing his "miracle" to the saint; the saint is angered, throws Sidi ʿAli out, and falls sick. Sidi ʿAli obtains the baraka by pulling the pail of vomit away from the blind woman and drinking it.[10]

It is suggested that the oral incorporation of baraka is analogous to insemination.[11] Indeed, material collected by free association related baraka to semen. It is rumored that some saints and their descendants cure sick women by having sexual relations with them; they give them their baraka directly. Semen is, according to the Moroccans of the Ḥamadsha's background, produced by a "vein" in the man's back which extends downward to the lumbar region. This vein converts

[9] Women—and not men—are, nevertheless, responsible for barren marriages, and must take measures to insure their fertility. A woman may affect a child during pregnancy. If she sees a dwarf or deformed individual, her child will be born with the same deformity; if her husband does not cater to her longings for special foods such as liver, and she should then scratch herself, her child will have a birthmark in the spot corresponding to the place where she scratched.

[10] The possible Oedipal implications of Sidi ʿAli's blinding the slave woman (the mother) for telling Sharqi (the father) of his (the son's) miracle (baraka, semen) will not be considered here.

[11] It may also be connected with nursing (milk is said to contain baraka) or fantasies of fellatio (which is not normally practiced in Morocco). In all of these instances, power is obtained by ingesting bodily secretions. This is a frequent fantasy.

blood into semen; blood itself is said to contain baraka and is frequently employed in Moroccan cures and magical practices.

The fact that Sidi ʿAli obtains his baraka by ingesting defilements is not as strange as it might first appear. It should be remembered that sexual intercourse, for the Moroccan Arab, is an act of pollution.[12] Undoubtedly the element of humiliation both on an individual level—man made woman—and on a religious level plays a role here as well. The saint, at any rate, becomes "pregnant with or by baraka" and is gradually recognized as a saint. This occurs during a period of *gestation* in the University of Fez where he remains immobile and spits,[13] or in Sidi Qasim's garden. In both instances the episodes end with his recognition as a saint. He alone is able to take the bread from the sultan; he has resisted the pomegranate. Sidi ʿAli "gives birth to himself" as a saint. It should be noted that during the period of gestation Sidi ʿAli performs manly tasks—meditation, prayer, spitting, gardening—and that at the end he does what even ministers and soldiers cannot do. Sidi ʿAli becomes a man. It is at this point that he retires to the Zerhoun and encounters (gives birth to) Sidi Ahmed, who is instrumental in the performance of his miracles and who finally, after bringing the female demon ʿAïsha Qandisha to the Zerhoun, inherits Sidi ʿAli's baraka.[14]

The legend appears to mirror two different developmental sequences. On the one hand, it mirrors the process of impregnation, gestation (birth),[15] the raising of a son and heir who is able to bring home a woman and to have offspring. On the other hand it mirrors the maturation of man from his acquisition of baraka—the hero's quest for his father—through a period of latency—the sojourn in the university or in the garden—to the performance of a number of miracles which establish his dominant position within society. It culminates in his death and the bequeathing of his powers to an heir. The legend of Sidi ʿAli appears to represent in a more manifest fashion the maturation of a

[12] It is curious to note that Sidi ʿAli obtains baraka—a theoretically impossible feat—by ingesting vomit. Vomit travels the wrong way on a one-way street.

[13] Saliva has been equated with semen by psychoanalysts. I have found no evidence for this symbolic equation in my Moroccan material.

[14] Although I do not pursue this line of thought, I should like to point out that many of the tasks performed by Sidi ʿAli during his period of gestation are of an other-worldly nature. In the end he becomes a saint who performs the ḥadra. Such periods occur frequently in the lives of saints and mystics throughout the world. The extent to which the sexual ambivalence expressed in the legend is related among Moroccan Arabs to the saintly role, the trance, etc., merits examination.

[15] Up to this point the sequence of events is also equivalent to Sidi ʿAli's rebirth as a saint who can pass on his baraka.

man, and in a more disguised fashion the birth cycle of a woman. The male maturation process and the female birth cycle are thematically intertwined and appear to be combined in the "rebirth" of Sidi ʿAli as a saint who has contagious and heritable baraka.

From a psychological point of view, the legend is concerned with the problem of male identity. It is a symbolic portrayal of certain sexual conflicts and, if Bettelheim's (1955) theory of the envious male is correct, may indeed be expressive of the male's desire for female characteristics and potentialities. It may serve as a schema—or partial schema—for these conflicts or this envy. The male child must be impregnated—feminized—in order to become a man. The child who *actively* seeks his father's power (semen, virility, manhood—baraka, miraculous power, saintliness) must play a passive role before the father. Fenichel (1966:334) notes, in discussing the passive homosexual, that the feminine man, who having identified with the mother becomes anally fixated, is an analogous mechanism.

Actually, "feminine" men often have not entirely given up their striving to be masculine. Unconsciously they regard their femininity as temporary, as a means to an end; they regard the condition of being a masculine man's "feminine" partner as learning the secrets of masculinity from the "master," or depriving him of his secrets. In such cases, the passive submission to the father is combined with traits of an old and original (oral) love of the father. Every boy loves his father as a model whom he would like to resemble; he feels himself the "pupil" who, by temporary passivity, can achieve the ability to be active later on. This type of love can be called apprentice love; it is always ambivalent because its ultimate aim is to replace the master.

Not only does the legend suggest that at least some of the Ḥamadsha are suffering from problems of male identity, but the parallels between the mechanism outlined by Fenichel and the legend of Sidi ʿAli suggest further a passive homosexual attitude toward the father and an identification with the mother (possibly with anal fixation). It is, of course, not possible from the analysis of a legend to deduce a psychology; the legend may serve only as a clue.[16]

The resolution of a possible Oedipal conflict in terms of passive homosexuality is a dead end for the man anxious to have heirs (to

[16] I am, at this point, less interested in the psychological implications of the legend—the legend as projective material—than in its symbolic-interpretive function for the individual born into a society in which the Ḥamadsha, their ceremonies, and their beliefs are a given.

obtain and pass on baraka): no children can be produced. Sidi ʿAli never gives birth to Sidi Ahmed. "Someone came up to Sidi ʿAli. His name was Sidi Ahmed." Nor does he bear any children, in legend or in fact. The saint must become a man.[17] After a period of latency which culminates in a manly act, he is able not only to perform miracles—the most notable is his resistance to the beheader, the castrator, Moulay Ismaïl[18] (again, curiously, through ingestion, this time of oil)—but also to raise Sidi Ahmed and bequeath him his power.

From a sociological point of view, the legend is an attempt to resolve the conflict between two different endowments of baraka: institutionalized baraka, which is passed from father to son (and daughter), and personal baraka, which is inherent in the individual and is not heritable. Personal baraka is in many ways analogous to Weber's conception of charisma (Gerth and Mills 1958:245–252). This problem is of central importance in much of Moroccan history. Clifford Geertz (1968:45) has written:

> The problem of who has baraka was indeed in some ways the central theological problem (if that is not too elegant a word for an issue which rarely rose above the oral and practical) in classical Morocco. And to it two major classes of answers were given: what we may call the miraculous and the genealogical. Maraboutism, the possession of baraka, was indexed either by wonder-working, a reputation for causing unusual things to occur, or by supposed lineal descent from the Prophet. Or, as I say, by both. But though the two principles were often, after the seventeenth century perhaps most often, invoked together, they were yet separate principles, and in the tension between them can be seen reflected much of the dynamics of Moroccan culture history.

Despite Sidi ʿAli's spiritual genealogy (*silsila*), which is not mentioned in the legends, it appears that he is endowed with personal, or miraculous, baraka, but not with the institutionalized and heritable

[17] Dundes, Leach, and Özkök (1970) suggest in their analysis of Turkish verbal dueling that "the shift from the boy's female passive role [in homosexuality] to the man's male active role is an intrinsic part of the process of becoming an adult male." Although homosexuality is perhaps not as common in Morocco as in Turkey, it is by no means uncommon. There is considerable scorn for the adult male who plays the passive role. Adolescent boys who play the passive role are teased and are expected when they are older to assume the active role.

[18] Freud (1963:109) notes that repudiation of the feminine attitude is "a result of the struggle to avoid castration; it regularly finds its most emphatic expression in the contrasting fantasy of castrating the father and turning him into a woman." (Cf. Miner and De Vos [1960] for their findings on castration anxiety among Algerian peasants.)

kind. His trip to Buʿabid Sharqi—and the other saints—is an active attempt to obtain the latter. This is by definition impossible. A man can obtain the baraka of a saint, but this is not heritable. A resolution is attempted: Sidi ʿAli becomes as a woman and is impregnated with the saint's baraka. If, by some miracle, he were able to bear a son and found a lineage, the lineage would not be his own since a woman, according to the Moroccan Arabs, cannot pass on baraka (or any other traits). To become lineage head he must again become man, but then he cannot father children who will inherit his baraka, since his baraka is not of the institutionalized sort. Self-inflicted androgyny has its ideological limits.[19] It is an attempted resolution, as Lévi-Strauss (1963b) might suggest, between two polar opposites. Another resolution is attempted: the master adopts a pupil.

Before examining the legend of Sidi Ahmed, it should be pointed out that the legend also attempts to resolve a contradiction between baraka per se and baraka that is a symbol for mystical learning. The former can be passed on only agnatically; the latter can be passed on to any willing student, despite his origin.

The most striking difference between Sidi ʿAli's acquisition of baraka and Sidi Ahmed's is that the former *actively* seeks it and the latter *passively* receives it. The two methods of acquisition are mirror opposites. Sidi ʿAli, the active seeker, must become a woman and passively receive it; once he has received it, he becomes a man again. To obtain baraka passively, Sidi Ahmed must be a man—this is symbolized in the errands he runs for Sidi ʿAli, by the fact that his stomach does not swell when he drinks ʿAbdelḥaqq's buttermilk, and that he brings back a female demon from the Sudan; once he receives the baraka, he becomes a woman. He slashes his head. Head-slashing, here, is the symbolic equivalent of castration. That there has been a displacement from penis to head is suggested by the fact that *ras* refers to the glans of the penis as well as to the head.[20] This equivalence—penis = head—is not infrequently encountered in psychoanalysis, also (Freud 1941).

The episodes dealing with Sidi Ahmed are much less ambiguous than those concerned with Sidi ʿAli. (I exclude here the legends relating Sidi Ahmed to the canonists of Fez and to Moulay Ismaïl, which were not

[19] The failure of this resolution is masked by certain hints at rebirth. Sidi ʿAli becomes pregnant with Sharqi's baraka and gives birth to himself as a saint who is capable of passing on his baraka to his children. This theme is not developed.

[20] This interpretation is supported by material collected by free association and in Rorschach tests. These will be treated in the sequel to this work. I have no evidence for an equivalence between blood from head wounds and menstrual blood, as Bettelheim (1955) might suggest.

part of the legendary cycle related by Muqaddim Touijer but were told to me by the descendants of Sidi Ahmed.) Sidi Ahmed—whether the son of Sidi ʿAli or a stranger—is treated like a servant or slave. This is indicative of the subordinate relationship of son to father which is characteristic of Arab society. The errands Sidi Ahmed runs for his master are tests of his manhood. He must overcome ʿAbdelḥaqq, the son of Moulay Ismaïl, the beheader; then he must go to the Sudan to fetch the ḥal. He brings back a female demon, a woman—only to learn of his master's death, according to the most frequently heard version of the legend, and his legacy of baraka. The sequence to this point appears to mirror the maturation of the boy under the tutelage of the father. Then there is an odd twist. Once having inherited his father's power, the son castrates himself, at least symbolically, despite the admonitions of his companions.

"You are lucky to be alive," they said. "You are lucky to have children. The children will carry on your blood and your baraka. You must not be angry or sad. You will always have children. They will always replace you."

At the moment when Sidi Ahmed's (and Sidi ʿAli's) presumed desire to found a lineage carrying on his baraka has been fulfilled, he renders himself a woman, and women cannot pass on baraka. A woman is, in a sense, like a man with personal baraka; she cannot pass on her traits, and he cannot pass on his baraka.[21]

Psychologically, the legend again appears to be concerned with masculine identity. The son has not followed in his father's footsteps. Although he has obeyed his father's commands, including the preparation of bath-water, which is usually a female task, he has remained a man. There are no indications of a passive, homosexual attitude toward the father; however, there are hints of his dependence upon the father. Each time Sidi Ahmed goes off on a mission, it is Sidi ʿAli who saves him—whether from the hand of Moulay Ismaïl, after he has killed the famed beheader's son, or from the soldiers of the king of the Sudan, after he has stolen the king's instruments and his woman. At one level of analysis, the head-slashing appears to symbolize the son's inadequacy—his lack of independence—once the father has been eliminated; he rejects the masculine role, the role of head of a lineage possessed of

[21] The passage of baraka from Sidi ʿAli to Sidi Ahmed is not as well developed as that from Buʿabid Sharqi to Sidi ʿAli. The fact that Sidi Ahmed is not the son of Sidi ʿAli is not played up.

baraka. The "masculine protest"—to use Alfred Adler's expression—has been unsuccessful. He renders himself a woman—the sign of frailty, weakness, and inferiority—and thereby incapable of passing on baraka.[22]

From a sociological (and an ideological) point of view, the episode appears again—but less clearly—to be an attempt to resolve the dilemma of the saint who is possessed of personal but not institutionalized baraka (and an attempt to resolve the conflict between the passage of baraka per se and baraka as a symbol for mystical learning). Sidi Ahmed, who is not the real son of Sidi ʿAli, plays the role but must depend upon his father. When his master dies and bequeaths him his baraka, he is incapable of receiving it—he is after all not the son of Sidi ʿAli—even though he is capable of bearing children. He is compelled to make himself feminine—to castrate himself—in order to receive it. Then as a woman he cannot pass it on. The dilemma remains unresolved. Once again self-inflicted androgyny is not a satisfactory answer.

The legendary cycle appears to have two principal parts, each of which attempts to resolve certain psychological, sociological, and ideological problems. Psychologically they are concerned with the problem of male identity and, if Bettelheim is correct, even with the male envy of the female. Specifically they treat of the son's relationship with the father; they reflect alternative attitudes toward the father. The son may either play the passive role, as Sidi ʿAli did, and receive his father's power; or, as Sidi Ahmed did, he may withstand the temptation to submit to the father and find himself inadequate to the power that is eventually bequeathed him. Having resisted submission, he has, nevertheless, become dependent. It is suggested that both the passive role and

[22] The extreme mourning probably reflects as well the ambivalence that the son felt for the father. As Freud (1963:106) notes: "The more ambivalent the relation has been, the more likely is the grief for the father's loss to turn into melancholia."

It is perhaps possible to argue that Sidi Ahmed slashes himself because he feels that bringing back ʿAïsha Qandisha is somehow responsible for Sidi ʿAli's death. Sidi ʿAli did not ask him to bring back ʿAïsha; he asked him to bring back the ḥal. ʿAïsha may be seen as a potential wife or as a mother; she is sometimes referred to as Sidi ʿAli's servant. This suggests to the psychoanalytically oriented that Sidi Ahmed's trip to the Sudan to fetch the ḥal involved intercourse with his mother. The trance state may be symbolic of intercourse. This intercourse may have been held responsible for his father's death. Head-slashing results—if this argument is pursued—from the guilt or remorse the son feels for having caused his father's death by sleeping with his mother.

It may even be argued—and such an argument would help to explain the curative value of head-slashing—that the mutilation libidinizes the head-penis and thereby renders the son (the patient) potent, virile, a man (cf. Bettelheim 1955: 81–82).

the dependency-inadequacy role of the son are symbolized *regardless of their genesis* in terms of woman. The female is stereotyped as frail, weak, inadequate, untrustworthy, and inferior by Moroccan Arabs, and as such she represents such self-feelings in the man. The therapeutic process will involve, as we shall see, an attempt to realize these feelings symbolically. It is a period of organized regression in which the individual symbolically plays out his female identity in order to become a man once more.

Sociologically, the legend attempts to resolve the problem of acquiring baraka which is inheritable from someone from whom one is not descended. In broader terms, it is the problem inherent in the Arabs' extreme agnatic principles. The son can acquire only what the father possesses; the mother can pass nothing on.[23] Self-inflicted androgyny is an attempted but, in the final analysis, unsatisfactory answer to the dilemma. Ideologically, the legends attempt again, through the symbol of androgyny, to resolve the conflict between institutionalized baraka, which can only be passed on agnatically, and baraka as a symbol for mystical learning, which can be conveyed to anyone who is willing to receive it.

Since baraka is the curative substance *par excellence*, it has been necessary to follow out these different levels of analysis in order to come to some understanding of its logic. At the same time, it has given us a means of considering how the problems of baraka transference are reflections of possible underlying psychological conflicts. It is suggested that such conflicts would be symbolized and worked through, at least for the Ḥamadsha, in terms of the logic of baraka and the other motifs in the legendary cycle.

[23] The lack of a well-developed mother figure in the legends is indicative of this. As a symbol of weakness, a woman is not able to mediate, ideologically at least, the son's relationship with the father. (Compare Lévi-Strauss' analysis [1956b] of the Oedipal myth.)

PART TWO

The following four chapters deal with the social and economic organization of the Ḥamadsha in three settings: the villages of Beni Rachid and Beni Ouarad, the madina of Meknes, and the shantytowns, especially Sidi Baba, of the same city. My discussion in Chapter Three of Beni Rachid and Beni Ouarad is, strictly speaking, concerned less with the Ḥamadsha as members of a religious brotherhood than with the descendants of Sidi ʿAli and Sidi Ahmed, who may or may not be members of a Ḥamadsha team but who are, by virtue of their birth, intimately related to the Ḥamadsha brotherhoods. In anthropological terms, membership in the *wulad siyyid* is ascribed and in the Ḥamadsha brotherhoods achieved. Only those aspects of the life and organization of the wulad sayyid which have a bearing on the Ḥamadsha complex are covered.

Attention is then given to the relationship of the saints' descendants both to the cult of their ancestors and to the brotherhoods. Examination of both of these relationships in the last chapter of this section, on social organization, involves an analysis of the passage of baraka and the passage of wealth, which complement and reinforce each other.

4

The Saints' Villages

The tombs of Sidi ʿAli ben Ḥamdush and Sidi Ahmed Dghughi are located, respectively, in the two neighboring villages of Beni Rachid and Beni Ouarad, on the south face of the Jebel Zerhoun. The Zerhoun itself is an irregular massif, covering an area of a little more than a hundred square miles and extending from the plains of the Oued Sejra, on the south, which separate it from the plateau of Meknes, to the Zaggota Pass and the Middle Sebou on the north; it lies west of Fez. The massif rises dramatically, like a giant bulwark, out of the rich Sais wheat and barley plains, to an altitude of 3,671 feet. Still wooded with holm-oak on its crest, it contrasts sharply with the characteristic plains and rolling hills of the area, which are often cultivated to their summits, and it is considered by both Moroccans and Europeans as one of the most beautiful mountains in the country (Boulanger 1966:232; ben Talha 1965:7; Herber 1923). The population of the Zerhoun has settled on the periphery of the mountain, and its wide crest has remained more or less uninhabited. Both the people of the south slope, who are primarily Arabized Sanhaja, and the people of the north slope, who tend to be of Rifian origin, live in clay-block (or sometimes stone) houses which are covered with terraced roofs of beaten earth.

The Zerhoun is said to produce the best olives in Morocco, and the sides of the mountain, particularly on the richer, south side, are covered with olive trees wherever there is sufficient soil for them to take root. The cellars of the larger houses in many of the villages—there are six principal villages on the south face alone—are equipped with oil presses resembling the presses found in the nearby Roman ruins of Volubilis, locally called the Pharaoh's Palace. The trees may be individually or collectively owned, worked by their owner or one of his hired hands, or rented out by individual agreement or to the best bidder in a village auction. Although occasional fig, carob, citrus, and other fruit trees can be found in the vicinity of the villages, the olive is the mountain's principal economic resource. (Prickly pears, which grow in the drier, rockier gorges and gullies, are also sold.) Many of the villagers, however, also own, or at least work, fields in the plains; they store their wheat and barley in underground granaries. There are also kitchen gardens, and many families have a few sheep, or even a cow, grazed by a son, grandson, or hired hand. The villages on the south face of the Zerhoun, like Beni Rachid and Beni Ouarad, are economically oriented to Meknes; those on the north face to Moulay Idriss, and to a lesser extent Fez.

Although the Zerhoun, located as it is between the imperial cities of Meknes and Fez, has long been part of the *blad l-makhzan,* or region under central government control and taxation, it has traditionally been a refuge for victims of war and famine, such as the Rifian Berbers who settled on the north face. The refugees were attracted to the mountain not only because of its strong defensive position but also because of its agricultural potential and its opportunities for work. They were drawn, too, by its sanctity, for the Zerhoun, accommodating the tombs not only of Sidi ʿAli and Sidi Ahmed but also of Morocco's "national saint," Moulay Idriss, and many lesser saints of merely local importance, is considered a sacred mountain, and its inhabitants are famed for and proud of their piety.[1] These migrations to the mountain have produced a heterogeneous population, both with respect to the Zerhoun as a whole and within many of the villages themselves. This is especially true of Beni Rachid and Beni Ouarad.

In the years immediately preceding the arrival of the French in Morocco in 1912, the Zerhoun was divided into two administrative units, one for the north, centered in Moulay Idriss, and the other for the south, centered in El Merhasiyne. Each district was headed by a

[1] They are proud of the fact that there are no Jews or Christians on the Zerhoun and that, despite the unusual number of pilgrimage centers, there are no prostitutes. Prostitutes have tended to gravitate to active pilgrimage centers like Moulay Brahim and Sidi Raḥal near Marrakech, and the baths of Moulay Yacoub near Fez and Sidi Sliman Mula l-Kifan near Meknes. It is said that the authorities will not touch them in the sacred area of the sanctuary. Ironically, the two baths are visited by those suffering from venereal diseases.

caid, or local administrator, who was responsible to the central government, and each village was headed by a muqaddim. The muqaddims of Beni Rachid and Beni Ouarad were responsible to the caid of El Merhasiyne; they were members of the saintly families but were not the leaders (*mizwars*) of these families. From what I have been able to gather from the older peasants, the traditional Moroccan Arab council of elders (*jmaʿ*) was of little importance in the two saintly villages even in the pre-Protectorate days, and village life was dominated, as it is today, by the leaders of the saints' children.

The French maintained this arrangement for some time after their arrival, but they eventually simplified it by placing a single muqaddim at the head of not one but three villages. Significantly, the muqaddim charged with Beni Rachid, himself a resident of the village and a descendant of Sidi ʿAli as well as brother-in-law to the caid of El Merhasiyne, was not charged with the administration of Sidi Ahmed's village of Beni Ouarad but with two other neighboring villages. This administrative separation probably resulted from the hostility and competition which has existed between the two villages for many years and which is, as we will see, dramatically portrayed during the annual pilgrimages to the saints' tombs.

Since Moroccan independence in 1956, a single caid has been responsible for the entire Zerhoun; his headquarters are in the town of Moulay Idriss. Moulay Idriss, however, falls under the separate charge of a pasha rather than under the jurisdiction of the Zerhoun caid. Beni Rachid and Beni Ouarad are under the more direct control of a sheikh, subordinate to the caid, who lives in the village of Hamraoua. (The former caid of El Merhasiyne lives in exile in France.) The villages still have different muqaddims, but the muqaddim of Beni Rachid is no longer a resident of the village or a descendant of its saint.

Beni Rachid and Beni Ouarad

Both Beni Rachid and Beni Ouarad, like the other villages on the south slope of the Zerhoun, are comparatively wealthy by rural Moroccan standards. Beni Rachid, which is much richer than Beni Ouarad, is located about a mile farther down the El Merhasiyne–Moulay Idriss road and is separated from Beni Ouarad by the hamlet of Qelaa, where some of Sidi ʿAli's descendants live. A narrow, winding path, frequented by pilgrims to the saints, joins the three villages. The houses of Beni Rachid are clustered on top of a rocky mamelon and are often supported by the walls of an old *kasba* (fortress), now in ruins, which is said to have belonged to one of Moulay Ismaïl's qaids, or pashas, called bel Shaqur. The villagers maintain that bel Shaqur, like his sultan, was notorious for his extreme cruelty and was finally flogged to death by the peasants of the nearby village of Beni Jennad after demanding the right of the first night from their virgins.[2] His kasba, they insist, was at least twenty kilometers in circumference; and although this is an obvious exaggeration, the kasba must have been an impressively large structure, since many of the houses of Beni Rachid lie within its confines. This gives the village a very tight, concentric look which contrasts with the narrow, elongated appearance of Beni Ouarad.

Sidi ʿAli's mausoleum, just above the basin and baths of the ʿAyn Kabir, runs lengthwise on a sort of land bridge that joins the mamelon of the village on the west with the Qelaa ridge on the east. It is one of the largest mausoleums in the country, measuring some 150 feet in length. The tomb, which forms an almost perfect square about 45 feet on each side, is located at the western end of the mausoleum complex and is covered by a hexagonal roof of glazed green tile. (Most of the qubbas in which Moroccan saints are buried are square with domed roofs.) An open rectangular court, about 110 feet by 45 feet, extends eastward from the tomb. One enters the court from the south and the tomb from the courtyard. Along the interior walls of the court there are little cubicles built by Sidi ʿAli's children for pilgrims who wish to spend the night, but these cubicles are not very popular. They are infested with fleas, ticks, and lice, and the pilgrims prefer to battle the insects in the sanctity of the tomb itself, where they can garner more of the saint's baraka. Sidi ʿAli lies parallel to the western wall of the mausoleum. His face is turned toward Mecca, and he is covered with a catafalque (*darbuz*) which consists of a simple wooden frame, covered with several layers of red, yellow, and white cloth (*ghota; kaswa;* or, if made only of cotton, *izar*). An alms box stands next to the door of the tomb room. At the southeastern corner of the complex is a yellow and white minaret, next to a more traditional qubba in which Sidi ʿAli's disciple—some say his son and others his brother from whom the children of the saint are, in fact, descended—Sidi l-Ḥafyan, the barefoot saint, is buried. The entire complex, which is usually referred to as the *siyyid*, has been under restoration for the past few years. The courtyard has been added, and the buildings have been plastered and whitewashed. The mizwar, who is responsible for the building,

[2] There are no legends relating bel Shaqur to either Ḥamadsha saint.

plans to tile the court, put a fountain in the middle, and illuminate the whole complex when electricity finally comes to Beni Rachid.

Although there are several other saints buried in Beni Rachid—the most notable is Sidi Musa, from whom many of the villagers claim descent—they do not play a significant role in the cult to Sidi ʿAli.[3] The ʿAyn Kabir and a grotto to ʿAïsha Qandisha are, however, important pilgrim stops. The waters of the ʿAyn Kabir flow from the rocky wall of the land bridge on which Sidi ʿAli's tomb is located. They are considered to contain much baraka, and are valued for their therapeutic effects. A few years ago the descendants of Sidi ʿAli attempted to build a basin for the water but, as the basin cracked open every time they completed it, they decided that Sidi ʿAli did not wish to have his sacred waters confined, and they abandoned the project. The water now drips down a stairway to the three-roomed, clay-block bathhouse which the saint's descendants built at the same time they tried to build the basin. They charge pilgrims an admission of 50 francs (or 100 francs during the musem) a bath.[4]

The grotto (*ḥufra*) to ʿAïsha Qandisha lies a few hundred yards east of the village proper. It is banked on one side by the root system of an enormous fig tree, which towers over it and is considered extremely powerful by local peasants who graft its branches onto their own young trees to make them fruitful. The grotto itself consists of two small hollows. In the larger outer hollow, the roots of the fig tree are tied with rags and ribbons and other bits of cloth which have been left by pilgrim women as a sign of a vow (*ʿar*) to sacrifice something, usually a black chicken, to ʿAïsha Qandisha if she grants them their wishes. The inner cavity, where an underground stream trickles to the surface, is dark and muddy. It is here that ʿAïsha is said to reside.[5]

The mausoleum of Sidi Ahmed, which is located at the end of the main road that separates the larger houses of the wealthy villagers on the south from the smaller houses of the poor on the north, is much smaller than Sidi ʿAli's tomb and, unlike it, is structurally integrated with the houses of Beni Ouarad. Not only does the house of the former mizwar actually share a wall with the mausoleum, but the square in front of the tomb is the scene of most village activity. Although Sidi Ahmed's descendants claim that their ancestor's tomb is

[3] There are no legends relating them to either Sidi ʿAli or Sidi Ahmed.

[4] There are 100 francs to the dirham. A dirham was worth 20 American cents at the time of my investigation.

[5] I have heard ʿAïsha's grotto called the fish spring (*l-ʿayn l-ḥut*) by women. It should be noted that *ʿayn* may mean both a spring and an eye. Fish are associated with other sanctuaries in Morocco.

also undergoing renovation, there are no signs of work, with the possible exception of a few dabs of whitewash around the "keyhole arch" door. The tomb itself, which can only be reached through the courtyard, is located to the northwest of the courtyard and is oriented from northeast to southwest. In the corner of the courtyard is a small hole, filled with muddy earth, which is called ʿAïsha's pit (*ḥufra*) because ʿAïsha Qandisha is said to appear there from time to time, especially when ecstatic dances are performed in front of the tomb. Sidi Ahmed's descendants are very sensitive about this pit, because it does not compare either in size or lucrativeness to ʿAïsha's grotto at Beni Rachid. They believe that since their ancestor brought ʿAïsha to the Zerhoun, they should obtain a share of the profits from the grotto, but the descendants of Sidi ʿAli have never agreed with them.

Population and Social Organization

The two villages of Beni Rachid and Beni Ouarad are about the same size. Beni Rachid, according to the census of 1960, has a population of 500 (89 households), of whom about 300 claim descent from Sidi ʿAli. Beni Ouarad, according to the same census, has 604 inhabitants (140 households), 200 said to be the children of Sidi Ahmed. Although the saints' descendants account for only 60% of the population of Beni Rachid and 30% of Beni Ouarad, they dominate village life both economically and politically and are treated with a mixture of respect and resentment by the other villagers. There are almost no marriages between the descendants of the two saints. Of 146 marriages recorded for the children of Sidi Ahmed, only two took place with inhabitants of Beni Rachid, and only one of these with a descendant of Sidi ʿAli. Although over 50% of the marriages recorded were with spouses from outside the village, and about 23% with inhabitants of other villages on the Zerhoun,[6] it appears that there is a great reluctance to form unions not only with the descendants of Sidi ʿAli but with any inhabitants of Beni Rachid. Despite the traditional Arab preference for parallel-cousin marriage, only two parallel-cousin marriages were recorded for Sidi Ahmed's children. And in spite of the obvious economic advantages of marrying a descendant of the saint—the saint's children receive a share of the proceeds from the saint's tomb and of the gifts of the brotherhood—only 20% of the marriages in the last four genera-

[6] It should be noted that no marriages with inhabitants of Qelaa and Beni Jennad, the next closest villages, were recorded. Qelaa is dominated by the descendants of Sidi ʿAli.

tions were endogamous.[7] Although my figures are not complete for Sidi ʿAli's children, who were quite resistant as informants, a similar pattern is discernible in even my fragmentary data. There are considerable differences in wealth and political influence among the descendants of each saint, but the children of Sidi ʿAli appear, on the whole, to be wealthier than those of Sidi Ahmed.

The descendants of Sidi ʿAli and Sidi Ahmed follow, at least ideally, the traditional model of segmentary society characteristic of the Arab Bedouin (Peters 1960; Evans-Pritchard 1949:29–61), and they are divided into agnatic lineages whose members orient themselves to a significant ancestor and refer to themselves as the children (*wulad*) of that ancestor. The particular ancestor chosen depends on the particular segment of the group the speaker wishes to call on and on what is demanded by the particular circumstances at hand. Since the descendants of both saints live, and have lived for hundreds of years, under central government authority, the corporate strength of the descent groups has been greatly—but not completely—reduced to the field of domestic relations (cf. Fortes 1953). The division of proceeds from the saints' tombs (*futuḥat*), the religious brotherhoods, and the saints' properties (*ḥabus*), as well as the administrative function of the mizwars as the heads of each of these saintly lineages and the brotherhoods, has preserved the corporate structure of the groups to an extent which is not apparent among the other inhabitants of the Zerhoun.[8]

The most distant ancestor, encompassing the largest descent group capable of joint action, to which the descendants of either saint make reference is either Sidi ʿAli or Sidi Ahmed. (Both descent groups appear to have no affiliation with any larger clan or tribal groups.)

[7] It is theoretically possible to argue that the high frequency of exogamous marriages resulted from the saintly children's desire to increase their political support. Given the complexities of political power within the saintly lineages and within the village itself, this seems unlikely. A better argument is that nonsaintly families are willing to accept smaller bride-prices and give larger ones for the prestige of marrying into a saintly family.

[8] "A group may be spoken of as 'corporate' when it possesses any one of a certain number of characters: if its members, or its adult male members, or a considerable proportion of them, come together occasionally to carry out some collective action—for example, the performance of rites; if it has a chief or council who are regarded as acting as the representative of the group as a whole; if it possesses or controls property which is collective, as when a clan or lineage is a land-owning group" (Radcliffe-Brown 1962:41). The descendants of the Ḥamadsha saints score on each count: they come together during the annual pilgrimage and for the division of proceeds; they have a chief, the mizwar; and they hold ḥabus lands in common.

Generally, they refer to themselves and are referred to as *wulad siyyid*, the children of the saint, when they wish to distinguish themselves from, say, the other villagers, or *wulad Sidi ʿAli* or *wulad Sidi Ahmed* when they wish to distinguish themselves from the descendants of another saint. Since every member of the wulad siyyid is at least theoretically capable of tracing his genealogical connection with every other member of the group from a known ancestor, the wulad sayyid is then, in anthropological terms, a maximal lineage (cf. Radcliffe-Brown 1962:39). The mizwar is the leader of the wulad siyyid, as well as of smaller lineage segments within it; and the permanence of his position, which is chartered by the "extra-familial hand" of the King as representative of the central government and the Moroccan nation, tends to give the group a more stable character than is usually found in "pure" segmentary systems. Even among the smaller segments of the wulad siyyid, there is a similar tendency toward permanency. The particular segments which play a decisive role in the lives of the saint's descendants are those concerned with the division of proceeds from the saint and the brotherhood. It is these that have more or less congealed.

All men, women, and children who are agnatically descended from either Sidi ʿAli or Sidi Ahmed are eligible for an equal share in the proceeds from the saint's complex and the associated brotherhood. The proceeds from the former include the alms, candles, sacrificial animals, and other gifts left by pilgrims at the saint's tomb or for ʿAïsha Qandisha, as well as the fees from the baths in the case of Sidi ʿAli's descendants. Profits from the ḥabus lands—lands donated to the saint by pious Muslims who are anxious to obtain by their good deeds much baraka and, thereby, easy entrance to heaven—are also divided. The teams associated with each saint are required to bring large gifts—theoretically all that they have received in the form of gifts and fees throughout the year—to their mizwar at the time of the musem. These, too, are traditionally divided among the saint's descendants.[9]

[9] A distinction is usually made between alms (*futuḥat*) left by pilgrims and the revenues of the sanctuary's ḥabus properties. The former are most often divided among the saint's descendants; their manner of distribution lies ultimately in the hands of the King. Revenue from the ḥabus properties is supervised by an official overseer (*nadir*). Conflicts concerning the distribution of alms were to be decided in the last instance by a decree from the King; those concerning ḥabus revenues by the religious courts (Anonymous 1927?). Such legal niceties were not generally recognized by the wulad sayyid at either Beni Rachid or Beni Ouarad. They claimed that not only alms but ḥabus revenues and revenues from the zawiyas and teams were traditionally evenly divided among them, and ought still to be so divided.

Among the descendants of Sidi ʿAli, there are four major lineages, each claiming descent from one of Sidi ʿAli's four supposed sons, which have traditionally played a role in this division. A single respected elder from each was always present at the division, which took place in the confines (*ḥorm*) of the saint's tomb. He received the shares set aside for his lineage and distributed them. Although the presence of the elders in the sanctuary assured each lineage of its proper share—barring of course collusion, which was unlikely in the sacred precincts (*ḥorm*) of the mausoleum—there was no institutionalized safeguard against cheating individuals, or individual family heads, within each lineage, and this gave rise to a great deal more suspicion and mistrust among the saint's descendants than probably occurred in most Moroccan Arab villages.[10]

To what extent this is a realistic portrayal of the division at Beni Rachid is impossible to determine, for the system has not been operative for several years. Judging from the complexities of the lineage structure among the descendants of Sidi Ahmed, about which my data are much more complete, it seems unlikely that the lineage structure was this simple or that it accounted, as I have been told again and again, for all of the children of Sidi ʿAli. The mizwar, assured of his position both by his wealth and by outside (government) authority, has not divided the proceeds from the saint's tomb in several years, but has claimed to have used them for the restoration of the mausoleum. This has given rise to even more suspicion and resentment among Sidi ʿAli's children, who do not feel that they were properly consulted and do not believe that the progress of restoration is in any way commensurate with the expenses claimed. Rumor has it that the mizwar pockets most of the proceeds and pays out the rest to the more influential of his relatives. Thus the major lineages, which had traditionally played an important role in the division, have lost their principal function. Still, when asked, the villagers assured me that the division took place in the prescribed way until very recently and that it will again take place as soon as the renovation is completed (or there is a change of mizwar).

The lineage organization of the descendants of Sidi Ahmed, which is diagrammed in Figure 1, is more complex. The lineages do not play as decisive a role in the division of proceeds as is alleged for the major lineages of the wulad Sidi ʿAli. Division is organized here

[10] Such suspicion and mistrust is probably characteristic of the descendants of other saints as well. It was, for example, very noticeable among the "children" of Moulay Brahim.

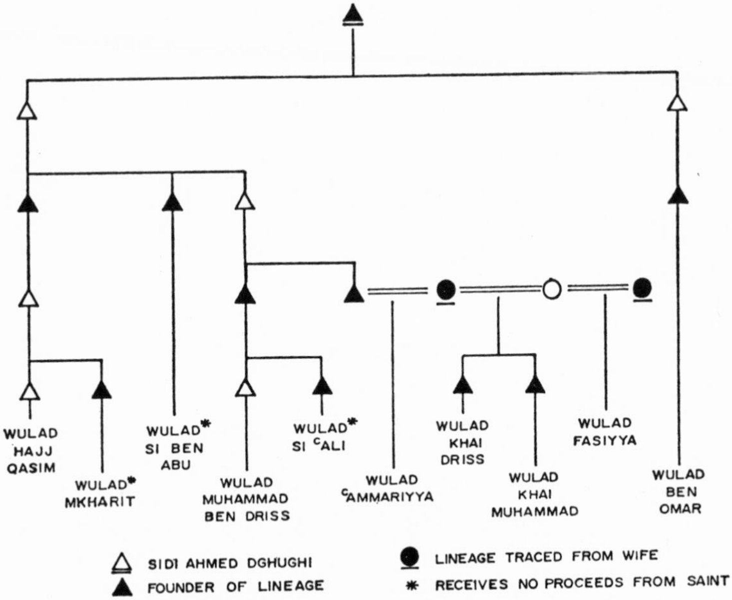

Figure 1. The lineages of the wulad Sidi Ahmed Dghughi

quite differently, and operates on chance. Each of the agnatic descendants of Sidi Ahmed—man, woman, and child—who qualifies for a share is in charge of the sanctuary for a day and receives all of the proceeds of the day with the exception of a bull, which is divided equally among the saint's descendants.[11] Rotation stops for the very active month preceding and including the musem; all of the proceeds for this month go to the mizwar, who uses them for preparing for and entertaining at the pilgrimage. The role of the lineages is limited then to the division of gifts from the brotherhoods (and whatever remains from the month of the museum). This division takes place not in the mausoleum but in the mizwar's house.

Among the ten lineages we find that three do not receive a share because they are said not to be "true" children of Sidi Ahmed. The members of two of these are no longer residents at Beni Ouarad. Of the remaining seven lineages, one is virtually defunct, having one last member, an old woman, who receives her share but does not participate in the division. Elders from only four of the other six lineages

[11] There are no special rules for butchering. The meat is distributed without reference to cut.

have supervised the sharing: wulad Hajj Qasim, wulad ʿAmmariyya, wulad Fasiyya (of whom the present mizwar is a member), and wulad khai Driss (who may have represented wulad khai Muhammud as well). The wulad Muhammud ben Driss, one of the largest, has not been represented recently but has received a share. It is from this lineage that the mizwars came before the position was preempted for his son by the father of the present mizwar, who was the wealthiest, most influential man in the village.

It must be emphasized that representation does not follow a hard and fast rule but depends more on local politics. The wealthiest and most influential elders, regardless of lineage affiliation, are chosen. There is a tendency for these elders to represent different lineages—which may be structurally justified by the fact that the largest possible number of descendants are, thereby, represented and appeased—but this is not always the case. The division the year before I made this study was supervised by two elders from the wulad Fasiyya and by representatives of the wulad Hajj Qasim and the wulad ʿAmmariyya. It appears that among the descendants of Sidi Ahmed, the lineage structure does not operate in terms of balancing opposing groups of equal size and status, as such segmentary systems are said classically to operate, but in terms of local political considerations. This probably results from the fact that the authority of the mizwar rests on his wealth and his influence with the outside world, and it has tended to render the structural balance of power ineffective, if indeed it ever was effective in a world as open to outside influence as that of Beni Ouarad.

The Mizwar

The mizwar of each of the saint's families is in complete control of the affairs of the saint's complex and is considered to have a greater endowment of baraka than the other of the saint's descendants, although the descendants themselves and the most pious of the followers do not make this assertion straightforwardly. Not only is the mizwar charged with the care and maintenance of the saint's tomb and associated cults, but he is the leader of all of the teams that claim to be followers of his ancestor. He also administers all ḥabus lands. Although his powers are officially limited to his descent group, where he serves as an arbiter in the case of disputes, he is in fact in control of the village because of his position as mizwar, his wealth, and his influence with the government.

The mizwar's political powers outside his maximal lineage and the village are restricted. Although he is charged with the administration of a network of lodges found in all of the principal cities of northern Morocco and in many rural areas as well, he does not have under his control a politically significant organization from either a formal (institutionalized) or informal point of view. The adepts were, and still are, without political influence. Moreover, the saintly families, unlike those of other similar complexes like the Ihansalen of the central High Atlas (Gellner 1963), have played almost no institutionalized political role in the surrounding tribal and village groups. This may be accounted for on two grounds. First, the descendants of Sidi ʿAli and Sidi Ahmed have lived in the center of the blad l-makhzan and have been subjected to the central authority of the sultanate from the time of the death of their saintly ancestors. Second, the tombs of Sidi ʿAli and Sidi Ahmed are located within the sphere of influence of the greater saint, Moulay Idriss. Thus, even asylum in the sacred confines of the mausoleum—asylum could be sought, as in the Christian churches of Europe, in many of the saints' tombs of Morocco (LeTourneau 1949:600)—was seldom preferred to that of Moulay Idriss, whose descendants had much more influence with the central government than those of either Sidi ʿAli or Sidi Ahmed.

There are no explicit rules for succession to the "mizwarship." All that is required is a testimonial letter signed by twelve of the saint's descendants, which is then presented to the government for ultimate approval by the King. Among the descendants of Sidi ʿAli, three elders from each of the four major lineages were said to have approved the choice of mizwar; among the descendants of Sidi Ahmed, the situation was more complicated. The mizwarship has tended to pass from father to son in both groups, however, and any break in this pattern is considered by both the saint's descendants and followers and by other villagers as a break with tradition (*qaïda*) which will incur the saint's disapproval. When Taik, the former mizwar of Sidi ʿAli, died, for example, he left a son and several grandsons. All of them were eligible for the mizwarship theoretically, but the present mizwar, Taik's younger brother, who was wealthier than Taik and had more influence with the government than his brother's sons and grandsons, obtained the position for himself by paying off twelve elders to witness his appointment. He was able then to obtain—at a price, it is usually claimed—a letter of charter from the King which insured his appointment. The fact that despite three marriages he had only a single son who was born before he became mizwar was taken by the villagers as a sure sign of Sidi ʿAli's disapproval, and it was not until he "arranged matters" by marrying his son to Taik's granddaughter that Sidi ʿAli's "approval" was gained. The mizwar then married still another woman and had six children by her.

The Endowment of Baraka

All of the men, women, and children who are descended through the male line from either Sidi ʿAli or Sidi Ahmed are endowed from birth with their ancestor's baraka. It is necessary once again to distinguish between the two different endowments of baraka: institutionalized and personal baraka. The former results from the status of the individual, and the latter from his personal merit. As agnatic descendants of a saint, all of the children of the saint are institutionally endowed with baraka, without regard to their personal merit. It is asserted, however, that as descendants they must *necessarily* be endowed with the qualities that are said to be in keeping with the possession of baraka. This baraka can never be lost. The second type of baraka, the personally achieved, depends not upon an individual's heritage but upon his character, his piety and spirituality, his moral fiber and his therapeutic gifts—in short, upon that "vividness" of which Geertz writes.

Although all of the agnatic descendants of the saints are possessed of baraka—their institutional endowment—some are considered to have more baraka than others. This greater endowment may also be institutionalized, as in the case of the mizwar, or achieved, as in the case of certain elders who by virtue of their personal qualities are said to have a lot of baraka. (Old people are generally said to have baraka.) The latter, since they are approachable, are often sought after by pilgrims for cures. The mizwars themselves usually keep a certain distance from the run-of-the-mill pilgrims, in keeping with their highly esteemed position. This distance not only safeguards their authority, but it also preserves their institutionalized endowment of baraka from any dilution by their lack of personal baraka.

Endowed from birth with their ancestor's baraka, the descendants of the saint have no need for any special ceremonies by which their endowment is made manifest or confirmed. Their attitude toward their ancestor is not qualitatively different from that of other Moroccans to the saint, except insofar as they regard him as an economic boon. They follow all of the religious practices of the average Moroccan of the Zerhoun (cf. ben Talha 1965), but invite the local team to perform at their name-day celebrations, circumcisions, and other life-crisis ceremonies more often than do the other inhabitants of the massif. They recite communal prayers in the mausoleum on the night of the twenty-seventh of Ramadan (*Lilat l-qadar*). They follow essentially the same procedures as other pilgrims when they visit their ancestor's tomb, but they do not give any alms.

Some of the saint's descendants belong to the local Ḥamadsha team, whose members are recruited primarily from the other villagers. Others, like the mizwars and the wealthier descendants, never participate in any of the team's dances and treat their activities with a mixture of scorn and respect. The teams of both villages, which are very loosely organized and poorly led, are rife with jealousy and factionalism. Members who are descended from the saint believe they should receive all of the proceeds; the other members believe that the proceeds should be shared equally; and the saint's descendants who are not team members think that all of the proceeds should be placed in the alms box and shared equally among them. Although some of the children of the saint do fall into trance and slash their heads, they categorically deny—and so do their pious followers—that this has ever occurred. They cite a proverb which may be roughly translated: "If a child of the saint falls into ecstasy, the followers of the saint will fall out of ecstasy." This proverb not only emphasizes the social differentiation between the children of the saint and the followers, but it also suggests that there may in fact be a qualitative difference between the children's endowment of baraka, which does not enable them to trance and slash, and the followers' endowment, which is the enabling factor.

5

The Lodges of Meknes

Within the city of Meknes the Ḥamadsha fall into two principal categories: those who are associated with one of the two lodges of the old town, or *madina*, and those who are affiliated with teams that have no special meeting place. Although the majority of teams are found in the bidonvilles that surround the city, there are a number of madina inhabitants, usually recent immigrants to the city like their confreres in the shantytowns, who are affiliated with them. This chapter deals with the Ḥamadsha who are associated with the two lodges, or *zawiya*s, of Meknes. They may be divided into the adepts (*foqra*), who are members of the lodges; the devotees (*muḥibbin*); and the *ghiyyata*, or oboe players. The members of one of these zawiyas are followers of Sidi ʿAli and are called *ʿAllaliyyin;* the members of the other are followers of Sidi Ahmed and are called *Dghughiyyin.*[1]

The City of Meknes

The city of Meknes is set between the Zerhoun massif on the north and plateaus on the south which extend down to the Middle Atlas and are populated primarily by Berbers. It lies on the great caravan route, the *tariq s-sultan*, that joined Algeria and other Islamic lands to the

[1] The distinction between the zawiyas whose members follow one or the other saint does not exist in all Moroccan cities. In some cities there is only one zawiya, and followers of both saints attend it; in other cities, like Marrakech, membership in the two zawiyas is mixed. The two lodges there are linked to rival quarters rather than to any one saint. Even in Meknes, many of the adepts of one lodge have transferred to the other.

east with the rich Atlantic plains of northern Morocco. These plains had been settled by Hilalian Arabs in the eleventh and twelfth centuries, and Meknes may be considered a sort of border town between Arab and Berber worlds. It is located about 35 miles from the imperial city of Fez, and with the exception of the long reign of Moulay Ismaïl (1672–1727), when the city was in its prime, it has been overshadowed both intellectually and politically by the great university city.

Originally a series of small villages, Meknes was first consolidated by the Almoravid sultan Yussef ben Tashfin in the second half of the eleventh century; but it was not until Moulay Ismaïl transferred his capital to Meknes in the seventeenth century that the city became internationally famous. Moulay Ismaïl, builder with grandiose aspirations, was determined to have *his* city outshine the cities of Fez and Marrakech, both of which he despised because of their resistance to his power. He personally supervised the work of about 2,000 Christian captives, 30,000 common criminals, and countless black African slaves who built his palaces, gardens, military quarters, and kasbas, and the more than fifteen miles of walls which surrounded the city (Julien 1966(II):237). The eighteenth-century English traveler John Windus (1725:115–116) has written:

> The Emperor is wonderfully addicted to Building; yet it is a question whether he is more addicted to that, or pulling down, for they say if all his Buildings were now standing, by a moderate computation, they would reach to Fez, twelve Leagues off; And those who have been near him since the beginning of his Reign, have observed him eternally building and pulling down, shutting up Doors and breaking out new ones in the Walls. But he tells them this is done to occupy his People; for says he, if I have a Bag full of Ratts, unless I keep that Bag stirring they will eat their way through; but he does not design to give them time.

It must be remembered that it was during the reign of Moulay Ismaïl that Sidi ʿAli lived and the Ḥamadsha first appeared. After the Sultan's death, Meknes declined rapidly; but it did retain its general plan until the French arrival in the beginning of this century.

The French made Meknes their principal military garrison, and the city soon developed into an agricultural center. The appearance of garages, retailers in trucks and farming equipment, canning and bottling factories, transportation and trucking services, pharmacies and moving picture theaters, had, however, only a gradual influence on the madina. Certainly the greater demand for madina products, both by Europeans and Moroccans, had its effect; but the tanners and coppersmiths, the enamelers specializing in the grey-black Meknes enamelware, the tile- and brick-makers, and the other artisans, continued their age-old manufacturing practices and went about their business as they always had. Although the French changed the bureaucratic structure of the city, this too had but little effect upon the average madina Arab, who retained his traditional dislike of dealings with the government. Even today, more than fifty years since the French first arrived in Morocco, madina life in Meknes is much as it was in pre-Protectorate days.

The contrast between these two economies and two life styles is illustrated by the contrast between the madina on the northern ridge of the Boufkrane and the new quarter, built by the French on the site of Moulay Ismaïl's olive groves on the southern ridge. The Hamriya, as the new quarter came to be known, followed the plan of the traditional French city, with broad, tree-lined avenues, carrefours, and modern, windowed houses and apartments. The madina followed the plan of the Muslim city, with its narrow, winding streets and twisted alleys, its specialized markets, and its ethnically-oriented residential quarters with windowless houses, all radiating out from the Friday mosque and central market (von Grunebaum 1955:154 et seq.). In the case of Meknes, the streets have been laid out according to the *qibla*, the orientation toward Mecca, or to its perpendicular (Planhol 1959:17). Moulay Ismaïl's enormous palace, now half in ruins, dominates much of the city.

The French changed the character of Meknes not only by the addition of the new quarter and their various military installations but also by attracting a huge rural population. In 1936 the population of Meknes was about 62,000—about 50,000 Muslims and the rest European and Moroccan Jews. By 1960 there were nearly 161,000 inhabitants, 150,000 of whom were Muslims. Thus the average annual growth rate for the Muslim population of the city from 1936 to 1960 was 4.35%, which contrasts with the Moroccan national average of 2.5%. This difference is readily accounted for by rural immigration to the city (Service d'Urbanisme n.d.).

Although the heterogeneous character of the population of Meknes may be attributed to this influx of rural peasants from both the Atlantic plains and the Berber plateaus and mountains, it should be remembered that the population had always been mixed. Not only was the city a sort of border town between the Arab and Berber worlds as well as a stop on the east-west caravan route; it was also a created city, to use the expression of the French urbanists, whose inhabitants were attracted to it or brought in by force from many parts of Morocco. It was not Moulay Ismaïl alone who was responsible for this; later rulers on occasion brought in whole tribes, or tribal segments, to protect the city from outside threat or from internal disorder. These groups settled in separate quarters of the city with which they are still identified, although over the years inhabitants have married out of their group and moved to other quarters.

Like other major cities of Morocco, Meknes is stereotyped by both Moroccans and Europeans. The Moroccans consider it to be one of their most beautiful cities, endowed not only with a temperate climate, clear air, and adequate rainfall, but with work opportunities both within the city and in the nearby rural areas. Prices are said to be lower there than in some of the other Moroccan cities. Meknes is not recognized for its piety as is Marrakech, for its learning as is Fez, for its "big business" and corruption as is Tangier, or for its international flavor as is Casablanca. It is considered, instead, to be the most "Moroccan" of the major cities.

To the European, particularly the French, the beauty of the city was taken more in stride, and it was recognized as a provincial farming center and military base which had excellent economic possibilities and was, despite its provinciality, not an undesirable city in which to settle. This picture, however, was greatly tarnished by the so-called *événements* which followed Independence. Then the inhabitants of Meknes rose up and rioted, and they stormed some of the European homes and factories and killed a few of the Europeans. These events, which seem to have been unique to Meknes, caused panic among many of the Europeans who left the city. Meknes, in fact, has had a rather violent history, from the time of Moulay Ismaïl to the present day. (It was the scene of one of the few violent incidents in Morocco during the six-day Arab-Israeli war in June of 1967.) In part, this "tone of violence" can be attributed both to the continued presence of military installations in the city—Meknes was always and still is an "army town"—and to the city's unusually heterogeneous population, which was subject to internecine conflict as well as to straightforward envy of the wealthier Jews and Europeans.

More than any other Moroccan city, Meknes is known for its popular brotherhoods, especially for the internationally famous ʿIsawiyya, who follow Meknes' patron saint Sidi M'hamed ben ʿIsa and who have lodges all the way across North Africa to Mecca. The ʿIsawa are known for their trances, in which they attack anything that is black or anybody wearing black and, like the worshipers of Dionysius, tear apart (the Bacchic, *sparagmos*) and eat raw (the Bacchic *omophagia*) their sacrificial victims (Jeanmaire 1951:259 et seq.; Dodds 1966:270–282). Although the ʿIsawiyya were the largest and best-known popular order in Meknes, many of the other Moroccan orders were and still are represented in the city. Not only are the ʿIsawa and Ḥamadsha still active, but the Jilala, the Miliana, the Tuhama, the Gnawa, and even the Heddawa continue to meet there. Among the "higher orders," the Tijaniyya and the Darqawiyya are still well represented. None of these orders are as active as they were before the arrival of the French. Some of them, like the Miliana, have lodges in the madina which are now closed; the zawiyas of others, including the Ḥamadsha, are moribund.

The Ḥamadsha Zawiyas

The two Ḥamadsha zawiyas are located a few hundred yards apart in one of the poorest sections of Meknes, not too far from the smiths' quarter. There are a number of butcher shops in the area, as well as shops where one can buy second-hand clothes, cord and rope, musical instruments, and odd bits of junk, or have an old jallaba mended or shoes repaired. It is not a specialized quarter, and the everyday needs of most of the local residents can be met within a radius of a few hundred yards. It is in easy walking distance of a little food market near Sidi ben ʿIsa's mausoleum before which the Ḥamadsha of the shantytowns often perform on Fridays, along with adepts from other popular orders.

Both zawiyas consist of enclosed courtyards in which grave plots have been sold to wealthy Arabs anxious to facilitate their entry into heaven by partaking of some of the baraka inherent in the place. This practice is not restricted to the Ḥamadsha. One finds graves not only in many of the lodges of the city, but also in the countryside in the vicinity of a saint's tomb. Usually the founding saint is reported to have spent some time at the site of the zawiya or one of his descendants is said to be buried there.[2] The latter is true of the Ḥamadsha zawiyas of Meknes. At about the turn of the century, both orders were able to obtain their lodges by promising the revenues from the sale of grave plots to their previous owners. Until then they performed in the open or in private houses, much as the shantytown teams do today. Members of the Ḥamadsha brotherhoods themselves are usually too poor

[2] Cf. pp. 25 et seq.

to buy the expensive plots, and only one or two of them are buried there. The ʿAllaliyyin's zawiya is slightly larger than the Dghughiyyin's, and has a room as well as covered porticos on two sides of the courtyard. The Dghughiyyin have only a portico on one side of their lodge. Both have fig trees in the center of the court which are dedicated to ʿAïsha Qandisha. As to the fig tree at Beni Rachid, bits of cloth have been tied to these trees as signs of various promises to the she-demon, most often a promise (*ʿar*) to sacrifice a chicken to ʿAïsha if a child is born. Many of the lodge members claim to have seen ʿAïsha in front of the trees.

The organization of both lodges is much simpler than that of many of the other Moroccan brotherhoods. The Ḥamadsha zawiyas come under the direct charge of their particular mizwar, who not only receives the money they collect for supposed distribution among the saints' children but acts as an arbiter in cases of disputes among the lodge members or between the lodges of his brotherhood. He approves the choice of a local leader, a *muqaddim*, who is selected by the adepts themselves, and provides the muqaddim with both a letter of authority and a flag. In the case of the ʿAllaliyyin, the mizwar also gives the muqaddim a handwritten copy of the *ḥizb* (sacred writings) allegedly composed by al-Shadhili. The mizwars of both orders exercise considerably more authority over their Meknes lodges, which are close to the Zerhoun, than to zawiyas in more distant cities. This breakdown in central authority is characteristic of most Islamic brotherhoods and has severely limited the political potential of such great orders as the Tijaniyya or even the ʿIsawiyya.

Ideally, the muqaddim is unanimously chosen by the foqra, or adepts, who meet at the zawiya about a month or six weeks after the death or retirement of the previous muqaddim. The lodge members discuss the possible candidates, who may be present but usually arrive later, after a decision has been reached. "The muqaddim must be intelligent, a good judge of people, and not overly powerful, and he must have the ability to speak to people at all levels," an adept of one of the zawiyas explained. When the adepts have come to an agreement—there is no formal voting—they say a *fatḥa,* or prayer, over their new leader, and send word of his appointment to the mizwar. A few days later, the new muqaddim usually sponsors a ceremony to celebrate his election.

In fact, the appointment of a new muqaddim usually involves considerable politicking, in the course of which various delegations of foqra visit the mizwar to press for their particular candidate. The mizwar then makes a decision based upon the popularity of the candidate, the strength of his loyalty, his knowledge of the litanies, his leadership qualities, and, above all else, his honesty. He lets word of his preference leak down to the adepts, who then meet to "decide" upon their new leader. The preferred candidate, who is well aware of the mizwar's choice, does not arrive until after the foqra have had a reasonable amount of time to make *their* decision, and he acts surprised when he learns of it. He declines at first but, upon the insistence of the lodge members, he finally permits them to say a fatḥa over him and declare him their new leader. The mizwar is then informed of the "decision" and sends the muqaddim a letter of congratulations and authority and the flag. The muqaddim is then expected to sponsor a ceremony in which litanies are chanted, the ḥadra performed, and a meal served. The ceremony serves to announce his appointment to important local personages like the muqaddim of the ʿIsawiyya and the foqra of the other Ḥamadsha brotherhood. It also helps the muqaddim consolidate his position in the lodge, for his rivals and their supporters, having accepted his hospitality—shared his bread—are obliged to befriend and support him.

In the spring of 1968, the muqaddim of the ʿAllaliyyin died. He had been leader of the zawiya for over twenty years and, well-established in his position, he had been able to cheat the children of Sidi ʿAli out of much of the zawiya's proceeds. Although some of the adepts respected the muqaddim, many others disliked him. Several of these, like Sidi Mohammed Touijer, had begun to attend the meetings of the Dghughiyyin. For several weeks after the muqaddim's death, there was much speculation among the adepts of both lodges as to who would become the new muqaddim. One group of ʿAllaliyyin supported the assistant (*khalifa*) to the former muqaddim, a seller of amulets and leather scraps; a second a man named Ahmed, a butcher's assistant; and a third, Touijer, a tanner. Touijer, a man in his thirties, was the youngest of the three. Each group of supporters sent a delegation to the mizwar at Beni Rachid to push their candidate and to disparage his rivals. The supporters of the khalifa argued that their candidate was older and more familiar with the traditions of the zawiya than either Touijer or Ahmed and that Touijer was a Dghughi at heart and Ahmed was a drunk. Touijer's supporters argued that their candidate knew the litanies best and that he was very honest. They maintained that the khalifa was as dishonest as the former muqaddim and that Ahmed was a drunk. Ahmed's supporters used similar arguments.

The mizwar told the different delegations that he would have to think the matter over and would let them know. He then went secretly to the muqaddim and khalifa of the Dghughiyyin and asked them their opinion.

They were very pleased that he had asked them. The mizwar himself was anxious to improve relations with them—relations had deteriorated ever since the former muqaddim had been appointed leader of the ʿAllaliyyin. The two leaders of the Dghughiyyin urged the muqaddim to choose Touijer. The mizwar decided finally to appoint Touijer temporary muqaddim (and Ahmed khalifa), and sent a letter to this effect to his lodge in Meknes. This served to avoid a "mock election" which, under the circumstances, might have been embarrassing. It served also as a test for Touijer. His appointment would be validated, the mizwar said, immediately after the musem. In other words, Touijer would have to collect enough money to make his appointment worthwhile to the mizwar. Touijer, who was a hard worker, was familiar with the ways of not only the conservative adepts of the madina but also with those of the rural immigrants to the city, who had until then gravitated toward the Ḥamadsha of the bidonvilles. Thus he was able to collect enough money to please the mizwar, and was appointed permanent muqaddim.

In August, about six weeks after his appointment, Touijer sponsored a ceremony to which he invited not only the ʿAllaliyyin but also the Dghughiyyin and the muqaddim of the ʿIsawiyya. The latter, an educated man who acts unofficially as the leader of all the muqaddims of Meknes, was unable to come but sent his khalifa. Midway through the ceremony, the khalifa of the ʿIsawiyya and the Dghughiyyin excused themselves and went into a separate room where, "much to their surprise," the muqaddim served them couscous and then handed a letter to the ʿIsawi to read. It was the muqaddim's letter of appointment. After the letter was read, all of the Dghughiyyin said a fatḥa over him, and the new muqaddim gave them the first proceeds of his night, which was a substantial offering of over 60 dirhams. They then returned to the ceremony.

The muqaddim is charged with administration of the lodge; the collection of alms; the organization and direction of ceremonies; curing the sick during ceremonies and at other times; and settling minor disputes between the adepts. He is the liaison between the zawiya and the mizwar and between the zawiya and the municipal government. He is considered an authority on Ḥamadsha lore and leads the foqra in the recitation of the litanies. He is assisted by a *khalifa*, who may act also as his messenger. The khalifa is charged with keeping the supplies of the lodge and with letting all of the foqra know the schedule of ceremonies. The muqaddim and khalifa of the ʿAllaliyyin both keep records of the alms and other proceeds from ceremonies that have been collected; the muqaddim safeguards the proceeds. Among the Dghughiyyin, a treasurer (*khzana*) keeps the money, and the muqạddim, the khalifa, and a registrar (*katib*) each keep separate records as a check on the treasurer and on each other. These records are shown to the mizwar when the proceeds are presented to him. Each zawiya also has two female caretakers who keep the lodge clean, care for the guests' slippers at the lodge, and take charge of female participants during the ceremonies. The muqaddim, the khalifa, the treasurer, the registrar, and the caretakers are the only "officers" of the zawiya, and they receive compensation in one form or another from the mizwar.

The Foqra

The *foqra*—today there are about 15 in each zawiya—are not organized into any hierarchy. They do not go through any form of initiation or receive any secret instruction.[3] They are simply men who attend the meetings at the zawiya and assist regularly at the ceremonies. They may, in fact, belong to other orders as well, although none of the present-day adepts do. They usually dance the ḥadra and fall into trance, but dancing and trancing are by no means qualifications for membership, nor is any detailed knowledge of the litanies. Many of them play the hourglass-shaped drum, the *gwal*. Most of the foqra will have invited their fellow lodge brothers to their homes for a *sadaqa*—a seance at which litanies are recited, the ḥadra performed, and a meal served—shortly after beginning to attend the lodge with any regularity. The sadaqa will usually have been accompanied by the sacrifice of a male goat or a ram. They all consider themselves to be foqra of the zawiya and followers of its founding saint, from whom they derive their good fortune and baraka which enables them to perform the ḥadra and experience the ḥal.

The nature of an adept's relationship to his saint is complicated. Many Moroccans feel tied to a particular saint who serves them as an almost personal intermediary with God. They speak of themselves as supported (*msannad*) by the saint. In some instances the relationship may be formalized, but this is not necessary. A man's hair may have been cut for the first time in the saint's tomb. His parents may have taken him (or her) to the tomb when he was first born and "given" him to the saint. If there are descendants of the saint, the child may be presented to their leader for blessing. The leader says

[3] Although there is no initiation ceremony in either the lodges or teams of Meknes, there may be initiatory practices elsewhere. Schoen (1937:12, fn. 1) claims that the muqaddim's spitting on the head of a new Ḥamdushi serves as an initiation.

the fatḥa over the child—he may spit or blow on it—in exchange for money or a gift from the parents. The presentation of the child to the saint or to his descendants usually occurs only if the child was born after the parents had made a pilgrimage to the saint to ask for one. If a man was never formally presented to a saint, he may still in later life obtain the saint's support by making a pilgrimage to his tomb, asking the saint to be his support, and leaving an offering. Often, the inspiration for this is a dream which occurs during a crisis in the man's life.

H. was apparently worried because he had publicly supported the King of Morocco during his exile and had been warned that he would be thrown into prison if he continued. He had a series of dreams about Moulay Idriss, the last of which involved a man who had appeared in earlier dreams. The man gave him a white candle. H. asked the man what he was going to do with the candle. The man said to bring it to him. The next day H. left for Moulay Idriss and prayed. He did not ask to become msannad, but when he left the tomb he found 7½ dirhams in front of it and has considered himself msannad by Moulay Idriss ever since. He stresses the fact that he did not choose Moulay Idriss but Moulay Idriss called him. The man in the dream was Moulay Idriss.

Although many Moroccans are not msannad by any particular saint, and although the formalization of such a relationship is neither required nor fixed, once a man is supported by a saint he cannot be msannad by another. This does not mean that he cannot visit other saints to ask their help. He is always privileged to do this.

Neither the descendants of Sidi ʿAli or Sidi Ahmed nor the foqra are necessarily supported by either Sidi ʿAli or Sidi Ahmed. Many of the saints' descendants have had their first haircuts in the tomb of one of the lesser Zerhoun saints. The foqra consider themselves to be followers (*tabaʿin*) or workers (*kheddama*) of one of the Ḥamadsha saints, but they may be msannad to other saints or to no particular saint at all. Those who are msannad to one of the Ḥamadsha saints usually come from a family in which there were already either Ḥamadsha or members msannad by the saint; they were most often presented to the mizwar for his blessing. Ḥamadsha who wanted their sons to become head-slashers occasionally brought them to the tomb of one of the saints and pressed their heads down on a miniature of the axe with which the Ḥamadsha traditionally slashed their heads.

The distinction between being supported by a saint and being a follower of one is not altogether clear. Ideally, one can obtain everything one wants, Allah willing, through either one's supporting saint or the saint one follows (or, for that matter, from any saint). The main difference appears to be one of focus and exchange. The follower works for the saint he follows; that is, he participates in (or at least attends) the Ḥamadsha ceremonies, the proceeds of which are given to the saint. He has unwittingly obtained the baraka of the saint, much in the same way that the Sufi mystic obtains the ḥal; it is descended from God (or the saint). It cannot be obtained by work; but once having obtained it, the recipient is obliged to work for the saint. He gives the proceeds from his work (the ceremonies) to the saint, or his descendants, in exchange for the baraka he has obtained from him. This baraka not only enables the follower to perform the ḥadra and experience the ḥal (in the Ḥamadsha sense of the word) but, so long as he works for the saint, it keeps him in good fortune and health as well. Strictly speaking, one does not work for one's supporting saint unless one is also a follower. There are many people msannad by either Sidi ʿAli or Sidi Ahmed who never perform the ḥadra or attend a Ḥamadsha ceremony. The person who is supported by a saint finds his saint to be a moral and psychological support in all the domains of his life. Although the saint theoretically is only an intermediary to God, for the average illiterate Moroccan he is the source itself of comfort and solace, help and support.

The position of the adepts in urban society is difficult to determine. Although LeTourneau has suggested that there is a correlation between membership in the Ḥamadsha brotherhoods and in certain professions (1949:366), I was able to find no evidence of this in Meknes.[4] The adepts do belong to the lowest economic strata of the madina—they earn less than five dirhams a day—and are engaged in occupations in which they not only use but often dirty their hands; they are either totally or nearly illiterate; but they are neither recruited from nor do they dominate any one occupational group. They themselves recognize no connection between being a Ḥamdushi and having a certain occupation. The diversity of their professional ties is illustrated in Table 1. And just as there appears to be no relationship between occupation and membership in the brotherhoods, so there seems to be no relationship between membership and place of residence or work. The lodge cannot be conceived of as either a "professional" or a neighborhood organization.

The foqra, like the Ḥamadsha generally, have been stereotyped by many wealthier, more literate Moroccans as being black, and many of

[4] LeCoeur (1968:98) claims that in Azzemour the blacksmiths, drivers, porters, and fishermen were affiliated with the Ḥamadsha.

TABLE 1

Profession	*ʿAllaliyyin*	*Dghughiyyin*	*Total*
Baker's assistant		1*	1
Barber	1	1	2
Butcher	1	1	2
Carpenter		1	1
Cloth merchant	1	1	2
Cook	1		1
Gardener	3	1	4
Grain merchant		1	1
Greengrocer	1	1	2
Jallaba merchant		1	1
Kefta salesman	1		1
Lime dealer		1	1
Pallbearer		1	1
Porter	1		1
Shoemaker	2		2
Tailor		2	2
Tanner	1		1
Weaver	2	1	3
	15	15	30

* The baker's assistant joined the army and now lives on a pension without working.

them are often considered to be black. They are, nevertheless, differentiated from the members of the so-called black confraternity, the Gnawa, who claim to be descendants or followers of Sidina Bilal, the Prophet's slave, and who until a few decades ago spoke African languages. Since Moroccan notions of race are social typifications and not biological ones, such statements as "The Ḥamadsha are black" must be understood not from a racial, or even an ethnic, point of view, but as a means of ascribing relative social status. In Morocco, a person's racial identity varies according to his own social status and to the status of the person classifying him.

It is possible—and there is some evidence for this—that historically many of the Ḥamadsha were recruited from among the black slaves who were brought north from sub-Saharan Africa, and that their stereotype as black also reflects this. The tribal affiliation of the two orders suggests this. (See Table 2.) The Filala, the Bukhara, and the Drawa, who make up 40% of the membership of both orders, may

TABLE 2

Tribe	*ʿAllaliyyin*	*Dghughiyyin*	*Total*
Berber	2	2	4
Bukhara	3		3
Drawa	2		2
Fez*		1	1
Filala	1	6	7
Gharbawa		3	3
Jbliya	3		3
Meknes*	1	1	2
Ouazzana	1		1
Taza*	1		1
Zrahna (Zerhoun)	1	2	3
	15	15	30

* No memory of tribal affiliation.

have come originally from sub-Saharan Africa. The Bukhara were brought to Meknes by Moulay Ismaïl as military slaves.

The fact that only two of the foqra consider their families to be from Meknes, and that these are unable to recall their tribal origin, is indicative of the recent arrival of the majority of foqra to the city. (Genealogies tend to be shallow; three ascending generations appear to be the limit.) But unlike the Ḥamadsha of the shantytowns, who are primarily first-generation arrivals the foqra of the madina are second or third generation.[5]

Since more than half of the ʿAllaliyyin and 80% of the Dghughiyyin are over 45, the families of the adepts appear to have been attracted to the city not by work opportunities created by the arrival of the French but by those created by pre-Protectorate city life in general. Many of the foqra explain that their parents or grandparents first came to Meknes because they were called in by the government to fill specific positions for which there was a shortage of men.

Membership in the Ḥamadsha brotherhoods is not hereditary. Since both orders were apparently loosely organized before they obtained

[5] Ten of the 15 ʿAllaliyyin were born in Meknes, as were 9 of their fathers; 9 of the 15 Dghughiyyin were born there, 4 of their fathers, and only one of their paternal grandfathers. Information concerning the paternal grandfathers of the ʿAllaliyyin is incomplete. Few, if any of them, appear to have been born in Meknes.

their zawiyas in the beginning of this century, and since many of the parents of the present-day adepts were not born in Meknes, it is impossible to determine whether or not zawiya membership followed family lines. There does appear to be a tendency for the adepts of both lodges to come from families in which at least one parent performed the ḥadra. This is true for 8 ʿAllaliyyin (7 fathers and 2 mothers, with an overlap of one) and 11 Dghughiyyin (11 fathers and 5 mothers, with an overlap of 5). Although my data for the second ascending generation are incomplete, they suggest that a significant number of paternal grandparents also performed the ḥadra. It should be pointed out, however, that there are 8 families among the adepts of both zawiyas in which the present-day adept is the only Ḥamdushi.

Four of the wives of the 9 married ʿAllaliyyin and 3 of the wives of the 13 married Dghughiyyin participate in the ḥadra. A smaller number of children appear to be following in their fathers' footsteps.[6] This is usually explained away as the result of education. The foqra themselves recognize that the Ḥamadsha come from among the illiterate, and it is not unusual to hear them say that so-and-so's children do not perform the ḥadra because they have been to school.

Apart from the regular adepts, who often play drums at a ceremony, there are professional musicians—*ghiyyata*, or oboe players—attached to the orders. The *ghita* is the most important instrument of the ḥadra, and playing it requires considerable skill and endurance. The exact status of the ghiyyata in the Ḥamadsha brotherhoods has been a source of confusion to other investigators. Although the ghiyyata have been affiliated with the zawiya for years, they are treated as distinct from the foqra, both because they receive remuneration for each performance and because they ply their trade elsewhere as well. (The ghita, usually a smaller version of the *ghita gharbawiyya* used by the Ḥamadsha, is played at marriages and circumcisions and at the ceremonies of other brotherhoods like the ʿIsawiyya and the Jilaliyya.) Moreover, their experience of the ḥal is different from that of other adepts, who may fall into a more frenetic trance called *jidba*. The ghiyyata, who must exercise great self-control, cannot enter such a state without disrupting the ḥadra entirely.

[6] At least one child of 3 ʿAllaliyyin—8 have children—and one child of 4 Dghughiyyin—8 have children—participate in the ḥadra. It should be noted that, considering the age of the adepts, an above-average number of ʿAllaliyyin (6 out of 15) are single and an above-average number of the married Dghughiyyin (5 out of 8) are childless.

There are two ghiyyata in each brotherhood; they play the guitar (*ganbri*) and recorder (*nira*) as well. Each of the four ghiyyata comes from a family in which members performed the ḥadra; one of them is a descendant of Sidi Ahmed Dghughi. Ghita playing is the only source of income for three of them; the fourth also sells rugs. The rug merchant comes from an old Meknes family. The other three come from the Jebel Zerhoun.

Each lodge also has a professional ganbri player. This role is not so well differentiated as that of the ghiyyata, and it may be unique to the Meknes orders. Usually, the ghiyyata also play the ganbri. The two ganbri players come from the Gharb and earn their living by playing and begging. One of them attends the ceremonies of both orders regularly. They, too, are paid for their performances and are not considered foqra.

The Muḥibbin

The last and largest group associated with the lodges is the *muḥibbin*, or devotees, of the order. The word "muḥibbin" is derived from the Arabic for love (*ḥub*), and refers to all the men, women, and children who are in some manner attracted to the ḥadra of the Ḥamadsha and who attend the performances—usually of one or the other of the two brotherhoods—whenever they can. They do not necessarily meet at other times or under other circumstances. They are, as it were, the tertiaries of the order. The ḥadra (and, to a lesser extent, other ceremonies of the lodges) is the focal point of the muḥibbin; it is the one activity in which they all engage. The devotees form a group, as it is classically defined by sociologists, insofar as there is social interaction between them, but they differ from the "group" insofar as there is no clear-cut boundary between member and nonmember. The fluid boundaries of the muḥibbin are typical not just of the Ḥamadsha but of other religious confraternities of the Islamic world.

There are definite differences among muḥibbin, which are recognized both by the foqra and by the devotees themselves. Although it is possible to speak of a particularly active devotee as a *muḥibb kabir*, a great devotee, there are no verbally differentiated categories of muḥibbin. Differences are expressed by tone of voice or by paraphrasis. There appear to be two distinct factors which determine what kind of muḥibb an individual is: the intensity of his involvement with the ḥadra, and the frequency of his attendance at the ḥadra. The latter can easily be measured. Some muḥibbin attend the ḥadra from three to four times a week; others, once or twice a year. Intensity of involvement is more difficult to determine. Some devotees perform the ḥadra, enter into a frenetic trance, and mutilate themselves; others simply like to attend the ceremonies but do not participate. Figure 2 presents a somewhat arbitrary summary of the degree of involvement of the

CATEGORY OF MUḤIBBIN	SELF-MUTILATION	FRENETIC TRANCE (JIDBA)	TRANCE (ḤAL)	COMPULSIVE PERFORMANCE OF ḤADRA NO TRANCE	VOLUNTARY PERFORMANCE OF ḤADRA NO TRANCE	COMPULSIVE ATTENDANCE OF ḤADRA TRANCING - NO DANCING	COMPULSIVE ATTENDANCE OF ḤADRA NO TRANCING - NO DANCING	VOLUNTARY ATTENDANCE OF ḤADRA WHENEVER POSSIBLE	OCCASIONAL ATTENDANCE OF ḤADRA	REQUIRED YEARLY INVITATION	VOLUNTARY YEARLY INVITATION	OCCASIONAL INVITATION
1	■	■	■							■		
2	■	■	■								■	
3	■	■	■									■
4		■	■									
5		■	■							■		
6		■	■								■	
7		■	■									■
8		■	■									
9			■							■		
10			■								■	
11			■									■
12			■									
13				■						■		
14				■							■	
15				■								■
16				■								
17					■					■		
18					■						■	
19					■							■
20					■							
21						■				■		
22						■					■	
23						■						■
24						■						
25							■			■		
26							■				■	
27							■					■
28							■					
29								■		■		
30								■			■	
31								■				■
32								■				
33									■	■		
34									■		■	
35									■			■
36									■			

FIGURE 2.

muḥibbin. There are 9 measures of intensity and 4 measures of frequency, providing 36 possible categories of muḥibbin. (An understanding of all of the significant measures will be possible only after an analysis of the ḥadra and patterns of trance has been made.) All of the factors listed are recognized by the Ḥamadsha themselves, although the compulsive quality of some of the activities is recognized by only the more perceptive.

There are no formal ties between the muḥibbin and the zawiya. The foqra know many of them and invite them to their ceremonies, but all of the devotees do not attend any one performance. They form clusters of individuals who attend one another's ceremonies. Only the most active devotees are present at all of a zawiya's performances. The composition of these clusters is informal; they consist of both patrilateral and matrilateral relatives, friends, neighbors, work associates, and other devotees respected for their piety, their devotion to the founding saints of the orders, or the intensity of their ḥadra (as measured by the factors in Figure 2). The clusters overlap and may best be conceived as an aggregate of individual networks in which there is a high incidence of recurrent membership (cf. Barnes 1968:118). A network—a primary order star in Barnes' terminology—is limited here to all of the devotees whom an individual will invite to ceremonies he sponsors. The network has, of course, no external boundaries and no clear-cut internal divisions.

Boualem and His Network

Boualem is a typical madina muḥibb of the Ḥamadsha, although at 30 he is perhaps a little younger than average. He was born in the madina of Meknes. His paternal grandfather, a member of the Chaouia tribe from the countryside around Casablanca, came to Meknes as a young man. Boualem still considers himself a member of the Chaouia, although he has never visited his tribal "homeland." He has been told that not only is there the belief in ʿAïsha Qandisha and other jnun there, but also a spot sacred to Sidi ʿAli ben Ḥamdush. It is said that Sidi ʿAli spent some time there on his way to Buʿabid Sharqi in Marrakech. This spot, which is marked by a qubba and a sacred fig tree, is visited by people suffering from headaches, paralysis, and other "problems" caused by the jnun. Women anxious to have children also visit it. Not only are there Ḥamadsha in the area but also ʿIsawa, Jilala, and Darqawa. Most of the members of Boualem's immediate family are Ḥamadsha, as the partial genealogy in Figure 3 indicates.

His parents often invited the Ḥamadsha to their house; his father, a peasant, was particularly prone to attacks of the jnun which took the form of paralysis, and could only be cured by the ḥadra.

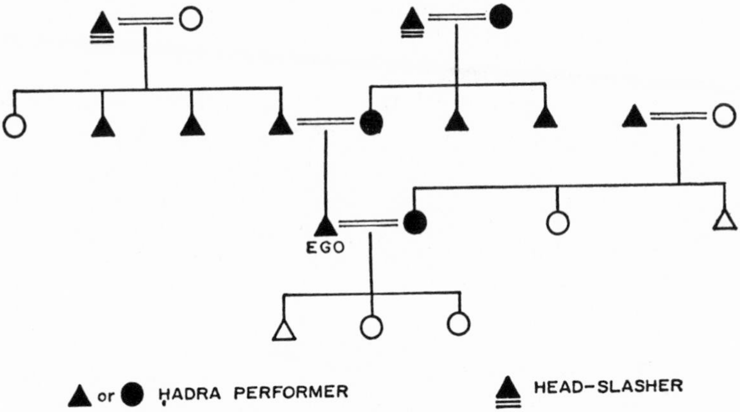

FIGURE 3.

Boualem went to Koranic school for only seven months, and he never attended government school. He is capable of signing his name, but can neither read nor write anything else. He works for a Frenchman in a wine cellar and claims that among the Frenchman's workers there are many muḥibbin. He never worked as an apprentice for a master artisan and, like other madina inhabitants, he works the harvest in the vicinity of Meknes whenever possible. Boualem, who has always lived in Meknes, now rents a house in the *mellah*, or Jewish quarter, of the city, to which many Arabs moved after the Jewish exodus in the late fifties. Rents are cheaper there. Boualem is married to a Berber who was born in Meknes. (Arab-Berber marriages are still the exception, even in the city.) He has three children, the oldest of whom is 7 and goes to school. They are too "small" to perform the ḥadra.

Boualem has made several pilgrimages to Sidi ʿAli and has experienced the ḥal and performed the ḥadra. He was 15 years old when he first danced. He had a fever at the time, his bones ached, and he felt as though "water were boiling in his head." He slashed his head. It had begun to sting and felt as though there were a "worm" in it. Since then, he tries to dance at least four times a month. (His *riḥ* is from the Zerhoun; his color is black; and ʿAïsha Qandisha is his *jinniyya*.)[7] He seldom slashes his head now. He attends the performances of the ʿAllaliyyin, but as they are not active enough today to satisfy his needs, he also attends performances given by a team from a little town just outside Meknes. If he does not perform the ḥadra often enough, his body begins to tremble, his hands become heavy, his knees shake, and he is vulnerable to attacks by the jnun. He, or his parents, invites the Ḥamadsha at least once a year.

[7] These terms will be explained later.

Boualem has a number of acquaintances who are muḥibbin. He invites them to his ceremonies, and they invite him to theirs. Fourteen devotees—those with whom Boualem immediately associates both socially and psychologically—were interviewed.[8] Two of them were his brothers. They all consider themselves muḥibbin; with one exception, they all fall into the first twelve categories of devotees. This reflects the fact that the term "muḥibbin" refers primarily to the most active—the most intensely involved—Ḥamadsha. No women are included in the group. Although there are undoubtedly certain women who usually attend Boualem's ceremonies, they are, owing to the segregation of the sexes, part of Boualem's wife's or mother's network. Boualem himself cannot invite them. Invitations must pass either through his wife or their husbands.

Figure 4 summarizes the significant facts concerning the members of Boualem's network. The members all live in the madina, but in no single quarter. With two exceptions they are all about Boualem's age and are probably somewhat younger than the average muḥibb. Their age also accounts for the high percentage who are single. The average muḥibb is married. The fact that only 5 of them were born in Meknes is also exceptional. Of the 12 devotees who are not related to Boualem, only one is of his tribe; the majority of them are not related either by blood or marriage. They tend to work in the same area of Meknes; tanners are well represented. It appears that occupational ties are here not altogether insignificant —even though, in this case at least, they are established not through the nodal figure of the network but through his brothers, both of whom are themselves tanners. It is possible then to state that the muḥibbin in Boualem's network are about his age and occupy social positions which are similar to his both in terms of the type of work and degree of integration into the urban milieu.

With one exception, all of the devotees perform the ḥadra; 6 of them slash their heads. They all appear to need to dance at least three times a month,

[8] These devotees may be conceived of as forming a network (a primary order star) with Boualem as the center (Barnes 1968:113). This network must not be reified or considered as an indigenous conceptualization of a social reality. It is an analytic device, employed by the investigator, and must be taken as such. Boualem is in no sense a leader of the network; he has simply been taken as a reference point for a particular investigation. The 14 persons interviewed do not comprise Boualem's complete network; a network is in the final analysis boundless. Rather they were chosen because they were the devotees he invites to his nights. (It was impossible to ascertain how frequently he invited them.) He gave the same names when asked who invites him to their nights; however, as a second question, this answer was, in a sense, prefigured. Boualem probably suspected that I would want to interview them and may, therefore, have chosen those with whom he was especially friendly. Although this method of inquiry is not altogether satisfactory, it does, in my opinion, give an adequate picture of the muḥibbin and their social relations. It is noteworthy that Boualem did not list his father, with whom he often sponsors ceremonies; he did name his brothers.

MUḤIBB	PLACE OF BIRTH	TRIBAL AFFILIATION	AGE	OCCUPATION	HARVEST WORK	PERFORMS ḤADRA	AGE OF FIRST ḤADRA PERFORMANCE	"SICK" AT FIRST ḤADRA PERFORMANCE	HEAD-SLASHER	RIḤ
EGO	MEKNES	CHAOUIA	25-30	WORKS IN WINE CELLAR	+	+	15	+	+	Z
BR-1	MEKNES	CHAOUIA	30-35	TANNER	+	+	22	—	+	?
BR-2	MEKNES	CHAOUIA	20-25	TANNER	—	+	13	+	—	GH
28	ZERHOUN	ᶜALAWA	25-30	TANNER	—	+	18	+	+	Z
27	TARA	BRANES	50+	PEASANT	+	+	45	+	—	Z
26	MEKNES	TSOUL	20-25	COPPERSMITH	+	+	13	+	—	Z
24	MEKNES	REHAMNA	25-30	BARBER	—	+	13	+	—	Z
23	MEKNES	FILALA	15-20	TANNER	—	—	na	na	na	na
22	ZERHOUN	SKHIRA	60+	BUTCHER	+	+	10	—	+	Z
19	ZERHOUN	HAMMADA	25-30	WOOL DYER	—	+	15	—	—	Z
18	MEKNES	CHAOUIA	25-30	TANNER AND COPPERSMITH	—	+	12	—	+	Z
16	ZERHOUN	OULED YOUSSEF	35-40	COPPERSMITH	—	+	18	—	+	Z
15	MEKNES	ZRAHNA	15-20	BARBER	—	+	10	+	+	Z
XI	MEKNES AREA	?	25-30	PEASANT	+	+	10	—	—	Z
X	MEKNES AREA	?	40-45	PORTER	—	+	20	—	—	Z

FIGURE 4.

and they all express the same symptoms of heaviness, depression, and lethargy if they do not dance. The ḥadra appears to invigorate them. Eleven of the 14 started to dance between the ages of 10 and 20; 17 is the average age. Six of them were, like Boualem, sick before they fell into trance for the first time. This sickness was said in all cases to be caused by the jnun. Thirteen report that other members of their family perform the ḥadra; 10 had at least one parent who danced. All of them have made pilgrimages to the founding saints of the Zerhoun. Most of them perform the ḥadra publicly as well as privately; they or their parents have all invited the Ḥamadsha to perform. It is significant that they do not all attend the

COLOR	JINN	PERFORMS PUBLICLY	VISITS ZAWIYA FRIDAYS	FREQUENCY OF ḤADRA PER MONTH	CATEGORY OF MUḤIBB	FAMILY MEMBER PERFORMS ḤADRA	FATHER PERFORMS ḤADRA	MOTHER PERFORMS ḤADRA	WIFE PERFORMS ḤADRA	WIFE'S RIḤ	WIFE'S COLOR	WIFE'S JINN
B	ᶜA	—	A	4	2	+	+	+	+	Z	B	ᶜA
B	ᶜA	+	A	3	3	+	+	+	S	na	na	na
G	ᶜA	+	A	3	7	+	+	+	S	na	na	na
B	ᶜA	—	D	3	2	+	—	+	S	na	na	na
R	ˢH	+	A	8	6	—	—	—	+	M	Y	M
R	ᶜA	+	A	2	7	+	+	+	S	na	na	na
B	ᶜA	+	D	8	7	+	—	+	S	na	na	na
na	na	na	—	na	32	+	—	—	S	na	na	na
—	—	+	D	3	4	+	—	—	+	?	?	?
B	ᶜA	+	D	3	12	+	+	+	S	na	na	na
B	ᶜA	+	D	10+	4	+	+	+	S	na	na	na
B	ᶜA	+	A	3	4	+	—	—	—	na	na	na
B	ᶜA	+	A	4	4	+	+	+	S	na	na	na
B	ᶜA	+	—	8	7	+	+	—	—	na	na	na
B	ᶜA	—	—	6	7	+	+	—	—	na	na	na

A	ᶜALLALIYYA
ᶜA	ᶜAÏSHA
B	BLACK
D	DGHUGHIYYA
G	GREEN
GH	GHARBAWI
M	LALLA MIRA
na	NOT APPLICABLE
S	SINGLE
SH	SIDI ḤAMMU
WI	WIFE
Y	YELLOW
Z	ZERHUNI

FIGURE 4.

ceremonies of a single zawiya. Many of them, like Boualem, go to the ceremonies given by other teams.

Perhaps the feature that the devotees have most in common is the Zerhoun *riḥ*[9] and devotion to ᶜAïsha Qandisha. It is curious that despite considerable tribal representation all of the members of Boualem's network, with the

[9] The *riḥ,* which is examined later in this study, is a tune, or musical phrase, that will send a particular adept or devotee into trance. Each person is believed to have such a tune, which is associated with a particular jinn and a particular color. The riḥs fall into several groups, named after tribal regions; but response to them is not restricted to tribal members.

exception of one of his brothers, have a trance-inducing tune from the same musical group. Whether this is accidental or caused by some social or psychological predisposition must be left an open but by no means insignificant question.

A General Picture

Boualem and the other members of his network are not unusual muḥibbin. They exhibit many of the social and psychological characteristics of the average muḥibb. Such a devotee, at least one who falls into the first 12 categories of Figure 2, refers to himself as a muḥibb and considers himself a follower of either Sidi ʿAli or Sidi Ahmed. He does not speak of himself as working for the saint, as the adepts do. He is usually devoted to ʿAïsha Qandisha as well.[10] He has made at least one pilgrimage to Beni Rachid or Beni Ouarad, and he makes every effort possible to attend the annual pilgrimage. He does not play an instrument. Occasionally he attends the Friday afternoon ceremonies (see below) at one of the zawiyas, and the private ceremonies of either zawiya whenever he is invited. If he must dance frequently—three times a month or more—he usually attends ceremonies performed by teams not affiliated with the zawiyas. He may even invite them himself. This results from the moribund condition of the zawiyas and the more spectacular performances of the teams.

He is usually born in Meknes, but can still state his tribal origin. If he is older than the members of Boualem's network, his family has come to the city at least a generation before him. He will have a trade in which he works with his hands and often dirties them. He earns about five dirhams a day and belongs to no particular guild or occupational group. If he falls within the age range of Boualem's network, he tends to be less integrated into the urban milieu. He is usually completely or quasi-illiterate. He goes to the mosque on Friday but, like many Moroccans, seldom performs his daily prayers. There are usually other members of his family who have performed the ḥadra, often one of his parents. His family comes from an area in which there was a belief in ʿAïsha Qandisha and in which there were Ḥamadsha, but from no one tribal group. Often—perhaps more often than in Boualem's network—he traces his devotion to the Ḥamadsha to an illness, usually conceived in terms of being struck or possessed by ʿAïsha Qandisha or other jnun, which was cured either by the Ḥamadsha themselves or by a pilgrimage to the tombs of the founding saints. This illness often appears to

[10] The exact nature of this relationship will be examined in Part Three.

the Western observer as hysterical in nature. If his trance dance has not been "a good one"—that is, a satisfying experience—or if he has not danced in a long time, he suffers a mild depression, a general malaise, and parasthetic pains which he describes as "pinching bones." Sometimes he experiences a recurrence of the symptoms which first caused him or his family to invite the Ḥamadsha to treat him.

The members of his network are all men and tend to be of his age. There is considerable variation in his relationship to them, although they often work in the same quarter as he and may often be members of his profession or a profession which is centered near his own. They may be members of his tribal group, and usually at least a few of them are related to him. It is impossible to state whether they, like the members of Boualem's network, share the same riḥ, although they have in common their devotion to ʿAïsha Qandisha.

The Ceremonies of the Zawiya

There are three principal ceremonies which are given by the adepts of the zawiyas and which provide the zawiyas with the funds necessary for their maintenance and for their gifts to the children of their respective saints. One of them—the *lila*, or night—often serves as a curing ceremony, and is treated in detail in the third part of this work.

Of the other two ceremonies, the first is the Friday afternoon meeting. It is very informal and subject to considerable variation. The doors of the zawiyas, which are usually kept locked, are opened every Friday afternoon—the Muslim Sabbath—to both the foqra and the general public. The regular members of the lodge gather there to drink tea, gossip, and chant a few of their litanies—whichever litanies they know best and like the most.[11] The adepts do not perform the ḥadra there because, they claim, the entire floors of both lodges are "covered with tombstones." It appears that the foqra used to perform the ḥadra on Fridays but that in recent years they have given up the practice, not only because of the tombstones but because of their age. Friday ḥadras are now performed by the bidonville teams in front of Sheikh al-Kamal.[12]

[11] The manner of recitation and the content of the litanies is discussed in the section on the night. Litanies recited at the zawiyas are the same as those recited at the nights, but they are repeated in a calmer manner. They are not designed to send the adepts into an ecstatic transport.

[12] Before the adepts had lodges, they used to meet in the cemetery near Sheikh al-Kamal on Fridays to perform. At this time there seems to have been no concern

There are usually some male visitors who stop to leave a few francs, a candle or so, or even occasionally a chicken, but the majority of Friday visitors are women who come to glean some of the baraka of the place, to have a prayer said for them by the muqaddim or another brother, and to listen to the litanies.[13] Apart from acting out general devotion to the saints and ʿAïsha Qandisha, who is often said to oblige an individual to leave something at the zawiya each week, the women also usually come to ask for something—a child, relief from stomach pains or "pinching bones," the preservation of a marriage, or simply good luck. They too leave candles, bread, sugar, or couscous. Often, especially at the lodge of the Dghughiyyin, they will tie bits of cloth to the branches of the fig tree as a sign of a vow (*ʿar*) to do something for the saint or ʿAïsha Qandisha—usually sacrifice a chicken—if what they asked for comes true. Such visits may be likened to the pilgrimage to the saint's tomb.

Although the Friday afternoon ceremonies are a constant source of income for the lodges, the second ceremony, the name-day ceremony, a regular feature of the Moroccan life-cycle which takes place seven days after a child's birth, is said to be the zawiya's chief source of income. The foqra of the Ḥamadsha brotherhoods—like those of other brotherhoods—are often invited to the name-day festivities of wealthy muḥibbin and other wealthy madina inhabitants who wish their children to be msannad by either Sidi ʿAli or Sidi Ahmed or, at least, to glean some of the baraka of the saints. The adepts repeat the fatḥa over the newborn child and often chant litanies. This is said to give the child some of the saint's baraka. The foqra usually attend the sacrifice of a male goat or ram and partake of the communal meal at the end of the festivities.

If a couple has been able to have children only after a visit to either Sidi ʿAli or Sidi Ahmed, the foqra who work for the particular saint held responsible for the child's birth may be asked to name him. This is considered a great honor by the adepts and a guarantee of continued good fortune for both parents and child. If an infant is born to an adept, his father will usually invite the foqra of his zawiya to perform the ḥadra as well as to recite prayers and litanies. The members of his

---

about dancing over the graves of the dead; the older adepts, however, maintain that the government stopped their performances because they took place in the cemetery.

[13] It must be remembered that women in the Islamic world do not attend the services at a mosque. Worship of saints and associated cults provides women with some "communal religious activity."

lodge will usually send him some sugar in the morning before the ceremony, to help him pay for it. He does not have to pay them, but the lodge receives all of the alms collected during the ceremony. Often, to feed all the guests, the adept will have to borrow money from the zawiya and return it when he can; he usually adds a few extra dirhams when he repays this loan. If a muḥibb or someone else not related to the zawiya invites the lodge members, they must pay the lodge between 20 and 50 dirhams for the ceremony.

Distribution of Income

The money and gifts collected at the ceremonies are theoretically for the children of the saint as a genealogical extension of the saint himself. They are held by either the muqaddim of the zawiya, as in the case of the ʿAllaliyyin, or the treasurer, as in the case of the Dghughiyyin, until the annual pilgrimage, when they are given to the mizwar for distribution to the children of the saint. In the course of the year, the money may be lent to foqra, or to friends of the foqra by way of a particular adept, to tide them through periods of financial strain such as a birth, a circumcision, a marriage, an illness, or a death in the family. Although no interest is charged for such a loan, it is expected that the borrower will return somewhat more than he borrowed. If the adept is particularly poor, he is given the money outright. In this way, the zawiya functions as a society for mutual protection.

In fact all of the alms and gifts received by the lodge do not go to the mizwar. Aside from the money given outright to the poorest adepts when they are in financial crisis, many of the gifts are perishable and so are distributed immediately to the foqra and the other poor. Each zawiya has its own rules, but the differences between them are of little importance.

The alms and gifts received by the Dghughiyyin are distributed in the following manner. The money given the adepts at the Friday meetings is left with the treasurer for safe-keeping; the amount is registered with the muqaddim, the khalifa, and the registrar. Usually, before counting it, a few francs are distributed to the poorest foqra. (In fact, all of the foqra receive a little.) The muqaddim, the khalifa, the treasurer, and the caretakers do not receive any. Couscous is eaten immediately by the adepts; bread is distributed among the poorest foqra and among beggars who come to the lodge on Fridays for alms. Chickens are given to the families of two of Sidi Ahmed's descendants who live in Meknes. Sugar is saved by the treasurer for ceremonies like the name-day ceremonies sponsored by the adepts. Candles are sent to Beni Ouarad once a month. Money collected at the name-day ceremonies is kept by the treasurer, although an adept is given a little if he is in dire need. The proceeds from the curing ceremonies are saved for the children of the saint, but a part is given to all of the foqra. The amount is decided by the muqaddim, the treasurer, and three witnesses.

A report is made each month, but it is never shown to the mizwar. Two days before the annual pilgrimage, the muqaddim, the treasurer, the registrar, and three witnesses meet in the zawiya under lock and key to decide how much they will give the poorest descendants of Sidi Ahmed and how much they will give the mizwar. It appears that each zawiya gives a little extra to the poorest of Sidi Ahmed's children. The exact amount is determined on the basis of individual need. (Envelopes containing the funds are given during the musem.) The remainder of the year's proceeds are given to the mizwar for distribution. The day before the musem, the muqaddim, the treasurer, the registrar, and the three witnesses all visit the mizwar at Beni Ouarad and give him the money. Before counting it, he gives a token amount (called baraka) to the registrar and the witnesses and says a fatḥa for them. Then he counts the money and divides it into four equal parts; he keeps three of these and gives the fourth to the muqaddim. The muqaddim divides his fourth into three parts; he keeps two and gives the third to the treasurer. Thus he receives one sixth of the year's proceeds, and the treasurer one twelfth. The mizwar does not say a fatḥa for them.[14]

[14] In 1968 the Dghughiyyin of Meknes collected 780 dirhams: 80 dirhams were divided among the poor descendants of Sidi Ahmed, and the mizwar received the remaining 700 dirhams. He divided nearly all of this into four parts. Each part, it is reasonable to assume, was about 170 dirhams. Thus, the muqaddim received about 113 dirhams for his year's work; the treasurer, about 57 dirhams; and the mizwar was left with about 510 dirhams to distribute to the 200 or so descendants of Sidi Ahmed. Each descendant theoretically received about 2.5 dirhams from the Meknes zawiya. (Meknes probably provided considerably more money than any other zawiya, with the possible exception of the Fez team.)

6

The Shantytown Teams

In Meknes in 1968 there were seven teams of Ḥamadsha which were not affiliated with the zawiyas of the madina and had no permanent meeting place. These teams, which were far more active than the urban lodges, operated throughout the city and nearby countryside; their members occasionally traveled as far as Fez, or even Rabat, to perform their ceremonies. Their center of activity was, however, the bidonvilles of Meknes, and both the team members and the muḥibbin attracted to their performances were primarily from these shantytowns.

The Bidonvilles

The population of Meknes, as we noted in the preceding chapter, has grown rapidly since the arrival of the French. Rural immigrants poured into the city seeking work; most often they came from the Gharb and from the countryside around Fez and Meknes—areas in which the Ḥamadsha were particularly active. At first they settled in the madina, often in the nooks and crannies of Moulay Ismaïl's walls or in the cellars of his palaces—which were so extensive and so labyrinthine that they lived there undetected, in some instances, for years. By the early thirties there was such a housing shortage in the city that the immigrants began to settle in vacant lots just outside the city limits.

Bordj Moulay Omar, the largest of these shantytowns, sprang up in the early thirties near El Minzeh, which had been a pleasure palace for one of Moulay Ismaïl's ministers. It was conveniently located just north of the new town of Meknes and within a mile of the industrial quarter. By 1935 the municipal authorities had begun to show some recognition of the shantytown's problems, particularly those concerning waste disposal. In July 1936 there were 400 households; in 1952 there were 3,104 (Franchi 1959:258); Bordj had then a population of 11,507. In 1960, four years after independence, there were nearly 19,000 inhabitants living on 36 hectares.

The other bidonvilles of Meknes have had similar histories. The population of Sidi Baba, where most of my shantytown research was conducted, jumped from 5,249 in 1952 to 12,758 in 1960. My own estimate for its population in 1968 was between 18,000 and 20,000. It covered 5.2 hectares.

The plans of the different shantytowns vary with the lay of the land. Sidi Baba and Bordj Moulay Omar are located on relatively flat terrain. They have large squares and appear more open than others which are built onto steep declivities. Some bidonvilles are considered poorer and less desirable than others. Sidi Baba is usually preferred. The larger shantytowns are divided into quarters named after some important center of activity such as a steam bath, a school, an oven, or a former football field.[1] The largest quarter of Sidi Baba is named after the Moroccan veterans of World War II and the French–Indochinese wars who settled there in the fifties and make up a large segment of the bidonville's population. Although I was not able to find any correlation between quarter or street and tribal area, Franchi found that the inhabitants of some streets or quarters in Bordj came from the same tribe or region of Morocco (Franchi 1959:264).

The houses of the bidonvilles may be made of wattle and daub, clay bricks, clapboard, reeds, tar paper, or scrap metal. Few if any of them have more than one story, and this gives the bidonvilles a more open quality than the madina, with its narrow streets walled in on each side by two- and three-story windowless houses. All but the poorest huts have an inner court, which is closed on the top with a grill to prevent robberies. Perhaps 40% of the houses in Bordj have three or four rooms; most of the rest are smaller (Franchi 1959:272). Only a handful have windows facing the street; these are covered with bars and shutters.

Although each household forms a separate and independent unit, usually consisting of parents and unmarried children and, occasionally,

[1] These quarters have no official status. Their names may, however, appear on mailing addresses.

paternal grandparents, unmarried siblings, or relatives from the countryside, rooms are sometimes let to strangers. The bidonville households are not closed-in and isolated from one another as are those of the madina; women, if only by necessity, are not as segregated as in the old quarter itself. The fountains at the end of each street, where women and children go for water; the ovens, where bread is baked for each household; the steam baths; and the local grocery shops are all centers of communal activity. They may be considered neighborhood centers.

Les commerçants et boutiquiers sont liés à leur clientèle qu'ils coudoient chaque jour et avec laquelle ils entretiennent d'excellents relations créant ainsi une communauté intime parmi tous ces gens. (Franchi 1959:271)

Although it is possible to speak of an intimate community, *une communité intime*, bidonville life is by no means as harmonious and peaceful as this phrase suggests. Rather, it is characterized by feelings of mistrust and suspicion. Hardly a day goes by without the spectacle of two or three women neighbors in a row—most often over their children.[2] Sometimes these fights become physical and require hospitalization of at least one of the participants. Men, too, fight—often brutally—and it is considered unsafe to walk the streets at night. There is much talk of robbery.

Urbanization

Although the bidonvilles have retained the more open quality of the countryside, they have lost its traditional controls—ties of kin and mutual obligation—in undergoing what Jacques Berque has aptly called *urbanisation sauvage*. The bidonville families have moved to the city as individual units. Often they had and still have no relatives in Meknes; or, if they do, their relatives may live on opposite sides of the city. Friendship among men is not limited to the inhabitants of single neighborhoods or quarters; but women, whose activities are far more restricted, usually find their friends and enemies in the vicinity of their homes. Often a neighborhood will split into two or more factions, which will then take sides in the many disputes that occur in such high-density populations.

[2] The ease with which women enter these tantrums reminds one of the ease with which they fall into trance.

The bidonvilles are administered by the municipal authority. They are usually headed by a *muqaddim*, to whom every individual must appeal if he has any affairs whatsoever with the government. The muqaddim is responsible to that *khalifa* (assistant) of the pasha of Meknes charged with the particular ward in which the bidonville is located. It was not my impression that neighborhoods or quarters formed political units from which leaders were likely to emerge. Such indigenous patterns of leadership are discouraged by the central government. It is said that there are more than a few "secret police" in the shantytowns. They can usually be spotted by their more expensive shoes, their trench coats, and by a style of behavior reminiscent of James Bond, who is a very popular movie hero among them.

The position of the bidonvilles with respect to both city and countryside is complex, and is reflected in the relationship between the Ḥamadsha of the urban zawiyas and those of the shantytown teams. The bidonvilles are not independent social entities. On the one hand, they fall under the municipal administration and, on the other hand, they are regarded by the inhabitants of the madina (and, to a lesser extent, by the inhabitants of the bidonvilles themselves) as outside the confines of the city and part of the countryside. Although it is tempting to consider this as a result of the rural origin of the shantytown denizens, it must be noted that in the Mediterranean world the city is seen to end at its walls. All that lies outside the walls of the city is countryside.

Jacques Berque (1958:11) has attempted to describe the division between the two groups, a division he considers, in some way, greater than that between the madina and the European quarter.

> Mais la violence du décalage qui oppose, de part et d'autre des murailles, le citadin à son compère rural, est excessive. Le langage, les habitudes, l'histoire, le mode de vie, la figure même et les vêtements ne les opposent moins l'un à l'autre. Le grand style urbain reste coupé du pays. Et cette discorde de style qui reflète une discorde économique et psychologique, l'appauvrit et l'expose en cas de crise, à s'étioler.

Although Berque is writing of Tunisia, his observations are applicable to Morocco as well (cf. LeCoeur 1969:118–120). To what extent this split affects the self-image and self-esteem of the rural immigrant to the city remains an open question. The bidonville inhabitant does joke about his rusticity and is critical of urban ways. He is proud of his ceremonies, his music and, if he happens to be a member of a popular brotherhood, of the endurance of the country folk in performing the ḥadra. He is, nevertheless, conscious of his poverty, his illiteracy, his lack of skilled profession, and the misery of his household. All of the shantytown dwellers whom I questioned assured me that they would prefer to live in the madina, which was cleaner, more peaceful, quiet, and nearer their marketplace and place of work. One woman added, "where the people are educated and more civilized."

The integration of the bidonville and madina is, nevertheless, to some extent facilitated by the very structure of Middle Eastern cities like Meknes. These cities are themselves composed of quasi-independent units, or quarters, often of distinct ethnicity, which are oriented toward the central marketplace and administrative center. Coon (1964:232) has employed a cytological simile for describing the city:

> . . . It might be said that the city itself has a cell-like structure with its own nucleus, its own mechanisms for withstanding shocks from within and without, and its own ways of absorbing and sloughing off foreign materials.

The bidonvilles show some signs of becoming quarters of the city, but they are, at the same time, developing and maintaining their own separate character. This is best illustrated by the recent appearance of a cult and musem to Sidi Maʿsud, who is buried in Bordj Moulay Omar. In 1968 there was some talk of a musem to another, as yet legendless, saint, Sidi Baba, whose burial place has not yet been discovered but is believed to be in the vicinity of the bidonville named after him.

The principal tie between bidonville and city is economic. Franchi (1959:267–268) found that in the late fifties only 14% of the working population of Bordj Moulay Omar worked in Bordj itself. Only 30% of the total population of the bidonville (54.8% of the potential working population) were employed then, 63% of these as day laborers. Although there have been a number of changes in the economic structure of Meknes since Franchi's study—it is possible that the percentage of employed has decreased since 1958—it seems that the majority of workers in Bordj are still journeymen and earn well under five dirhams a day. Because of the large number of veterans who receive pensions from the French government, the situation in Sidi Baba is more complex. Nevertheless, the majority of workers there are laborers who do not work locally. This pattern also appears to hold for the other bidonvilles.

The shantytowns are also tied to the madina commercially. Although the larger ones have little vegetable and meat markets as well as grocery shops, many of the inhabitants of the bidonvilles prefer to do their marketing in the madina, where prices are lower. The bidonville markets, which maintain a very small inventory, are stocked each day, except Wednesdays and Saturdays, from the madina markets themselves. Wednesdays and Saturdays are the days of the "wholesale market" just outside the city limit. The mark-up in the bidonville is considerable. There are a few small shops in the shantytown where one can buy tobacco or mats or have clothes mended or shoes repaired; however, it is impossible to buy most standard household goods in the bidonvilles. At least one member of the average shantytown household—even those in which no one works in the city—visits the madina once a day. There is a bus service from Bordj Moulay Omar, but from Sidi Baba it is necessary either to walk, bicycle, or take a taxi.

Although the average bidonville inhabitant is tied to the madina economically, he is not integrated into its social life. As a newcomer to the city, he has in most instances married a woman from his own family or tribe. Second marriages—after divorce or death—are made more often with other bidonville inhabitants in a similar situation. Children who have been born and educated in Meknes are now beginning to marry other inhabitants of the shantytowns, regardless of tribal or family affiliation. Marriages between bidonville dwellers and members of old madina families are still rare. Marriage ceremonies are not those of the city but of the country. Patterns of friendship follow the same lines as marriage. Tribal and occupational relationships are the foremost determinant.

The "religious ties" with the madina are the most difficult to determine. Although the larger bidonvilles have their own mosques—often shacks with clapboard minarets—those men who pray regularly prefer to attend the madina mosques whenever they can, and especially on Fridays. They seldom belong to any of the old-quarter zawiyas; if they have an affiliation with a brotherhood, it is with one in the bidonville. Indeed, there is considerable hostility between urban and slum brotherhoods. Saints' tombs in the madina, especially Sheikh al-Kamal, are visited regularly by both men and women, although the majority of bidonville inhabitants seem to have greater faith in Sidi ʿAli and Sidi Ahmed. They visit and often invoke the saint of their countryside, by whom they are frequently msannad. The square in front of Sheikh al-Kamal is filled each Friday afternoon with inhabitants of the shantytowns who have come to attend the ḥadra of the Ḥamadsha, the Miliana, the Jilala, and the ʿIsawa, or to listen to storytellers, musicians, holy fools (*majdubin*), and the like.

The Shantytown Teams

The Ḥamadsha of the shantytowns differ from those of the madina zawiyas, as would be expected, in terms of their beliefs, their ceremonial style, and their organization. They may be divided into two groups: the team members and the muḥibbin. The team members are professional Ḥamadsha—they earn their living by performing the ḥadra—and appear to be much more explicitly concerned with the jnun and with sickness than the adepts of the madina, who are primarily concerned with the saints. Their ceremonies are simpler—they do not recite litanies—and more violent and spectacular. The public ones fall midway between spectacle (*fraja*) and religious ceremony (*krama, sadaqa*). The private ceremonies are primarily curing ceremonies and not homages to the saints.

Not only are the performances designed—often crudely—to maximize profits, but the team members actively seek out muḥibbin and threaten them with illness if they do not sponsor a ḥadra. Usually these threats are made in a joking, offhand way, but they leave their mark on a group of people who are highly susceptible to such suggestions. The bidonville Ḥamadsha are "exploiters," and they are seen as such not only by the descendants of Sidi ʿAli and Sidi Ahmed and the foqra of the madina but also by their "victims," the muḥibbin themselves, who stoically accept their dependence as their fate. The devotees conceive of their attraction to the Ḥamadsha as the will of ʿAïsha Qandisha and the other jnun, whose ways are neither to be questioned nor understood. Like the team members, they are concerned primarily with the jnun, who constantly interfere with their lives, and only secondarily with the saints, who are seen as providing the means (*baraka*) for managing the jnun. Baraka is not conceived in its more abstract quality as plenitude, well-being, and completion, but in its more concrete sense of material well-being, good health, and luck in everyday affairs. The devotees perform the ḥadra to obtain *something*, and are not at all unwilling to pay for it—even to men they recognize as charlatans, quacks, whoremongers, and money-grubbers.

The seven teams are dedicated to either Sidi ʿAli ben Ḥamdush or Sidi Ahmed Dghughi. The allegiance of the members, however, may be mixed. The teams usually have seven members, although there is technically no limit to membership or particular virtue in this number. Indeed, the number seven is popularly considered unlucky. The teams are not as strictly and as formally organized as the zawiyas, and on occasion—especially during the public performances on Fridays and holidays—two or more teams will combine. Often, too, individual members of a team which is not performing on a given night will join the ḥadra of another team. They may receive a small gift for this, but their unexpected arrival is usually regarded as an intrusion and is resented. There is considerable friction between the different teams.

Each of the bidonville teams is headed by a muqaddim who, like the muqaddim of a zawiya, receives a letter of charter from the mizwar of the saint he follows and carries the saint's flag. He is charged with the administration of the team, the scheduling and organization of ceremonies, and the division of proceeds; he acts as a dance leader during the ḥadra and cares for the sick. The mizwar's control over the muqaddim of a bidonville team is not as great as his control over the head of an urban zawiya. He does not choose, or even confirm, the election of the muqaddim. Usually the muqaddim was a team member or an active devotee who felt that he had enough baraka to attract a following and who conducted a few trial performances before presenting his case to the mizwar. Often he replaces an old or deceased muqaddim. The mizwar grants the new muqaddim a letter unless there is active opposition from other teams in the area.

Both mizwars hold the bidonville Ḥamadsha in some contempt, consider them cynically as a good source of income, and term their letters to them acts of charity graciously given to help a group of poor wretches earn a living. The letter is the mizwar's only hold over the muqaddim; the muqaddim must then present it to the municipal government, which grants the team permission to perform its lucrative public performances.

The other members of the team are musicians and dancers. There is usually one snare drummer (*tabbal*), who is familiar with the words of the various trance-inducing musical phrases (*riḥs*), three gwal players, and two ghiyyata who also play the recorder (*nira*) and the guitar (*ganbri*). Each muqaddim tries to have at least one *sharif*—descendant of the Prophet—in his team, because a sharif, who is endowed with baraka, attracts a following and will bring in more money. The sharif may play an instrument; he usually aids the muqaddim in caring for the sick.

There is no formal initiation: "The muqaddim notices that you are a good muḥibb and invites you when one of the regular team members is unable to make it. Or he may ask you to dance because he has seen that you are a good dancer." If the novice is young, he is left with all the dirty work of the team—running errands, carrying the instruments, and informing team members of a ceremony—and is the object of a great deal of teasing. He may be required to shave his head, leaving only a small pigtail. The Ḥamadsha of Meknes do not have a single hair style, and the novice will usually let his hair grow long again.

The ghita players are considered part of the team, even though they receive greater compensation than the other musicians and perform at other ceremonies as well. They do not, however, play for more than one bidonville Ḥamadsha team. The difference in status between the ghita players of the zawiyas and those of the teams must be understood in terms of the division of wealth. The foqra do not divide the proceeds of a ceremony among themselves; theoretically, only the poorest of them can expect to receive a part of the small portion of total proceeds allotted to them. This allotment is referred to as alms (*sadaqa*), or baraka, or bread, a symbol for baraka, and is considered as an act of charity. The team members, however, divide all of the proceeds among themselves and do not normally consider their part alms.

The importance of the ghiyyata, who control the progress of the ceremony by playing the appropriate riḥs, often undermines the position of the muqaddim, whose authority, aside from what personal charisma and esoteric knowledge he may have, lies with his possession of the mizwar's letter. The teams tend, therefore, to be very fragile. The members of the seven teams operative in the bidonvilles of Meknes in 1968 were constantly shifting their allegiance from one muqaddim to another. Whatever stability there was resulted from the economic success or failure of a particular team. Ghiyyata perform at marriages and circumcisions; and during the period immediately following the harvest, when the majority of marriages and circumcisions take place, the Ḥamadsha seldom perform the ḥadra because they are unable to find ghiyyata for the occasion. This is the period of the greatest tension within the teams. They often break up, to be reintegrated later in the year.

The position of the ghiyyata in the larger social setting must be distinguished from that of the other team members. They form an occupational group and, as ghiyyata, are treated with respect. The majority of them come from illiterate, peasant Gharbawi families which usually included some Ḥamadsha. The fathers of the majority of them were not ghiyyata. The musicians learned to play the ghita from a *mʿallem*, or master, in their home villages, who may have noticed their musical ability and taken an interest in them, teaching them first to play the nira and then the ghita and ganbri. Most of them, much to their parents' disapproval, then joined a troupe of wandering musicians (*sheikhat*)—these travel from village to village, usually accompanied by a prostitute or two, performing at name-day celebrations, circumcisions, marriages, and other festivities—before coming to Meknes. Although many of the ghiyyata were familiar with the music of the Ḥamadsha, as well as that of the ʿIsawa, the Jilala, and the Gnawa, they were seldom affiliated with a team of Ḥamadsha before their arrival in the city. Usually, they joined one shortly afterward. The team provides them not only with a means of earning a living but also with the chance to form contacts with families who would later invite them to perform at family celebrations. They regard themselves and are regarded by others as professional musicians who are members of the guild of all ghiyyata, including those not attached to any brotherhood. They are proud of their profession.

The other team members do not form as homogeneous a group. Like the ghita players, they are younger than the foqra of the madina and have almost all been born in the countryside, where they performed the ḥadra. Like many of the madina Ḥamadsha, they began to dance in their early teens. They too did not become team members until coming to Meknes. The motive was usually financial. The majority of them come from areas in which the Ḥamadsha were active, and many of them report that other members of their families perform the ḥadra. It is not unusual to find families, especially among the head-slashers, in which every member of the immediate family has performed the ḥadra. But it is also not unusual to find team members who report that no one in their immediate or more distant families has danced. The majority of the members I interviewed came from the Gharb or from the region around Fez and Meknes; very few come from the Zerhoun. Most of them are illiterate and, as they put it, have no other "occupation" beside the ḥadra. They will take odd jobs whenever they can and will work the harvests, preferably around their old homes. Those who work have menial jobs—selling doughnuts or candies or working as garbage collectors or street cleaners—or make a little money by preparing magical amulets and formulae, predicting the future, or giving advice to the jinn-possessed, the jinn-struck, or those suffering from the evil eye or a magical curse. A few of them—they usually come from the Wulad Khalifa in the Gharb—claim to be descendants of the Prophet and earn some money reciting fatḥas, massaging aching limbs, or spitting into water which then, filled as it is with their baraka, is drunk by the ailing client.

There is considerable ambivalence in the attitude of the average bidonville inhabitant toward them. Although the shantytown dwellers regard them with a certain awe and treat them, in face-to-face encounters, with respect, the team members are never as respected and as admired as the ghiyyata (or the foqra of the zawiyas). In private, they are often referred to quite disparagingly. Most of the bidonville dwellers, including the team members themselves, do not want their children to become team members or even muḥibbin. There is little prestige associated with their role, although within their own ranks there appears to be a hierarchy of prestige. Those who abandon themselves most dramatically to excesses of self-mutilation and those who have access to the jnun have the most prestige. They are all treated with great condescension by the educated of the madina, and the foqra consider them "worthless Ḥamadsha."

The Devotees

The vast majority of the bidonville Ḥamadsha are devotees (*muḥibbin*); and like the devotees of the city, they are difficult to trace socially. They may be scaled with respect to intensity of involvement or frequency of performance in the same manner as the madina devotees. The most intensely involved—those who fit into the first 12 categories of Figure 2—have the most prestige; they form networks which are centered around a particular team member. Usually, this is a muqaddim or ghita player. He invites them whenever he gives a performance, especially if the performance is near their homes. Often the members of the network come from the same tribe or region as the muqaddim or ghita player; however, one muqaddim, who had a very large following, came from a region of Morocco which had produced very few immigrants to Meknes.

Most significant is the fact that the devotees of the bidonvilles are centered around particular team members whom they follow. The pattern is in this respect different from that of the madina. The team members, who are constantly sponsoring ceremonies themselves, play a much more active role in inviting the muḥibbin to ceremonies than the foqra do. There is an incipient, albeit restricted, form of leadership. Were the teams themselves more *stable*, one might expect to find a rudimentary association of muḥibbin around each team. This is not the case. One reason for the more active role of the team members in the invitations is economic. The more devotees present at a ceremony, the more money the team can hope to collect and use for its own devices. I do not mean to imply that the foqra are not sufficiently motivated to maximize their profits, but simply that there is a greater degree of urgency in earning money when one's very existence depends on it. A bidonville ceremony is much more a business affair than a ceremony in the madina.

Some of the muḥibbin of the bidonville teams do not live in the shantytowns but in the madina itself and in the villages in the vicinity of Meknes. Although devotees who live in the madina are, like their confreres in the shantytowns, usually newcomers to Meknes, there are a few who come from more established families. Unlike the devotees of the shantytowns, they usually have affiliations with one of the Ḥamadsha zawiyas of the old quarter; but, like Boualem, they require the ḥadra more often than the zawiyas perform. There is, in short, no complete division between the muḥibbin of the madina and those of the bidonvilles. Although they tend to split into two groups along an urban–bidonville (rural) axis, the split is not complete. They *do* share their devotion to the saints and ʿAïsha Qandisha, and their performance of the ḥadra.

There are many more female muḥibbin in the bidonvilles than there are among the zawiya-affiliated devotees; and the women, who are not as restricted as women in the old town, play a more active part in the ceremonies. The wives of most, but not all, of the team members also perform the ḥadra; this cannot be said for the wives of the male devotees. One often finds a devotee whose wife not only is not a devotee but disapproves of the Ḥamadsha altogether. Similarly, there are muḥibbin with husbands who are not only not devotees but who tolerate their wives' performances with the usual superiority of an Arab male toward an Arab woman. Spouses of either sex, however, frequently report becoming devotees after marrying a devotee.

The average male muḥibb resembles the average bidonville inhabitant. He is illiterate, an unskilled laborer of peasant background who may or may not have full employment and who leaves the city to work the harvests in the spring and summer. He is a newcomer to Meknes and was born in a part of the countryside where the Ḥamadsha were active: the Gharb and the regions of Fez and Meknes are the most common. I have found far fewer from the Zerhoun than I did in the madina. This may be the result of continued contact between the Zerhoun population and Meknes, which has provided the Zrahna with "better contact" in the madina. Like the muḥibbin of the cities and the foqra and team members, the devotees of the shantytowns usually report at least one other family member who performs the ḥadra. Like the other Ḥamadsha, they usually started to perform the ḥadra in their teens after a sickness—most often paralysis—which was interpreted as an attack by the jnun. From that time on they have felt the need to dance, and they suffer from depression, general malaise, and pinching bones if they do not dance for a prolonged period of time. Sometimes they become paralyzed again. Their first performance usually preceded their arrival in Meknes.

Finances

The economic organization of the bidonville Ḥamadsha is different from that of the zawiyas. Unlike the foqra, who "work" for their saint, the team members of the bidonvilles work for themselves. Their public and private ceremonies are always considered curing ceremonies, and they do not recite litanies or attend name-day celebrations. Just after each performance, they divide all the money and gifts—if there should happen to be any—among themselves. Nothing is left for the saint. During the weeks immediately preceding the musem, however, a part of the proceeds from each performance is put aside for the saint. Often, at this time, the teams will go from house to house begging alms for their saint. At the musem, this money is given to the mizwar, who renews their letter of charter without saying a fatḥa over them. The whole exchange is conducted like a business transaction with much bargaining, complaining, and cursing, and it does not have the sacrosanct quality of a zawiya's presentation of proceeds to its mizwar. The team members are simply renewing their contract.[3]

[3] During the musem of 1967, one team was not able to give the mizwar of Sidi ʿAli as much as was their custom (125–150 dirhams) because K., the muqaddim, fell sick shortly before the musem, and his team was unable to perform for several months. The mizwar of Sidi ʿAli did not consider this to be an excuse and threatened to withdraw his letter and inform his relatives in the municipal government of the change in K.'s team's status. When K. still refused to pay, the mizwar cursed him and called K.'s wife a pagan, a very strong insult. He did not in fact withdraw the letter, but sent his son to K.'s house several times during the year to collect as much money as he could. K. threatened to switch allegiance to Sidi Ahmed, but was urged not to "abandon his saint" by the other team members. K. ended up by giving the mizwar's son about 10 dirhams at each visit—40 or 50 for the year. In 1968 K.'s team was more active and was able to collect enough money (160 dirhams) to satisfy the mizwar. K. and the other team members do not hesitate to curse the mizwar and his son—not the saint; and K. who is reputed to have great knowledge of magic, claims to have made much evil magic against the mizwar, his son, and his brother.

7

The Circle of Exchange

The three levels of Ḥamadsha organization considered in the last three chapters are interrelated in a way that is typical of all levels of Ḥamadsha organization and that receives ritual expression during the annual pilgrimage to Beni Rachid and Beni Ouarad. They form an *exemplary complex,* the analysis of which provides an understanding of the "internal workings" of the organization as a whole and of its relation to the larger social scene. Only those aspects of the "external relations" of the Ḥamadsha bearing on the therapeutic process are considered here.

The Ḥamadsha organization under consideration may be summarized as shown in Table 3.

The Ḥamadsha are seen to fall into two structurally parallel organizations—the descendants and followers of Sidi ʿAli and the descendants and followers of Sidi Ahmed—between which there are certain ritualized ties. Both organizations are divided into two distinct levels: the *wulad siyyid,* who form a bounded group with explicit rules of membership—agnatic descent from the ancestral saint—and the adepts (*foqra*) and devotees (*muḥibbin*) of the brotherhood, divided into a series of teams whose organization varies from town to country. (The bidonville teams tend to follow the organization of the countryside.)

Membership in the teams is achieved. There are no explicit rules for recruitment. Each team is surrounded by a number of devotees, who may be scaled with respect to the intensity of their involvement. Acknowledgment of one's devotion to the Ḥamadsha saints and to their cult is the only criterion for being considered a muḥibb. Al-

TABLE 3

Sidi ʿAli		*Sidi Ahmed*	
Zerhoun	*Mizwar Wulad Siyyid (Ta¨fa)*	*Mizwar Wulad Siyyid (Ta¨fa)*	
Madina	*Bidonville*	*Madina*	*Bidonville*
Zawiya	Taïfa	Zawiya	Taïfa
(foqra)	(team member)	(foqra)	(team member)
(ghiyyata)		(ghiyyata)	
muḥibbin	muḥibbin	muḥibbin	muḥibbin

though the various teams are distinct from one another, the devotees are often affiliated with more than one group. Often, one finds a muḥibb who is connected not only to the zawiya of one saint but also to one or more bidonville teams, and who does not hesitate to attend the performances of the other zawiya.

The mizwar, who may be considered the direct representative of the saint, is in complete charge not only of the descendants but of the followers of his ancestral saint. He is the nodal point of the organization, and his importance to the organization is ritually reconfirmed every year at the annual pilgrimage.

The Musem

Each year, on the sixth and seventh days after the Prophet's birthday, or *mulud*, the component organizations of the Ḥamadsha complex come together for the musem at Beni Ouarad and Beni Rachid. Tens of thousands of pilgrims—foqra, team members, muḥibbin, as well as the curious, the pious, and the bored—from all over Morocco gather together to pay homage to Sidi ʿAli and Sidi Ahmed.[1]

On the days immediately preceding the musem, pilgrims arrive and set up tents in the village of the saint to whom they feel closest. Traveling vendors, entertainers, hawkers, and pickpockets who make the round of pilgrimages each year also arrive to ply their trade. Team members settle down in groups and begin to perform the ḥadra almost

[1] I estimate that there were between 35,000 and 50,000 pilgrims at the museum in 1968. This was also the estimate of the chief of the Gendarmerie Royale at Moulay Idriss. Schoen (1937:91) estimated 35,000 for the musem in 1935.

immediately on arrival. Their dancing continues intermittently for three or four days, until the musem ends. The foqra of Meknes and Fez, as well as the leaders of other important urban lodges, are given special housing by their mizwar. It is at this time that the various taïfas bring the year's proceeds to the mizwar and make the rounds of other saint's descendants to whom they feel especially bound. A constant stream of pilgrims visits the two saints' tombs, the baths at Beni Rachid, and the shrines to ʿAïsha Qandisha, leaving a few dirhams, a candle or two, or some other gift at every stop. (The mizwars usually grant charge of the baths and the shrines as concessions to the highest bidders in the villages a few days before the musem.) Numerous chickens are sacrificed along with the rams, he-goats, and bulls that are usually—and traditionally—brought by the urban zawiyas.[2] Each year one of these zawiyas brings a special cover for the catafalque and parades up and down the road with it.

The musem of Sidi Ahmed takes place on the sixth day after the Prophet's birthday. All morning and afternoon, teams from all over Morocco dance their way—in trance and often slashing their heads—down the narrow main street of Beni Ouarad to the saint's tomb; and there, in front of the mausoleum, they dance even more violently, some of them slashing with a halbard (*shaqria*). The mizwar and the other saint's descendants do not participate in this part of the pilgrimage; they stay in their houses, entertaining important guests.

The mizwar of Sidi ʿAli is invited to dine with the mizwar of Sidi Ahmed, if relations between the two permit this. (The musem is one of the rare occasions on which the mizwar of Sidi ʿAli will allow himself to be seen in Beni Ouarad.) Toward sundown, when all the teams have paid a visit to the saint's tomb and all the pilgrims are anxiously awaiting his appearance, the mizwar leaves his house, mounts a white stallion,[3] and parades down the main street of Beni Ouarad to the tomb of Sidi Mejmaʿ at the opposite end of town.[4] Bread and spoonfuls of couscous—both said to contain baraka—are given to the pilgrims just before his appearance. He pays homage to Sidi Mejmaʿ by circumambulating the tomb and then returns to his ancestor's mausoleum,

[2] For the musem of 1968 the mizwar of Sidi Ahmed required 4 cows, 20 sheep, between 300 and 400 chickens, 200 kilograms of honey, 100 kilograms of butter, 800 kilograms of couscous, and over a ton of flour. I have no figures for tea, sugar, coffee, and mint. It is said that the mizwar does not collect enough during the musem to pay for all this.

[3] It is explained that ʿAli, the Prophet's son-in-law, rode a white stallion.

[4] I know of no legends about Sidi Mejmaʿ or his relationship to Sidi Ahmed.

which he is supposed to visit but is seldom able to reach because of the crowds. He is followed by various teams of Dghughiyyin, who perform the ḥadra in tight separate circles (*ḥalqat*). The foqra of Fez, whose muqaddim is related to the mizwar by marriage, follow immediately behind him. The foqra of Meknes end the procession, accompanied by two or three men on horseback playing a long brass (or copper) horn called a *nafaᶜ*.[5]

On the seventh day after the Prophet's birthday, much the same sequence of events is repeated at Beni Rachid. The mizwar of Sidi Ahmed is asked to lunch, but then he returns to his village, mounts his stallion, and rides back down to Beni Rachid, followed by thousands of pilgrims. The Dghughiyyin perform the ḥadra. Traditionally, the mizwar followed a path through the olive groves between the two villages and stopped at the two palm trees, to the north of Beni Rachid, to be greeted by the mizwar—also on horseback—of Sidi ᶜAli. The mizwar of Sidi Ahmed would then dismount and, on foot, follow the other mizwar—still on horseback—to Sidi ᶜAli's tomb and back.[6] In recent years, however, the mizwar of Sidi Ahmed has refused to follow the traditional path, preferring the tarred Zerhoun road. He no longer enters the village. Instead he stops just short of the palm trees, waits for the mizwar of Sidi ᶜAli, greets him perfunctorily, and immediately rides back to his own village. The mizwar of Sidi ᶜAli returns to *his* house without visiting his ancestor's tomb. Thousands of tired pilgrims who have looked forward to this meeting for several days now pack up their belongings and prepare to leave that night or the following morning.

The musem, which is part of a complex cycle of pilgrimages to various saints' tombs in northern Morocco, is an amorphous affair with many different functions. It may be said to consolidate the various components of the Ḥamadsha complex by reaffirming their position within the Ḥamadsha scheme of things and by justifying the exchange of wealth and baraka which takes place both at this time and throughout the year. Traditionally, it reconfirmed the relative status of Sidi ᶜAli and Sidi Ahmed and their children and followers. Today, it pro-

[5] The nafaᶜ is rarely used at Ḥamadsha ceremonies. I once saw it played by the Dghughiyyin at a circumcision ceremony for their mizwar's son. It is often played at circumcisions.

[6] The descendents of Sidi ᶜAli insist that this is as it should be. The leader of the descendants and followers of Sidi ᶜAli's "slave" should follow Sidi ᶜAli's most important descendant afoot.

vides a vehicle for the expression of tensions that exist between the two economically vying groups. The mizwar's position, as representative of his ancestor and as leader both of his lineage and of the brotherhood devoted to his saintly ancestor, is reaffirmed symbolically—reinforced behaviorally, one might say, given the heightened suggestibility of the exhausted and often entranced pilgrims. His hospitality, which is symbolized by the distributing of spoonfuls of couscous and handfuls of bread from his kitchen, demonstrates to the pilgrims a magnanimity and generosity commensurate with a vast endowment of baraka.

Baraka and the Exchange of Wealth

It must be remembered that bread is also a symbol of baraka, and baraka is one element in the ideal exchange system that unites the various levels of Ḥamadsha organization. The muḥibbin (and general population) give money and gifts—wealth—to the adepts of the order and to the saint—by extension, to his children. In return for their gifts, the donors obtain baraka. The adepts who have worked for the saint give what they have collected to the saint—via the mizwar. In return, *they* receive baraka. The mizwar, as representative of the saint and his descendants, distributes the wealth he has received from the adepts and from the muḥibbin directly to the children of the saint (including himself), who are considered to be poor.[7]

It is incumbent upon the mizwar and the children of the saint to provide for individual pilgrims to the shrine and for pilgrims at the annual musem. The system of exchange is, then, a system of redistribution of wealth through a series of transfer agents from the muḥibbin who have wealth to those who do not, the poor and ailing who visit the shrine. This redistributive system is schematically represented in Figure 5. The thin lines indicate the direction of flow of wealth and the thick ones that of baraka.

The fact that the wulad siyyid and the foqra are considered to be poor—*foqra* is derived from the Arabic for poor—enables them to reap some of the benefits of the alms they receive. This is not considered a salary, or even as their due. The gifts are received as a blessing and are called baraka. It is noteworthy that the gifts to the "poor foqra" are given before the proceeds of any one night are counted, and that the

[7] Contrast Gellner 1969:74 et seq.

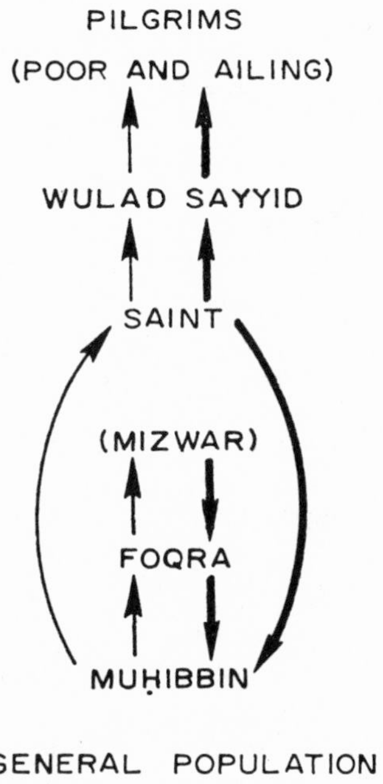

FIGURE 5.

mizwar gives a gift to the three witnesses who accompany the muqaddim and other officials of the zawiya to his house with the year's proceeds before he counts them. He says a fatḥa for the witnesses but not for the muqaddim, the treasurer, and other officials. His gift is referred to as baraka, or bread.

A detailed examination of the "logic" of baraka[8] is necessary for an understanding of this system of exchange. Baraka, as Geertz has pointed out, may be an attribute of an individual or may reside in an object. Westermarck and others have looked to the object itself for reasons which qualify it as endowed with baraka. They have failed, however, to consider the object as symbolic of a group or of some social or psychological process. It is indeed possible, and even likely, that the extraordinary quality of the object renders it a fit receptacle

[8] Here I refer to baraka within the Ḥamadsha context only. The term is widely used in Morocco for many different things, all of which are related in differing degrees to Geertz' gloss.

for baraka, but this does not necessarily enhance our understanding of the logic of baraka and its relation to social and psychological processes. These objects—sand, water, henna, and the like—which the Ḥamadsha believe to contain baraka are in fact extensions of the baraka of the saint. They possess no unique or extraordinary quality in themselves, and need not concern us here.

As an attribute of human beings, baraka may be either institutionalized or personal. The former is passed agnatically; the latter is a personal endowment which is not heritable, though it may be contagious. Among the Ḥamadsha, the descendants of the saints are endowed with institutionalized baraka. They are born with it and defined by it. In this sense, baraka is symbolic of the agnatic principle of descent—the rules of group membership. It does not reflect any particular quality in the saint's descendants, nor does it provide them with good fortune, good health, or any of the other more or less concrete benefits associated with baraka. It is contagious.

The baraka of the foqra and team members is personal. Here we must be careful to distinguish between the baraka an adept obtains from the saint in the same manner as a pilgrim—baraka which is translated into some concrete potential or actual state of being—and the baraka he possesses as a follower of the saint. The latter he cannot obtain by his own devices. It is descended from God via the saint. It is contagious. Possession of it may be said to define the group. In this case, working for the saint—performing the ḥadra—is the principle of membership.

Baraka is always ascribed to someone or something other than self. It is always possible to refer to someone or something as endowed with baraka, but it is impossible to refer to oneself as possessed of baraka. A man who is endowed with institutionalized baraka might make such a statement, but this would be considered gross immodesty and almost never happens. A man who is endowed with personal baraka is equally incapable of making such a claim. In fact, were he to state that he possessed baraka, his endowment might well vanish.

Baraka is also contagious. It may be passed from an endowed object or person to a supplicant by a number of ritual practices. The moment the baraka has passed to the supplicant—except in extraordinary circumstances like Sidi ʿAli's ingestion of Buʿabid Sharqi's vomit—it is no longer contagious. It ceases to be itself. The individual to whom the baraka has been passed obtains something—the state or potential state of good health, good fortune, business success, or fertility. A transformation analogous to the conversion of energy into matter, of semen into infant,[9] has occurred. Baraka is thus a potentializing force which in the process of transference is actualized into that which is sought. It should be noted that the specific desire for the baraka must precede its transfer. It is impossible under normal circumstances to hoard it and then decide upon its use.

In the Ḥamadsha scheme, baraka is passed from the saint—the inexhaustible source of baraka—through a series of transfer agents: the wulad siyyid, who are extensions of the saint himself and who have received their endowment biologically (through the semen of their ancestor), and the foqra, whose endowment is weaker than that of the saints' descendants, and must be continually renewed through work. The saint, his descendants, his followers, and the ritual paraphernalia associated with him, all possess baraka which is passed to those who do not possess it in exchange for wealth. The passage of baraka mirrors—and, in a sense, potentializes—the passage of wealth in a redistributive system which serves *ideally* to care for the poor and ailing and is congruent with a fundamental tenet of Islam: charity. It is seen to reside in precisely those ideologically selfless individuals, living in self-imposed poverty, who act as transfer agents in the redistributive system.

The ideal exchange of baraka and wealth is not, however, consistent with what I was told, or with what I observed.[10] What I observed is this: The nuḥibbin were the donors of wealth and the recipients of nontransferable baraka. They would either give directly to the saint or to the adepts of the order. They would always speak of receiving baraka from the saint if they left something at his tomb. They usually referred to receiving baraka when they gave to the adepts of the madina; when they gave something to the bidonville Ḥamadsha, they were generally more concrete in their demands and, or so it seemed to me, less likely to refer to baraka. The exception was when the adepts of the bidonville were in trance. Then they would refer to baraka. While many of the devotees referred to the baraka of the foqra, they seldom referred to the baraka of the team members. The

[9] The passage of baraka is in many ways analogous to the sexual act.

[10] The difference between what all Ḥamadsha expected to happen ideally and what in fact happened—that is, between the normative statement of the exchange system and a realistic one—created a dissonant situation to which the Ḥamadsha reacted, as we shall see, in accord with their vested interests and their structural position within the Ḥamadsha complex. The explanation offered in the text is indebted to Festinger's (1956) theory of cognitive dissonance.

foqra kept no money except the little that they divided among their poorest members; actually, each of them received a small share. These allotments were called bread, or baraka. In fact, the majority of the proceeds were given to the mizwar.

The team members, on the other hand, kept the majority of proceeds and gave the mizwar the bare minimum necessary for the preservation of their team. The mizwars—and here I am simplifying—kept for themselves as much of the wealth from both the saint's tomb and the brotherhoods as they could. What wealth they distributed to the other wulad siyyid fell into the hands of the most powerful and influential. Neither the mizwar or the other saints' descendants cared for the pilgrims to the tomb except on rare occasions when the pilgrims were influential. The leaders of the saintly lineages were usually careful to entertain important foqra who visited their ancestor's tomb. Both the mizwars and other saints' descendants made an exaggerated

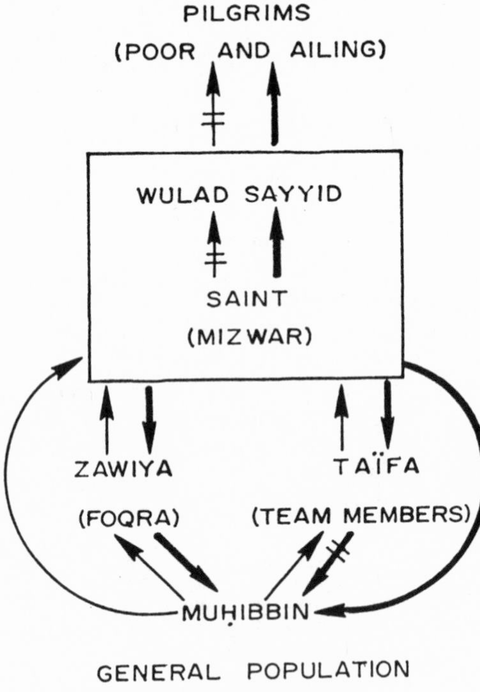

FIGURE 6.

display of their hospitality during the musem, but although they did distribute bread and couscous and fed the important foqra, they actually entertained only important visitors.

The exchanges may be represented in Figure 6. Once again the thin lines indicate the direction of flow of wealth, and the thick ones that of baraka. Double bars represent an interruption in the flow. As can readily be seen, the redistributive system is interrupted by the mizwar and the team members, resulting in their accumulation of wealth. Although there may be a corresponding playing down of the team member's baraka, baraka from the saint and his descendants is still distributed.

Indeed, it is precisely the conceptualization of the saint—and, by extension, the mizwar and other children of the saint—as a continual and inexhaustible source of baraka which enables the mizwar and the most influential of the saint's descendants to exploit the system for their own ends. The social and concomitant ritual organization supports their institutional endowment of baraka. It provides the mizwar with sufficient role distance to prevent his own personality, his selfish motives, and his prosaic character from interfering with his status as mizwar and his image as a selfless individual, highly endowed with baraka, who lives up to the highest ethical standards of Islam. Moreover, the mizwar reconfirms his status during the musem not only by riding through the crowd of pilgrims but also by taking advantage of a dramatic opportunity to demonstrate his hospitality.

The extent to which the mizwar is able to admit to the fact that he does not live up to the standards ideally expected of him is impossible to ascertain. It was my impression, however, that both mizwars were unable to accept fully the contradiction between their actual behavior and the behavior ideally expected of them. It has to be remembered that they themselves are members of the culture, subject to its values and standardized fears, and hold their ancestor in awe. This, I think, accounts in part for their exaggerated show of hospitality during the musem—a display which functioned for them as well as for the other pilgrims as a reconfirmation of the fact that they were living up to the ideal standards of mizwar behavior.

Structurally insulated and ideologically supported by the widespread faith in their ancestors' baraka, the mizwars were able to maintain their economically advantageous position without losing, at any rate outside their descent group, the image of pious and charitable men endowed with great baraka of their own. Within their own lineages, however, their images were far from pure. The wulad siyyid were well aware of the mizwars' duplicity, but, as interested parties—eligible, theoretically, at least, for a share in the proceeds—they were not so anxious to cast aspersion on the mizwars' image, and preferred to vie one with another for their favor.

Outside the saintly descent group, there was, however, comparatively little acknowledgment of the mizwars' failure to live up to the obligations of their role. The few team members who knew the facts were able to accept them quite readily. In fact, this became a good excuse for them not to give to their mizwars. The foqra who knew were much more reticent in admitting it. Even allowing for the image of their organization they wanted to communicate, their fear of their mizwar, and other considerations, there was resistance on their part to the realistic acceptance of the situation. Perhaps, were they to have accepted fully the mizwars' failure to distribute the proceeds according to custom, their belief in the system would have been shattered by the dissonant situation thus created, and they would have been unable to justify pouring their earnings into the mizwars' hands. They chose, instead, to accept the ideal rather than the real.

Beyond the positive injunction to give to the saint because one has received baraka from him, there are, as we have seen, certain negative consequences associated with the failure to give to him: business losses, paralysis, disease, and general misfortune. Here, the foqra's belief was also threatened by the bidonville teams, which did not give to the saint as they should have and suffered no such dire consequences. The teams made no secret of their refusal to give all they could to the saints, but they were not in the same structurally advantageous position of insulation as their mizwars. The foqra argued that the bidonville team members were not true Ḥamadsha and that their failure to give to the saint accounted for their abject poverty. A few insisted that the team members were insane (*ḥmqin*). This, again, is a typical reaction to a dissonant situation.

Only partially successful in resolving it, the foqra expressed a great deal of resentment toward the team members and refused to identify with them. The team members, who preferred their own economically advantageous status, had no desire to join the foqra. The mizwars, callously manipulating the team members for what they were worth, encouraged the foqra's resentment and discouraged any liaison between the two groups. The situation was, in part, responsible for the continuing split between the foqra of the madina and the team members of the bidonville.

The muḥibbin, on the whole, were less interested in the intrigues within the Ḥamadsha organization than in the efficacy of the performances. (One could also add, the dramatic quality.) They would often criticize both the team members and the mizwars, but in critical situations they would always accept the baraka of the mizwar and the ḥadra of the team members. Often, they believed that ʿAïsha Qandisha or another jinn had caused their "initiating" illness because they had scoffed at the Ḥamadsha.

Although the muḥibbin were not as partisan as the adepts or the team members, they tended to affiliate themselves with either the lodges of the madina or the teams of the shantytowns. The madina devotees, whose families had lived in the city for a few generations and who did not need to perform the ḥadra very often, would have nothing to do with the shantytown teams. They found their performances crass, spectacular, and not particularly pious. They accepted the prejudices of the foqra. The bidonville devotees, as well as the newcomers to the madina, preferred the teams. They explained that the foqra did not perform often enough, that they did not know the songs (*riḥs*) of the country, and that they chanted too long and danced too short a time. Some added that the foqra were not particularly friendly. By this, they meant that while the foqra treated them hospitably during a ceremony, the same foqra tended to ignore them on other occasions. The bidonville dwellers and the newcomers to the city seem to have expected more from their affiliation with the Ḥamadsha than the townspeople did.

The Organization of Devotees

There is also a significant difference between the organization of the madina devotees and that of the bidonville devotees. Team members in the bidonvilles play a much more active role in initiating ceremonies either directly or indirectly (through warnings to muḥibbin said in a joking manner), and in determining the composition of ceremonies, than do the foqra. In the bidonvilles, clusters, determined by the frequency of invitations to one another's ceremonies, tend to be focused on a member of one of the teams—usually the muqaddim or ghita player. He is, then, the core, or essential member of the cluster (cf. Barnes 1968:118). It is around him that much of the cluster's activities takes place. In fact, each muqaddim or ghita player is the essential member of a number of clusters which are differentiated primarily by location. In the madina, clusters tend not to focus on an adept of a zawiya or any other single individual. The foqra are invited to perform, but they do not usually sponsor or invite other devotees to ceremonies in which they participate. The difference may be represented schematically, as shown in Figure 7. The center of each star is either the team or zawiya or a member of either organization. The points of the star represent devotees who sponsor ceremonies from time to time. The arrows indicate the direction of invitations (cf. Barnes 1968:113).

This difference in organization can be explained in part in terms of the greater economic stake the team members have in their performances. Since they are economically dependent on the ḥadra, it is to their advantage to maximize their incomes by sponsoring ceremonies and by making sure that as many devotees as possible attend each of their performances.

A comparison of the two muḥibbin groups suggests another, latent function for this organizational difference. The devotees of the madina are, in fact, integrated into urban life. They have usually lived in the city all their lives, as did their parents and often their grandparents. They have professions, family, friends, neighbors of long standing, and other more or less permanent relationships. These relations tend to be specific, for specific ends. They are, as Max Gluckman puts it, single-stranded. The people of the bidonville are not integrated into urban life—they are in fact quite outside it—and they are not yet part of an established shantytown community. The shantytowns are too recent a phenomenon to provide their inhabitants with complete social networks. The average bidonville dweller and his family came from the countryside without a profession that was in demand and without family, friends, or other contacts in the city. He often settled into a neighborhood in which he had no contacts and looked for work wher-

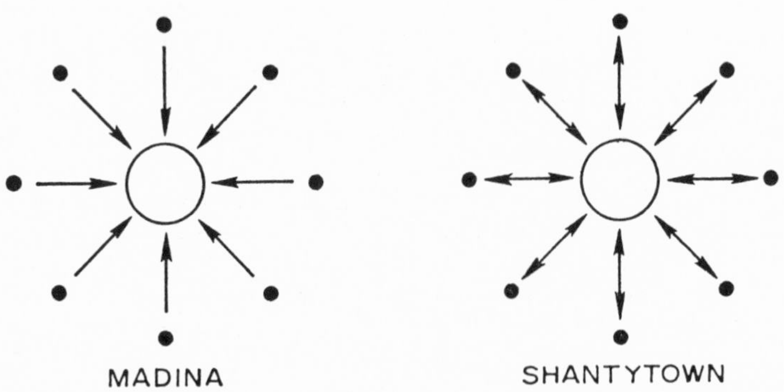

FIGURE 7.

ever he could find it. The single thing he had in common with other people in his bidonville was devotion to the Ḥamadsha. It is not unusual to find that many of the shantytown devotees were actually inactive as Ḥamadsha before coming to the city. Although their sudden recommitment can be explained away on psychological grounds—increased tensions and pressures, feelings of isolation, loneliness, and unworthiness—the facts suggest that the status of devotee provided the newcomer with a means of enlarging his social network.

While the devotees of the madina depend upon their own contacts for inviting and being invited to the ceremonies, those of the shantytowns depend less on their own personal contacts than on the contacts of the team members for their ceremonial attendance. The team members, who are professional Ḥamadsha, have a wide range of these contacts and serve, if you will, as mixers. They provide the devotee with a large number of contacts with whom he will develop reciprocal relations—mutual invitations and the like—not only within the Ḥamadsha frame of reference but also within the broader social setting. Again and again, analysis of the life histories of the bidonville Ḥamadsha reveals that their most significant contacts outside family and kin within the city of Meknes were other Ḥamadsha. The links between the devotees of the bidonville are not as single-stranded as those of the madina. They tend to be multiplex. They satisfy many more needs of the newcomers, who come from the country where multiplex links are predominant, than do the single-stranded links of the madina dweller.

The reluctance of the bidonville devotees to affiliate themselves with the madina zawiyas is, moreover, a reflection of the breach between city and country—city and bidonville—discussed in the last chapter. Certainly there are ritual differences between the two muḥibbin groups, but the rituals themselves are not rigid and could easily be modified. Rather, the concern for ritual differences seems to symbolize the difference between madina and bidonville inhabitants which the bidonville dweller senses. He prefers the bidonville teams because their devotees are very much in the same position as himself. Often, too, the teams' performances are near his own home and provide him with regular occasions to perform the ḥadra. Even newcomers to Meknes who have settled in the madina and attend zawiya performances prefer performances in the bidonvilles and go to them whenever they can. The foqra, who consider themselves city people, have never been anxious to develop a large following of bidonville muḥibbin, despite the obvious increase in income these devotees would bring. Whether this reflects a fear of economic takeover or the desire not to be identified with the newcomers cannot be determined. The foqra themselves, it has to be remembered, are comparative newcomers to the city too. One point is obvious—the majority of foqra are elderly, and they cannot, physically, perform the ḥadra as often as a large following would require. With such a large following, the foqra would see their position gradually usurped by the bidonville teams. The team members would not only pose a threat to the foqra's status within the organization; but, as we have seen, they would affect the very basis of their belief and practice.

The muqaddim of a Ḥamadsha team.

The mausoleum of Sidi 'Ali ben Ḥamdush in Beni Rachid. The tomb is located under the cupola; the wing, to the right, contains cubicles for pilgrims wishing to spend the night.

Pilgrims entering the mausoleum of Sidi Ahmed Dghughi in Beni Ouarad. The tents belong to pilgrims.

The musem at Beni Rachid in 1968. The two palm trees are those at which the mizwars of the saintly lineages meet. The mizwar of Sidi 'Ali entertains guests in the black tent. The mosque of Beni Jennad, a neighboring town, is in the background.

Circles of dancing pilgrims following the mizwar of Sidi Ahmed, hidden by flags, as he makes his way to the tomb of Sidi Mejma'. Musem, 1968.

Pilgrims at the bread ovens at Beni Rachid during the musem of 1968. Bread is symbolic of baraka and is said to contain it.

Pilgrims at the ‘Ayn Kabir in Beni Rachid during the musem of 1968. The stairs lead down to the bathhouse, where women bathe in the holy waters .

The ḥadra at Beni Ouarad. The man in the center of the circle has heard his riḥ and is about to enter jidba. Note the clay drums (*gwals*).

The Hamadsha ḥadra before the mausoleum of Sheikh al-Kamal in Meknes. Note the long ghita in the upper lefthand corner of the crowd.

Dghughiyyin of the madina of Meknes recite the dikr.

The zawiya of the Dghughiyyin in Meknes. Note the fig tree, to which bits of cloth have been tied as promises of a sacrifice (*'ar*) to either Sidi Ahmed or 'Aïsha Qandisha. The floor of the zawiya is covered with tombstones.

A performance of the ḥadra by a bidonville team. The man with his head exposed is slashing it with a barely visible knife in his right hand. Note the varying responses of the audience. Note too the snare drum.

A blow-up of the head-slasher.

The "line" at the performance on the previous page. The men are in ḥal. The woman in the striped jallaba has joined the line "to come down."

Country Ḥamadsha performing the ḥadra in Meknes. The woman with flying curls is in jidba. The boy in the foreground hits his head with a shoe in imitation of a head-slasher.

Part Three

The following chapters are concerned with Ḥamadsha therapy. I have chosen to present my material within a framework that will be familiar to readers of Western medical and psychiatric literature, because such a framework provides both a means of describing the Ḥamadsha system of therapy with minimum distortion and a suitable vehicle for comparison with both Western medical and psychiatric theories and those of other societies. It has to be remembered, however, that this presentation is not the Ḥamadsha's, nor would the Ḥamadsha feel altogether comfortable with it. As participants in a system which they have found to be more or less successful therapeutically, they have not felt the need to organize their beliefs and practices into a consistent whole. Were they to attempt it, they undoubtedly would not delimit their "therapeutic system" in the same way I have done. Their axis of orientation would be quite different. It would probably emphasize many more elements of what the Westerner would call religion or folk theology.

The Ḥamadsha system of therapy is not an isolated, secular system of beliefs and practices; it is embedded in and indivisible from the entire culture of the Moroccan Arab. The lines between secular and sacred have not been drawn, and Moroccan culture has not experienced the fragmentation resulting from specialization and overspecialization that Western culture has undergone. Throughout my presentation I have had to bring in data from other areas of Moroccan cultural life. The Ḥamadsha's therapy, like all therapies, is a legitimating apparatus—"the application of conceptual machinery to ensure that actual and potential deviants stay within the institutionalized definitions of reality" (Berger and Luckmann 1967:112–113)—and their psychology, like all psychologies, presupposes a cosmology (Berger and Luckmann 1967:175).

8

The Theory of Therapy

Ḥamadsha therapy is but one of many therapies within the Moroccan world, a point which has to be emphasized. Although in the Western world there are a number of quasi-legitimate therapies (fringe medicine) such as chiropractic and osteopathy, there is only one standard system of therapy—medical therapy—which has received the "charter" of the society. When a Westerner is sick, he will almost invariably have recourse to some product or some practioner within the medical field. The doctor of medicine, particularly the specialist, is the final authority.

In Morocco, there is no single, socially chartered therapeutic system with final authority. There are the *fuqaḥa*, or Koranic teachers, who specialize in writing amulets and talismans; the herbalists, who may be either Arab, Berber, or Jewish; the specialist in traditional Arab medicine; the barber, who, among other things, lets blood; the *aguza*, an old woman who is familiar with many herbal and magical brews and practices and who may be a midwife; her male counterpart; the exorcist, who may be a Koranic teacher or an adept of a brotherhood; the brotherhoods themselves—Gnawiyya, ʿIsawiyya, Raḥaliyya, Ḥamdushiyya, Jilaliyya, and the like; and Western medical practitioners. Even the Western medical practitioners are not popularly organized into a hierarchy of authority, and the Moroccan's decision to go to one rather than another is as significant as his decision to go to an herbalist rather than a Koranic teacher. There is, then, the choice of going to a French or Spanish doctor, to a Moroccan doctor who has studied Western medicine, to a pharmacist, to a male nurse who conducts a medical practice on the sly, to a European missionary, or to a local infirmary or hospital. The Moroccan may also visit any number of saints' tombs or sacred grottos, springs, pits, trees, or baths.

Although symptomatology plays a definite role in the choice of therapy, it is not the only consideration, especially since several different types of therapy are usually believed to be efficacious for the same complaint. Other factors are of equal, if not greater, importance. These include notions of what has caused the illness, the availability of the specialist, the cost of therapy,[1] the nature of the relations the patient or his family has with various practitioners, the past experiences of the patient and his family with various cures, the urgings of friends and neighbors, the advice of diviners and seers, the current popularity of a particular practitioner or type of therapy, the strength of belief in a particular saint, shrine, or brotherhood, and the seriousness and urgency of the complaint. The wide range of options leaves considerable room for unconscious as well as conscious factors in the choice of cure.

The Moroccans do not make the same distinction between physical and mental illness that the Westerner does. Just as they have many different forms of therapy, so they have many theories of causation. Their "pathologies" are often self-contradictory. They appear to be an amalgamation of various folk beliefs and popularizations of traditional Arab and modern Western medicine. Since theories of causation vary from tribe to tribe, city to city, and family to family, it is impossible to form a systematic Moroccan pathology. Still, although a supernatural element will enter either directly or indirectly into the Moroccan's explanation of any disease, it is possible to divide Moroccan theories of causation roughly into two categories: naturalistic and preternaturalistic explanations.

The naturalistic explanations are usually mechanistic. Syphilis is said to be caused by menstrual fluid. Gonorrhea is said to be caused by semen backing up into the kidneys, if a man is not careful to urinate after making love. Tuberculosis is caused by, among other things, not wearing a shirt in the heat, especially when riding a bicycle. Certain heart diseases are said to be caused by eating salt. Poisoning by one's enemies is a frequent explanation for wasting diseases.

Preternatural explanations can be divided into those involving the jnun and those that do not. The latter include magical poisonings, magi-

[1] Pilgrimages to saints' tombs and other traditional therapeutic practices are often chosen over Western therapies because of cost. This is not just true of Morocco but of other countries in North Africa and the Middle East (cf. Howell 1970).

cal curses, witchcraft, and the evil eye. The former have to do with being struck or possessed by a jinn.

It is for illnesses caused by the jnun that the Ḥamadsha are called, and it is with these that we will be primarily concerned. It should be remembered, though, that the cults to Sidi ʿAli and Sidi Ahmed have a broader range of efficacy. Although visits to the tombs of the Ḥamadsha saints are considered particularly helpful for illnesses caused by the jnun, these visits are also held to be beneficial in curing illnesses for which the jnun are not responsible. The pilgrim to the tombs obtains the baraka of the saints and somehow always benefits thereby, even if he is not entirely cured of his complaint.

I wish to emphasize, too, that illnesses caused by the jnun are not the sole province of the Ḥamadsha. Throughout Morocco, the *fuqaḥa* are considered to have special control over the jnun. They provide men, women, and children with talismans to protect them from the jnun, and are often called in to exorcize devils who have taken possession of a person. The members of the other fraternities—most notably the Gnawa, from whom the Ḥamadsha have borrowed heavily—also specialize in the cure of the jinn-struck and the jinn-possessed. The determination of which particular cure to undertake varies from case to case. Often, the patient will try one cure after another until he happens upon the one that "satisfies the jinn"—that is, the one that offers him relief.

The Theory of Pathology: The Jnun

The term *jnun*, the Moroccan Arabic plural of *jinn*, which is itself a plural in Classical and many dialects of Arabic, has both a general and a specific meaning. Generally, it refers to a wide variety of poorly differentiated "spirits" which are believed to inhabit the universe, but which are distinct from the ordinary beings of everyday life. These spirits are of a different ontological status from the objects of the phenomenal world. The exact nature of this difference is not clear. Their existence is attested to in the Koran, where it is written that God created man "of clay like the potter's" and the jinn "of smokeless fire" (LV, 13–14). The Westerner would classify them as supernatural or elemental spirits.

There are many terms for jnun in Moroccan Arabic. Some of them refer to specific classes of jnun—*ʿafarit*, *ghwal*, and *shayatin*—while others, as Westermarck has noted, are the result of fear of mentioning them by their proper name. "To pronounce their name would be to summon them" (Westermarck 1926(I):263). I have heard them referred to as *mluk* (the plural of *malik*, king), *muselmin* (Muslims), *muwalin l-ard* (the masters of the earth), *muwalin l-makan* (the masters of the place), *rjal al-blad* (the men of the country, a term that is used most often for saints), and *mu'minin*. The term *l-aryaḥ*, which is the plural of *riḥ* (wind, or, in the case of the Ḥamadsha, the particular trance-inducing musical phrase of a person), is very commonly used. Westermarck (1926(I):263) found that its usage was restricted to disease-causing jnun. Most often, however, references to the jnun are oblique: "those people there," "those people who are below the ground," "those people who are below the river," "those who shun salt," or "those who are hidden or invisible." French-speaking Moroccans refer to the jnun as *les diables* or *les invisibles*.

Not only are the lines of distinction between the various classes of jnun unclear, but the jnun themselves are often confused with other spiritual beings such as angels (*malaïka*) and Satan (*Shitan*, *iblis*), as well as with the saints themselves. Several of my informants confused the jnun with the two angels which are believed to live on a person's right and left shoulders and to count, respectively, their good and bad activities. Saints, angels, and jnun are often lumped together, as when the expression *rjal al-blad*, which commonly refers to saints, is used for the jnun, too, especially for those which I call named-jnun. Westermarck (1926(I):389) has noted this confusion between saints and jnun. He writes:

> Saints rule over *jnun* and have Muhammadan jnun as their assistants: and Mulai ʿAbdelqader [Jilani] is the sultan of all the saints and *jnun*. The term *rijal allah* comprises both saints and Muhammadan *jnun*, and in the *jenn* saints the borderline between *jnun* and saints is wellnigh obliterated.

Westermarck goes on to list animals such as frogs and snakes which may be considered either saints or inhabited by jnun, and the shrines associated with them.

Although the term *jnun* may be used for the *ʿafarit*, *ghwal*, and *shayatin*, most Moroccans readily acknowledge a difference, properly speaking, between these creatures and the jnun. The shayatin are associated with Shitan, or Satan, and have been called his children. Like Shitan, their status in the spirit world is not certain. The Koran refers to Shitan as both a jinn (XVIII, 48) and an angel (II, 32). Most Moroccans hold the shayatin responsible for mischievous thoughts and deeds, especially those deeds that appear to be more or less spontaneous and are against the better judgment of the man who perpetrates them. The shayatin are often blamed for sexual misconduct.[2] A man will speak of his amorous adventures with reference to the shayatin, or he will refer to women as shayatin when he reflects on their supposedly inexhaustible appetites and their inability to counter their libidinous desires. The transgressions for which Shitan or the shayatin are held accountable do not inspire strong feelings of remorse or guilt; the shayatin are not responsible for diseases of any sort.

The jnun, in the restricted sense of the term, also have to be distinguished from the huge, cannibalistic spirits known as *ʿafarit,* and the *ghwal,* or ogres. Although the Koran takes notice of the jinn and Shitan, it refers neither to the ʿafarit or the ghwal.[3] Both the ʿafarit and the ghwal appear to have a more substantial existence than the jnun, whose bodies are said to be made of vapor or flame. The ʿafarit are, perhaps, more powerful, clever, and evil than the "run-of-the-mill" jnun. Westermarck refers to them as the "aristocracy of the jnun." It is my impression that they occupy space more often, at least, than the ordinary jnun, and are capable of being perceived by man's ordinary perceptual faculties. They seem to differ in scale and capacity from both man and the other jnun. They may be giants with tremendous, often anthropophagous appetites; they may be capable of traveling great distances with extraordinary rapidity; or they may be endowed with great strength. They are always malignant and terrifying. They have the ability to be in more than one place at a time, to fly, and to render themselves invisible. They may possess a person, thereby rendering him a maniac with extraordinary strength.

The *ghwal,* or ogres, may be either male (*ghul*) or female (*ghula*). Belief in them is widespread in the Arab world. The ancient Arabs believed that they lived in the desert and, assuming the shape of women, led travelers astray. They appeared, and still appear in Morocco, more often as women than as men. Usually they are giant women with long pendant breasts and the feet of a goat. They are sometimes covered with hair. Although they are usually ugly, they have the ability to change their shape and become beautiful, enticing women, who lure their victims into deserted places and eat them up. Westermarck (1926(I):397) has written of them:

[2] The association of the shayatin with sexual activity is exemplified by the idiomatic expressions for sexual intercourse during dreams: *darab sh-Shitan* and *ja sh-Shitan.*

[3] Line 39 of Sura 27 refers to an "ʿifrit of the jinn," but this is probably a figure of speech which means a very powerful jinn.

> The *ghwal* are said to live in the Sudan or Sahara or in a thick wood from which they come out in the shapes of animals or who knows where? They have black faces and eyes like flaming fire and are fond of human flesh. Some people maintain that *ghwal* are not *jnun* but a species by themselves or a kind of men or wild animals, whereas others, who seem to be particularly well-informed, are of the opinion that they are of the *jenn* kind.

The female ghwal possess many of ʿAïsha Qandisha's features, and I have heard her called a ghula. Usually, however, she is referred to as a jinniyya or, especially by her most constant devotees, as simply *Lalla ʿAïsha,* a creature different from all other creatures.

The jnun—again in the more restricted sense of the word—are a race of spiritual beings, created before man and said to be composed of vapor or flame. They are not normally extended over space, but they do exist over time. They are intelligent creatures, resembling human beings, but they have no bodies and are usually imperceptible to man's ordinary senses. They are, however, capable of rendering themselves visible, and often take on various animal forms: snakes, frogs, wasps, cats, camels, donkeys, and jackals. They sometimes appear as female temptresses or male seducers. The jnun are capable of marrying humans, and their legal status has been discussed in all respects by Muslim theologians and canonists. They are also capable of appearing in more than one place at a time. There is, in Morocco, mixed opinion as to whether or not the jnun are mortal. Most Moroccans believe that Muslim jnun are capable of salvation.

The jnun are said to live underground, although some of them are believed to inhabit the air between the earth and the sky. They are said to like water and to gravitate to damp or wet places: marshes and bogs, streams and rivers, springs and wells, and the sea. They are frequently found near fountains, baths, toilets, and drains. Often, too, they live in grottos and caves or around unusual trees and rocks. All the areas where jnun are said to live are treated circumspectly. A Moroccan who approaches such a place will usually say *bismillah r-rahman r-rahim,* in the name of God the merciful and compassionate, or simply *bismillah,* to rid the area of their presence. He will also sprinkle salt, to which the jnun have a special aversion, around toilets and drains. The jnun have an equally intense dislike of benzoin (*jawi*) and other incenses,[4] and of iron and steel, silver, and tar.

[4] Nevertheless, under certain circumstances, as we shall see, the jnun are attracted by or pleased with jawi and other incense which normally drive them off (Pâques 1964:559–563).

The jnun do not usually have characters as well-developed as, say, the Zar of Ethiopia (Leiris 1958) or the Vodun spirits of Haiti (Metraux 1959). They cannot be equated with natural phenomena such as lightning and thunder or stars and comets, although certain of the ʿafarit are held responsible for these phenomena. Some of the jnun are named, and their names are well-known to all Moroccans. Westermarck (1926(I):49) has called these jnun "jenn saints." Others—the majority—are named, but their names are the secret of a few privileged individuals who have access to their world. There is much power in the name, and the discovery of the name of a jinn possessing a person is one of the first steps in exorcising it.

There are male and female jnun; Muslim (Arab and Berber), Jewish, Christian, and pagan jnun. The pagan jnun are especially dangerous. All jnun are capable of marrying among themselves and bearing children. It is claimed, in fact, that the jnun are organized into a world which mirrors the Moroccan world. There is a king of the jnun, Sidi Shamharush, who is venerated as a saint in some parts of the country, around Marrakech,[5] as well as a court of ministers, pashas, and other traditional civil servants. A Moroccan does not push the parallel very far, however, and members of the jnun world do not normally have relations with their counterpart in the phenomenal world.

Sidi Shamharush is said to have a complicated communications network that is likened to a river with a thousand tributaries, each of which has a thousand subtributaries. There is a jinn responsible for each of these rivers, who runs errands and carries messages for the king of the jnun to the farthest reaches of the world. The jinn of a river is named after the river; the names of these jnun are known only to a few, the Koranic teachers and magicians, and their knowledge gives them a certain control over the jnun. These magician-scholars are said to use their power to find buried treasures—a very frequent theme in Moroccan folklore—and to work magic and exorcise demons.

Often the jnun make their appearance in dreams, but it is possible by various practices involving blood, to which the jnun have a special affinity, to obtain a view of them. The jnun are frequently said to carry men and women off to their world and reveal its workings. It is not unusual to hear of a man suddenly disappearing from his village and then returning many years later to tell of his adventures among the jnun. Many of the magician-scholars are said to leave the phenomenal

[5] He is believed to be buried at the foot of the Jebel Toukhal.

world for varying periods of time and to descend into the rivers, where many of these spirits gather. They return with considerable power and are treated with care.

The jnun are not necessarily evil or harmful. They *are* whimsical and arbitrary, capricious and revengeful, quick-tempered and despotic —and therefore always potentially dangerous. If they are wounded or insulted, they are quick to retaliate by striking their adversary or taking possession of him. The man, or woman, who has injured a jinn is usually quite ignorant of his misdeed. He may have brushed against it accidentally, trampled it inadvertently—particularly when the jinn has taken on the form of an animal such as a snake or a frog—or scalded it with boiling water which he, or more commonly she, has carelessly thrown out. It is often said that where a jinn is injured, there will his injurer suffer.

Men and women who are angry or frightened are particularly liable to attack by the jnun; so are people in liminal periods associated with change in social status. Hence pregnant women, newborn children, boys about to be circumcised or just circumcised, couples about to be married, and the dying are particularly vulnerable. There are periods when the jnun are especially active—after mid-afternoon prayers, for example. There are also periods when the jnun are especially inactive—during Ramadan, the month of fasting, when the jnun are said to be imprisoned.

The jnun are always treated with the greatest respect, and they are generally feared. Moroccans take all kinds of precautions to keep them at bay. They may burn candles in the dark, sprinkle salt in areas to which the jnun are known to gravitate, utter apotropaic phrases, when crossing streams or thresholds, entering caves, automobiles, and unfamiliar places, or simply feeling the presence of a jinn; and they usually wear phylacteries containing words from the Koran as well as charms to protect themselves (cf. Westermarck 1926(I):302–324). The jnun's constant interference with man's daily life is accepted fatalistically, however, as one of the givens of wordly existence.

Named-Jnun

There are, as I have said, certain jnun whose names are common knowledge and whom I have chosen to call "named-jnun." They are not linguistically distinguished in Moroccan Arabic, as far as I know, but are always referred to by their proper names.[6] Westermarck has classified many of them as individual spirits. Because the named-jnun, especially ʿAïsha Qandisha, play an important role in Ḥamadsha therapy, it is necessary to consider them and their relationship with human beings in detail.

With the exception of the belief in ʿAïsha Qandisha, belief in the named-jnun in Morocco is associated primarily with the Gnawa. The Gnawa, like the other so-called black brotherhoods of the Maghreb, have an elaborate hierarchy of demons, which are associated with special colors, incense, dance steps, and musical phrases.[7] There is some character differentiation among them (Dermenghem 1954; Pâques 1964). The named-jnun are also associated with the Jilaliyya—the more "popular" and spectacular of the two brotherhoods that claim to be followers of al-Jilani. (The Jilala, however, are often confused with the Gnawa in Morocco.) Brunel (1926:145 et seq.) mentions the belief in named-jnun among the ʿIsawa. The Ḥamadsha themselves, as well as most other Moroccans of their background, recognize the Gnawa origin of many of their named-jnun.

Westermarck has argued (1926(I):379 et seq.; also see Pâques 1964) that the belief in these named-jnun was brought north from sub-Saharan Africa by black African slaves. The word "Gnawa" is said to be derived from Guinea. Tremearne (1914) has traced similar Tunisian beliefs to the Hausa; Andrews (1903) found them among the Songhrai immigrants to Algiers. I myself was told both by members of the

[6] In many of the religions of Northwest Africa, south of the Sahara, a distinction is made linguistically between the named and unnamed spirits (Greenberg 1946; Ortigues 1966).

[7] Viviana Pâques, in her extraordinary monograph, *L'Arbre Cosmique* (1964: 568), examines the symbolic significance of these associated elements in terms of an esoteric "African" cosmology. She considers the dances symbolic, recalling the first mythic and cosmic events which brought about the formation of the world in which we live. Bastide (1958:175) has argued similarly for the *condomblé* of Bahia. "La transe religieuse est réglée par les modèles mythiques; elle n'est qu'une répétition des mythes. La danse devient un 'opéra fabuleux'; l'expression célèbre de Rimbaud 'colle' exactement au phenomène."

Among the Ḥamadsha, and among other Moroccans of their milieu, I have found no such symbolic associations—and no knowledge even of the existence of such estoteric beliefs of which Pâques writes. The Ḥamadsha consider their dances as work for the saints they worship and as an appeasement of the jnun. They recognize of course that they fall into trance and mutilate themselves as Sidi Ahmed (and Sidi ʿAli) did. This is inevitable. It is the will of Allah, and perhaps the will of the Ḥamadsha saints and the jnun, even. They see it as a mark of devotion, of worship, even of obligation, but not as the symbolically significant reenactment of the practices of the saints they worship.

Gnawa order and by nonmembers living in the Valley of the Sous (at Sidi Ahmed ou Mousa and at Illergh) that the belief in these named-jnun came from the Sudan. Legends like that of ʿAïsha Qandisha suggest a Sudanese origin. Parallels between the religions just south of the Sahara—the religions of the Hausa, the Songhai, and the Zar worshippers in Ethiopia—and the belief in named-jnun among the Gnawa, Jilala, Ḥamadsha, and ʿIsawa are striking.

The extent to which the belief in named-jnun and the development of specific relationships to them is restricted to the followers of these brotherhoods cannot be determined. Michaux-Bellaire (1913:294) found belief in them current among the women of the Gharb in 1913. In fact, he suggested that this belief was restricted to women; but it exists today among both men and women affiliated with the Ḥamadsha and other similar brotherhoods. Still, it is claimed that more women than men have intimate relations with the named-jnun, especially with the female ones. The section of the ḥadra devoted to these demons is said to be for women. One of my best informants suggested that belief in them is restricted to Arabs of the northern countryside: Gharbawa, Beni Hsen, Shrarda, Hajawa, and Zrahna. Although there certainly is such a belief among these people, I am not certain that the belief is restricted to them.

The named-jnun have all the attributes of ordinary jnun. Their character traits and personalities are more elaborate, but they are not as well worked out as those of the Vodun and Zar spirits. Some of them, like ʿAïsha Qandisha, have legends associated with them. Having names, they all have sexual identities. The majority are female, but there are a few males. Some of the males are married to the females and may even have children. The named-jnun often appear as incubi and succubi. (Often the unnamed do, too.) Unlike the ordinary jnun, they establish definite relations with men and women and make certain demands on them.

The relationship between a man or a woman and his or her named jinn or jinniyya is complicated. Such a man is said to be the follower (*tabiʿ*) of the jinn and to lean on (*muttakil*) or rest against (*muwali*) the jinn. *Msannad* may also be used to describe the relationship between a man and his jinn, although it is usually restricted to his relationship with a saint. A man can decide—but does not necessarily decide—to become msannad to a saint; he cannot decide to become a follower of a jinn. It is the jinn, as we shall see, who always decides this. Once the relationship has been established, the jinn makes certain demands on his follower. These usually involve wearing a certain color, burning a special incense, and performing the ḥadra to a special musical phrase (*riḥ*). The jinn may also require special food and sexual taboos, visits to shrines, periodic sacrifices, or the sponsoring of ceremonies, especially those given by the Ḥamadsha, the Gnawa, and the Jilala.

ʿAïsha Qandisha[8]

Of all the named jnun, ʿAïsha Qandisha is the most important for the Ḥamadsha. They consider themselves to be her special devotees. Often they refer to her as "ʿAïsha Sudaniyya," "ʿAïsha Gnawiyya," "Lalla ʿAïsha" (Lady ʿAïsha), or the great female muqaddim. I have also heard them call her "our mother." Westermarck (1926(I):395–396) identifies ʿAïsha Qandisha with Astarte, the goddess of love of the ancient Eastern Mediterranean. He suggests that "Qandisha" is related to "Qedesha," the name for the temple harlot in the "Canaanitish cults," and that belief in her was brought to Morocco by the early Phoenician invaders. He further suggests that Ḥammu Qiyu, ʿAïsha's jinn-husband, can be identified with the Carthaginian god Hamam. While the belief in ʿAïsha Qandisha and the Ḥamadsha practices do show parallels with ancient Mediterranean beliefs and practices, there are equally strong parallels between the belief in ʿAïsha Qandisha and current beliefs in other female demons and ogresses throughout the Mediterranean basin and in sub-Saharan Africa (Frazer 1961).

Although ʿAïsha Qandisha is generally referred to as a "jinniyya," her exact status in the Moroccan demonology has never been determined specifically. To the coastal Arabs she is a siren, and to those of the interior she is a sort of chthonian mother associated with earth, mud, water, and rivers. She is always libidinous and quick-tempered. She never laughs, and she is always ready to strangle, scratch, or whip anyone who insults her or does not obey her commands. It is said that she prefers the morning air for her walks. Like Kali-Parvati, she may appear to believers either as a beauty or as a hag with long pendant breasts. Usually, even in her beautiful manifestations, she has the feet of a camel, a donkey, or an ass. Sometimes she appears with the legs of a woman and the body of a goat with pendant breasts (Westermarck 1926(I):392). Throughout northern Morocco there are places sacred to her. These are usually pits, grottos, springs, and fountains, as well as other spots where someone is said to have seen her or where some-

[8] See also pp. 43–45.

thing uncanny has taken place. The Ḥamadsha, particularly Sidi ʿAli's followers, say she resides principally in the grotto of Beni Rachid. However, she too is capable of appearing in many places at the same time.

When ʿAïsha Qandisha presents herself to a man as a beautiful woman, a seductress, that man will have no defense against her power unless he immediately plunges a steel knife into the earth. He is then privileged to reject her entirely or to make a "marriage contract" with her that is to his own advantage. (This is infrequent, since Lalla ʿAïsha invariably hides her camel's feet under a flowing caftan.) If a man has been unfortunate enough to sleep with her before discovering her identity, he becomes her slave forever and must follow her commands explicitly. Otherwise, she is sure to strangle him.

A man is walking along a road, and suddenly his vision blurs. He thinks there is something wrong with his eyes, but in fact it is Lalla ʿAïsha Ḥasnawiyya [one of ʿAïsha Qandisha's manifestations]. He sees only her in front of him, and he looks on and sees only her. When he comes to an isolated crossing or path, she takes him by the hand. She asks him why he is following her and where he knows her from. The man tries to excuse himself and says that he thought she was a woman he knew. She says, "Fine. Welcome. Come with me. But we must go into a garden, and not into a house." "I'll even go beyond the garden," the man answers. Lalla ʿAïsha agrees and tells the man to follow her. Because he follows her, he sees only clouds. He alone sees her. Suddenly they find themselves in a big garden with a lot of food, near a well-furnished house. Lalla ʿAïsha takes the shape of a woman the man loves and desires. She has the same features as the beauty, but they are slightly exaggerated. Her bust is eighty centimeters. They make love. Afterward she asks him what he wants to do. The man says he is single and wants to marry. Lalla ʿAïsha says she wants to do the same. "We'll make a vow [*ahd*] to God," she says. She tells him not to tell anyone, not even his mother. If he does, she'll have his throat. She tells him that she will sleep with other men. "I'll help you with money," she says. "You must not wear European clothes except if they are covered with a jellaba." Then she asks him if he knows her. She tells him who she is. "If you do not do what I say," she says, "then you'll not have me or any other woman." The man asks for three days to think it over. Lalla ʿAïsha gives him four. "If I don't do this," the man thinks to himself, "then I'll have to dress in a *darbala* [a ragged and patched cloak]. I may even lose my life. I'll marry her. Everyone knows me. I don't want them to see me change." [9]

[9] This example of ʿAïsha's ways was given me by one of my best informants, a born storyteller, who spent hours entertaining friends with his tales. He was not a Ḥamdushi but was very familiar with their ways. He was popularly thought to

Often ʿAïsha will demand that the man wear old and dirty clothes regardless, and that he never cut his hair or fingernails. She will usually restrict his sexual life too. She may forbid him to make love to any woman but herself and his real wife, or to any woman who is not on her side, her follower. Such men are said to be married (*mjawwej*) to ʿAïsha Qandisha, and they are treated circumspectly. This special relationship to ʿAïsha seems to bear no relation to membership in the Ḥamadsha brotherhoods. In fact, only a few of ʿAïsha's husbands are Ḥamadsha.

ʿAïsha Qandisha requires her followers—and not necessarily her husbands—always to wear red, black, or chartreuse green, or any combination of these colors. Red and black are the more common. Her incense is black *jawi* (benzoin) or *ḥasalban* (?), which is used to placate her, especially when she takes possession of her follower. She prefers the music of the Ḥamadsha, and often requires her followers to perform the ḥadra. Her special riḥ has the following words:

O ʿAïsha! Rise and place yourself in the service of the cause of Allah and the Prophet.
O Sire! Greetings to the Prophet. Welcome, O Lalla ʿAïsha.
The altar is prepared. O Lalla ʿAïsha! O Gnawiyya!
Welcome, O Daughter of the river. Allah! Allah! Lalla ʿAïsha!
She has come! She has come! She has come! Lalla ʿAïsha!

There is some variation in these words.[10] This riḥ is played at the peak of the Ḥamadsha ḥadra. The lights are turned out, and ʿAïsha is said to rise from the earth under the dancers and dance with her devotees. People claim that whenever and wherever the Ḥamadsha perform their ḥadra, ʿAïsha Qandisha is under them in the earth. She is particularly fond of blood, and often requires her followers to make sacrifices (*dabiḥa*s) to her. Black and red chickens are her most common demands. She also makes certain that her followers slash their heads when they hear her special riḥ or another riḥ that pleases her. Still other of her followers are made to imitate pigs or camels when they perform the ḥadra. Such theriomimetic behavior is even more common among the ʿIsawa (Brunel 1926:168 et seq.).

Sometimes ʿAïsha Qandisha fragments into a number of different

be married to the she-demon, and he considered himself to be tormented by her. This tale, which is considerably embellished and not without humor and suspense, was told to me in front of several Ḥamadsha devotees who were very impressed by it.

[10] Westermarck (1926(I):393) records a verse employed in the area of the Dukkala tribe: "ʿAïsha Qandisha is sitting and smears herself with henna."

jinniyyas, each with a slightly different personality: Lalla ʿAïsha Sudaniyya, who is also called Lalla ʿAïsha Gnawiyya and is the "basic" ʿAïsha Qandisha; Lalla ʿAïsha Dghughiyya; Lalla ʿAïsha Dghugha; and Lalla ʿAïsha Ḥasnawiyya. It is sometimes said that these jinniyyas are the daughters of ʿAïsha Qandisha, but most often they are simply named and their relationship to ʿAïsha Qandisha is left unquestioned. They all require their followers to wear black or red, but they appear to be placated by different incenses. Lalla ʿAïsha Dghughiyya likes red jawi; Lalla ʿAïsha Dghugha likes harmal (*Paganum harmola*); and Lalla ʿAïsha Ḥasnawiyya likes tar (*qatran*). I have been told that these "ladies" have different favorite times of day for taking walks. Lalla ʿAïsha Dghughiyya likes the hours immedately following afternoon prayers; Lalla ʿAïsha Dghugha prefers the hours after evening prayers; Lalla ʿAïsha Ḥasnawiyya only the first few hours after evening prayers. Lalla ʿAïsha Dghughiyya supposedly comes from Sidi Ahmed's village, and Lalla ʿAïsha Dghugha from the village of Sidi ʿAli. (Lalla ʿAïsha Dghugha is said to be particularly fond of houses.) Lalla ʿAïsha Ḥasnawiyya comes, as her name indicates, from the Beni Hsen. There is considerable variation in the extent to which these manifestations of ʿAïsha Quandisha are developed. Many of the Ḥamadsha do not believe in them, and some have never heard of them.

Ḥammu Qiyu and Sidi Ḥammu

According to some reports, ʿAïsha Qandisha is married to a jinn called Ḥammu Qiyu. Like most of the male jnun, his character is relatively undeveloped; however, the Ḥamadsha insist that he must be distinguished from still another jinn called Sidi Ḥammu. Sidi Ḥammu likes red jawi and is particularly fond of blood. In fact, he lives around slaughterhouses and slaughter blocks, and is said to have a particularly intimate relationship with butchers. He has a number of followers among the Ḥamadsha, and is known to have sexual relations with some of the female devotees. The words of his riḥ are:

> Sidi Ḥammu, forgive us.
> O, Our Prophet, forgive us.
> Messenger of God, forgive us.
> Men of God, forgive us.

Lalla Malika

Lalla Malika, the daughter of the king, has the most elaborate personality of the remaining she-demons popularly believed in the Meknes area. She does not respond to the ḥadra of the Ḥamadsha—she responds instead to the dances of the Gnawa and Jilala—but she is often referred to by Ḥamadsha and has relations with many of them. Lalla Malika is very beautiful and dresses, as they say, with a lot of chic. She demands the same elegance of all her followers. She is a flirt and quite promiscuous, and she especially enjoys relationships with married men. I have been told she speaks only French and that she lives in clothes cabinets.

When Lalla Malika sees someone she likes, she goes up to him and passes her hand in front of his eyes. The person then sees only clouds. He sees nothing but Lalla Malika. He cannot remember his house. Lalla Malika remains next to him. When she sees him standing off to the side, she calls him by name and tells him that she is next to him and asks him to accept her wishes. The man agrees. "I want you to marry me," she says. "I want you to sleep with me." The man agrees, say, on condition that he has the liberty to have intercourse with other women. Lalla Malika agrees. Once they have come to an agreement, the man asks to see her. (He has not seen her up to this time.) She appears in front of him with clothes embroidered in gold, sometimes with long hair, sometimes with short hair. Then she says all right. The man agrees. "I'm in your hands," he says. He can then marry her or sleep with her. It is all the same. She tells him to wear perfumes, to shave often, and to wear new clothes. "Then you'll have your liberty," she tells him. "I'll even help you escape prison." [11]

Lalla Malika is always gay, and she does not attack her followers. She likes to laugh and tickle them, and she is responsible when a group of women suddenly begin giggling. She prefers the color pink, and requires her followers to wear eau de cologne and burn santal (*l-ʿud qamari*). Her riḥ is usually played by the Gnawa or Jilala, but it may be played by the Ḥamadsha if, as happens occasionally, she should take possession of one of the dancers in their ḥadra. The words of her riḥ are as follows:

> Welcome, Lalla Malika! Welcome, O ʿAlawiyya!
> Welcome, Lalla Malika, to the ḥadra of Lalla Malika.
> Allah! Lalla Malika! I beseech Lalla Malika.
> Allah! Lalla Malika! He who beseeches can have no fear.
> Allah! Daughter of the Prophet.

Lalla Mira

After ʿAïsha Qandisha, Lalla Mira has perhaps the greatest following among the women of Meknes. She makes them wear bright yellow or

[11] This example was given by the same informant who told me of ʿAïsha's ways.

orange and burn yellow jawi. I have been told that she comes from the Beni Mtir, a Berber tribe, and she is often called Lalla Mira al-Mtiriyya. She lives in houses and takes her walks after afternoon prayers. Her character is poorly developed. She makes people laugh, but also attacks and takes possession of them. She is unmarried.

Sometimes a woman visits another and begins to gossip. Lalla Mira listens to them. If one of the women should criticize her, then she will attack her. Then the woman must wear yellow, the color of Lalla Mira, and perform the ḥadra. Lalla Mira can attack someone who is laughing or crying a lot. Sometimes a woman who is crying is suddenly paralyzed. She continues to cry as long as she is paralyzed. You must then put henna in her hands, in her mouth, and in her nose. She may recover or waste away. Lalla Mira also attacks women who do not perform the ḥadra correctly.

She responds to the ḥadras of the Ḥamadsha and the Jilala. Her riḥ is:

Allah! Lalla Mira! O, Gnawa! O, my eye!
I am your loyal servant.
I wish God to grant me my desires.
O, Our Prophet, forgive me.
O virtuous saints, forgive me.

Lalla Mimuna

Lalla Mimuna, some say, comes from the area of the Guerouan, a Berber tribe to the south of Meknes. She lives in wells and old deserted houses. She makes her followers wear blue and burn ḥasalban, and has been likened to "a woman who does not get on with her husband." She often attacks both men and women. She responds to the ḥadras of the Gnawa and the Ḥamadsha. I have been told that she likes to seduce men when they are traveling.

Other Named-Jnun

The female jnun play a much more active role in the lives of the Ḥamadsha than do the male jnun. The male jnun are less developed as characters, and their demands are not so clearly formalized. Sidi Mimun, Moulay Brahim (who is sometimes identified with Moulay Brahim, a famous saint buried near Marrakech), Sidi Musa, and Sidi Ḥammu are all important to the Meknes Ḥamadsha. Their riḥs are played at nearly every ḥadra.[12] In other parts of the country, other

[12] The words of the riḥ of these three jnun are:

jnun play important roles in the Ḥamadsha ceremonies. They are known to the Ḥamadsha of Meknes, but they have neither influenced, attacked, nor taken possession of them.

The Problem of Diagnostics

The Ḥamadsha—and other Moroccans of similar background—employ a not entirely consistent taxonomy of diseases which appears to be based on three principal factors: etiology (pathogenesis), symptomatology, and responsiveness to cure. These factors are interrelated, and no attempt has been made to isolate any one of them or give it priority in the construction of a consistent disease taxonomy. There is little interest in disease classification per se. What is important is the efficacy of the cure. The Moroccans are pragmatists. They operate on the basis of hunches—hypotheses—the validity of which is confirmed by the efficacy of the cure. A man falls ill. His general symptoms, both physical and mental, as well as certain social considerations which would receive scant attention in Western medical therapy—Does he have an enemy? Is he better off than the other members of his social group? Has he more than one wife?—suggest a cause for the disease. The man may have been poisoned; he may be the victim of the evil eye; he may be suffering the effects of witchcraft. For each etiological hunch, a certain remedy or series of remedies is appropriate. If one of them proves successful, then the hunch has been validated, and the disease appropriately interpreted and classified. It should be pointed out that each of these hunches "formulates" the disease. This is, of course, particularly true of those diseases which the Westerner would consider psychogenic, but it affects at least the psychological dimensions of all illnesses.

Sidi Mimun

Allah! O Sidi Mimun the Gnawi! O my eye!
Pardon, O our Prophet. O messenger of God, pardon.
Sidi Mimun, pardon. The virtuous of the Sahara, pardon.
Prophet of Allah, pardon. Messenger of God, pardon.

Sidi Musa

The saint! Sidi Musa!
Pardon, Sidi Musa. O, Allah!
O, Door of Musa in the Gnawa.
Sidi Musa!

Moulay Brahim

O, Moulay Brahim, pardon.
O, Moulay Ḥasan, pardon.
As well as the virtuous men of Allah, pardon.
I have come as a guest, pardon.

Symptomatology, however, is by no means insignificant. It provides a limit to the range of possible etiological hypotheses. A man whose lips turn blue after drinking a glass of mint tea and who is then unable to retain any food is not to be confused with a man who suddenly falls into a convulsion and awakes to find the left side of his body paralyzed. The blue lips immediately suggest poisoning and a whole range of cures. The paralysis indicates that the man has been struck by a jinn, and suggests another series of cures. Social considerations, which are not necessarily articulated or even conscious, may encourage a particular explanation or even limit it. Thus, if the hemiplegiac is known to have prevented his son from attending Ḥamadsha performances, it is reasonable to assume that ʿAïsha Qandisha is responsible for his paralysis. The range of possible cures is limited thereby to a pilgrimage to Beni Rachid or an invitation to the Ḥamadsha. If the hemiplegiac recovers after having tried either or both of these cures, it is assumed that ʿAïsha did in fact strike him. If the cures prove ineffective, a new hypothesis is formulated and new cures are tried.

Symptomatology provides, then, diagnostic guidelines. Diseases, however, are classified less on the basis of symptoms than on etiological considerations, and the correctness of these considerations is validated by the efficacy of the appropriate cure. Since etiology provides the key to disease classification, its underlying structure has to be uncovered. Here I will limit my analysis to those illnesses which are said to be caused by the jnun.

The jnun are held accountable for a wide variety of diseases that the Westerner would consider physical, and others that he would consider psychological. The illnesses for which the jnun are etiologic agents fall into two principal categories. In one, the jnun are said to have caused the illness, but they do not play a role in its treatment. In the other, the jnun are also said to have caused the illness, but here they are explicitly involved in the treatment of it. These categories are not distinguished by the Moroccan. I have chosen to term the particular way in which the jnun are held accountable for the first category of illness the *explicative mode of responsibility;* the second category, the *participational mode of responsibility*.

The Explicative Mode of Responsibility

The jnun serve simply as an explanatory device for phenomena which cannot otherwise be explained within the cultural system as a whole—or, more specifically, within the individual's own cultural reality. The individual does not immediately associate the illness with the jnun. He refers to the jnun only when he is hard-pressed to find an explanation for the illness. For example, in discussing the reasons why a man goes crazy (*ḥamiq*), one of my informants told me that a man becomes crazy when he has lost all of his money or all of his children in some disaster. I then asked him about a particular man who was considered crazy. This man had neither lost all of his money nor all of his children, nor suffered any similar disastrous experience. "Ah," my informant said, "it is those people there." He assured me that he had no idea why "those people there" chose to make the man crazy. It was written. Similarly, he had no idea of how the jnun made the man crazy. There was nothing to be done, he said. The Ḥamadsha, the Gnawa, or even the Koranic teachers who specialize in exorcism could do nothing. True, the man's family could take him to a saint's tomb; there was always the chance that a saint could help him, but this was doubtful. The man was sure to end up in Berechid, the government's mental hospital.[13]

The jnun function in the explicative mode of responsibility as a full stop in the speculations of an individual. They may serve to explain why or even how that individual fell ill. They set a limit to the causal chain; there is nothing more to add but to say that it is written, that it is the will of God. In this mode of responsibility, the jnun do not represent, reflect, or symbolize a dynamic process within the disease. They are, rather, a logical construct whose symbolic function is much more diffuse.

The Participational Mode of Responsibility

Here, too, the jnun function as an explanatory device for phenomena which cannot otherwise be explained either culturally or personally. No other explanations will be offered first, however; the jnun do not serve in this case as a full stop to speculation about the illness. The illness is related immediately and dynamically to the jnun. Not only have the jnun—or, more often, a single jinn—caused the illness, but they "participate" somehow in the illness itself and must be appeased to bring about a cure. In this mode of responsibility the jnun are more than a logical construct. They represent, image, or symbolize an etiological factor or a dynamic process within the illness it-

[13] When a man goes crazy because he has lost all his money or all his children, it is usually not the jnun who are responsible for these disasters. They are attributed to the evil eye—to the jealousy of someone within the man's society.

self (see below). It is precisely with this category of diseases that the Ḥamadsha are concerned.

A Taxonomy of Jinn-Produced Illnesses

The Ḥamadsha—I am restricting myself here to the Ḥamadsha in and around Meknes, since there are considerable dialectical differences in Morocco—recognize several different ways in which the jnun can cause an illness in their victims.[14] The mode of attack is usually suggested by the symptomatology. The person who exhibits the symptoms of a possession state is said to be "inhabited" (*maskun*) by a jinn, whereas the person who suddenly is paralyzed is said to have been struck (*madrub*) by a jinn. These distinctions in attack, however, only partially correspond to symptomatic differences. Thus, while it is possible to differentiate linguistically between a blind man and a paralyzed man, it is also possible to refer to both of them as *madrub*, as "having received a severe blow by a jinn," if both the blindness and paralysis occurred under certain circumstances—suddenness of onset, for example—and if the men exhibit no counterindicative symptoms—such as, in the case of the blind man, a cataract. In only one instance is a category of the jnun-produced illnesses symptom-specific: *matrush*. The word *matrush* refers to a sudden, unilateral paralysis of the face, usually on the left side. It is believed to be the result of a slap in the face by a jinn.[15]

The jnun attack in two principal ways. They may strike a person, or they may take possession of him. If the victim is struck, he usually suffers from some detrimental bodily change: blindness, deafness, mutism, paralysis of the limbs or face. If the victim is possessed, he exhibits all of the classical symptoms of "possession states": falling unconscious; syncope; convulsions; tremors; speaking in tongues; sudden and abrupt, often meaningless, changes in conversation or activity; flights of thought; and so forth. The jnun are believed to enter the body of both the possessed and the struck. They remain with the possessed; with the struck they enter and leave almost immediately.[16]

While the terms describing individuals who have been attacked by

[14] Although there is a difference in terminology, I do not believe that the basic distinction between being struck and being possessed is ignored in any dialects.

[15] It should be noted that the Moroccan Arab is particularly sensitive to slaps, which he finds far more insulting and humiliating than blows of the fist.

[16] Just as possession states must be distinguished from states of being struck, so must they be distinguished from trance states (Bourgignon 1968; Wallace 1959). Possession is an interpretation of a syndrome which can occur in everyday life or during the trance dance. All trances are not interpreted as possession states, as

the jnun are often used loosely to refer to either or both modes of attack, they do suggest the mode of attack and qualify its intensity. They may be arranged as shown in Figure 8.

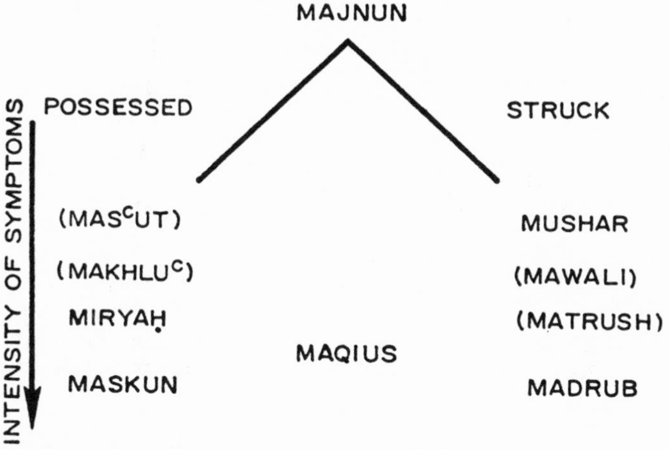

FIGURE 8

Majnun appears to be used most often as a generic term for anyone who has been attacked by a jinn. It may refer either to someone who has been struck or to someone who is possessed. When used more specifically, it refers to someone who is possessed, and not struck.

Masuʿt and *makluʿ* are descriptive of a person who is temporarily possessed by a jnun but not in need of any treatment. *Masuʿt* refers to someone obsessed with an idea; it may be translated as monomaniacal. So long as the jinn is in the person, that person is obsessed with an idea of activity. *Makhluʿ* refers to someone who is afraid, transfixed with fear, or even paralyzed with fear. It is the jinn who, entering him, has caused this state of fear (*khalʿa*) (Westermarck 1926(I): 276). These terms are used to describe sudden and unexpected moods which come over a person and for which he does not feel himself fully responsible. References to the jnun in explaining these and other similar states are frequent.[17] Although the person who is either masuʿt

we shall see. Possession in everyday life, which may involve trance-like (dissociative) states, is considered an illness. During the trance dance, it is considered part of the course and of therapeutic import. As a given in the Ḥamadsha's world, possession serves not only as an interpretation of a particular syndrome but also as a model for behavior.

[17] Compare this function of the jnun with "the intervention of nameless and indeterminate daemon or 'god' or 'gods' " in the *Iliad* (Dodds 1966:11).

or makhluʿ does not usually require the ḥadra of the Ḥamadsha, both terms are often used to describe the prodromal condition of a man who later becomes possessed or is struck and requires the ḥadra or some other treatment. The Ḥamadsha, particularly those who trance frequently, will usually feel the need to perform the ḥadra after experiencing such states of fear or obsession.

Maryaḥ is used to describe a person who is possessed.

Maskun is more specific than *maryaḥ*, since it refers to an individual who is actually inhabited by a jinn. It is the strongest word that can be used to describe someone possessed. Here the jinn is well lodged in the person, who exhibits the classical symptoms of possession.

> The *maskunin* [pl. of *maskun*] talk with you normally and then suddenly they appear to be in flight. Sometimes they talk and agree with what you are saying, then suddenly they will not agree with anything. Sometimes their brain changes. Sometimes there is something [the jnun] that takes hold of their brain and their head turns. Then they are all right again. They only felt something pinching their brain.[18]

The Ḥamadsha consider sudden changes in conversation or activity, as well as convulsions, to be the significant symptoms of a person called maskun.

Maqius is the term most frequently used to describe a person who is attacked by the jnun. It may refer both to someone who is possessed by a jinn and to someone struck by a jinn. The jinn is usually considered to be in the person. The person may also suffer some bodily change. One of my informants explained the term to me as follows.

> A person is maqius by the jnun. He feels absent [*ghaïb*]. It is as though someone is in front of the person, and the person is outside his body. Sometimes he falls and trembles. [I asked him where the jinn is.] God only knows where the jinn is. It is possible that the jinn is in the body. But this is not sure. There are some who are ghaïb and tremble and fall, and others who are sick and remain seated and immobile in the corner [*mqallesh*].

Ghaïb is often used to describe the condition of a person in trance. It is usually translated as "absent" but, as my informant seems to suggest, it refers to a state of dissociation.

Another of my informants explained maqius this way.

[18] This description and the one that follows were given to me by an older Ḥamdushi who has been involved in the treatment of many of the devil-struck and the devil-possessed. He himself has been maqius on more than one occasion. His descriptions were confirmed by many of my other informants.

There are people who are walking normally and suddenly their foot stops. They cannot move it. It always happens to people who are crossing a stream and to not say *bismillah r-rahman r-rahim* [in the name of Allah the merciful and the compassionate]. When you say this the jnun will not approach you. Only one of the man's legs is paralyzed—the one that steps on the other side of the stream first. A hand can be maqius if you throw a rock and hit a jinn by accident. The jinn is only in the part of the body where the person is sick. He can talk normally. The jinn is wounded in the same place. The person is not maskun.

A person who is maqius may perhaps best be described as in a state of partial possession.

Mushar is derived from the verb *shir,* to point, to point a finger at, to signal. It is the weakest of all the expressions used to qualify a person struck by a jinn. I have been told that the jinn does not even graze his victim; he simply points at him. The victim seldom bears a mark of the jinn—manifest bodily harm or malfunctioning. At most, he undergoes a slight, often temporary paralysis. The more usual symptom is general malaise. The term often refers to the very first contact a person ever has with a jinn.

Matrush has already been considered.

Madrub, derived from the verb to beat (*darb*), qualifies a person who has been severely struck by a jinn. This usually involves paralysis of the legs, feet, arms, or hands—most frequently on the left side—but it may also refer to sudden blindness, deafness, or mutism. "The person has an arm or leg that does not work. He cannot clench his fist quickly. Sometimes you see someone who has a string around his slippers to hold them on. Such a person is madrub." "To be madrub is more dangerous than to be maskun. It is stronger. The moment a person who is madrub falls, you think he will die. He can fall off a tree or a mountain."

All of these terms, in one grammatical form or another, are used frequently by Meknes Ḥamadsha to describe victims of the jnun. Occasionally, they refer to these victims as slaves (*mamlukin*) of the jnun. There are, however, many other ways of referring to the victims, to their condition, and to their relationship with the jnun. Often these involve complex paraphrases.[19]

[19] The most common expressions—many of which do not indicate so neatly whether the victim is struck or possessed—are as follows: *fih l-aryaḥ* (l-aryah are in him); *fih ej-jnun* (the jnun are in him); *bih ej-jnun* (the jnun are with him); *shadduh l-aryaḥ* (l-aryaḥ have seized him); and *tiyuh l-aᶜdam* or *tah bi-l-aᶜdam* (fall into epileptoid convulsions).

It should be noted that *aᶜdam* may mean bones. The relationship between bones and attacks by the jnun and the need to trance is discussed later.

There is considerably more fluidity in the use of the terms to describe the jinn-struck and the jinn-possessed than my paradigm suggests. The fluidity stems not only from the normal looseness of everyday speech but also from the type of relationship the jnun maintain with human beings. This is subject to considerable variation. Often a person who first is struck (*madrub*) will later become possessed (*maskun*). Moreover, these terms are used to describe various conditions of an individual in trance who may be possessed, paralyzed, or rendered blind, deaf, or mute by a jinn. One Ḥamdushi put it this way, after we had discussed the meaning of the words in my paradigm:

All of these words can be used in the same way. To be *madrub* is to have been given a good blow. *Maqius,* a much lighter one. *Matrush* is from a slap. *Maskun* occurs when the jnun are in the body. Sometimes when the maskun talks he is all right, and at other times he confuses everything. A person is *mushar* when the jnun have reached out but have not touched the person they want to slap. It is the least strong. *Muwali* is a light touch. [I have not discussed muwali in my paradigm, because it is more often used to describe a relationship with a jinn or jiniyya.] A person who is *madrub* may be distinguished from a person who is *maqius* by the fact that he (the former) always has a mark—a black-and-blue mark, a scratch, or a swelling, paralysis, drooling, a tight mouth. The person who is *maqius* is always sick, but he does not know where. *Matrush* is always the face. *Madrub* refers to other parts of the body. *Maskun* refers to a person who is inhabited for a long time. *Muwali,* just struck. *Mushar,* never before struck, just touched.

Diseases of the Named and Unnamed Jnun

The Ḥamadsha and other Moroccans of their background do not distinguish between illnesses caused by the named-jnun and those caused by the unnamed ones, just as they do not distinguish between named and unnamed jnun. However, in their etiological theories there seems to be a difference between the two types of illness, and these differences are reflected in their choice of treatment. (There is not, to my knowledge, any difference in manifest symptoms.) It has to be remembered, nevertheless, that the distinction between diseases caused by named-jnun and those caused by unnamed ones is analytical and as such implies a certain consistency and rigidity which is not found in as pragmatic a therapy as the Ḥamadsha's.

While it is possible for the jnun, both named and unnamed, to attack a human being for no apparent reason, it is rare. Most illnesses for which the jnun are held accountable are the results of transgressions committed by the sufferer against the jnun. Both the named and the unnamed jnun, being sensitive to insult and injury, are quick to retaliate for wrongs committed against them. In the case of most illnesses for which the unnamed jnun are held accountable, the victim is unaware of his transgression. Often it is suggested that the victim inadvertently trampled on a jinn while walking at night or that he threw boiling water or fire on it, particularly if he threw the water or fire into a drain, a spot popular with the jnun.

The initial attack by a named-jinn—attack is one of the most common ways a named-jinn establishes a relationship with a human being —resembles an attack by an unnamed jinn. Often, the victim does not know how he has offended the jinn. Speculations about the cause of the illness are similar to those for illnesses caused by the unnamed jinn. Once the name of the jinn is uncovered (see below), and the victim has been appropriately treated, most, if not all, subsequent "attacks" are interpreted as an attack by that particular jinn. The victim is considered to be dependent (*muwali*, *muttakil*) on the jinn from that time on. If the victim, without ever having been previously attacked, is already dependent on a named-jinn, symptoms of an attack by the jnun are also interpreted in terms of the jinn he follows. This sort of dependency relationship is formed most often during the ḥadra, when a person who is not ill is thrown into trance by a riḥ known to be the favorite of a particular jinn.

Attacks by a named-jinn on someone already dependent are interpreted as the result of some act that incurred the rage of the jinn. Most often the jinn's rage is said to be brought on by his follower's failure to obey one of his commands. The follower may have neglected to wear the appropriate color or to have burned the appropriate incense on schedule. He may have failed to sponsor a promised ceremony, or he may have tried to postpone a sacrifice. More generally, he may not have lived up to the standards of propriety expected of the followers of a jinn. The point to be emphasized is that the follower had displeased his jinn and "the jinn—they are not like human beings—do not go in for any nonsense."

Therapeutic Theory

There are a number of possible remedies for a person who is struck by a jinn. The purpose of these remedies, according to Westermarck (1926(I):324), is to drive the enemy out. In fact, this is only partially true. There seem to be two basic approaches to the cure of victims of the jnun. One of these *is* to drive the jinn out permanently, but the other is to establish some sort of a "working relationship" with him. The first approach—exorcism, properly speaking—is considered by the French classicist Jeanmaire as characteristic of those countries in which the possessing spirit is considered evil; the second is to be found in North Africa, the Sudan, and among the ancient Greeks.

Il semble qu'on puisse valablement caractériser le processus en observant qu'à la différence de l'exorcisme proprement dit, tel qu'il se pratique dans un milieu où la possession est comprise comme l'effet de l'intrusion d'un esprit maléficient par nature et où l'exorcisme tend, par suite, à l'expulsion de ce principe mauvais pour produire la délivrance du sujet, la méthode de traitement appliquée ici [in North Africa and the Sudan] vise moins à la suppression des états affectifs et délirants qui résultent de l'état de possession (supposé ou suggéré) qu'à leur transformation par élimination du facteur dépressif et à leur utilisation en vue de réaliser un équilibre nouveau par une sorte de symbiose avec l'esprit possesseur devenu esprit protecteur et par une normalisation, sous forme de transe provoquée, de l'état de crise. (1951:121; quoted from Jeanmaire 1949)

In Morocco, both exorcism and the establishment of a symbiotic relationship with a jinn are popular. Although no hard and fast rule can be established, it appears that most often exorcism (*ʿazima,* lit. incantation) is employed when a person is attacked by an unnamed jinn,[20] and the establishment of a symbiotic relationship is effected when one is attacked by a named-jinn (cf. Westermarck 1926(I):155–156). I would suggest, further, that the two modes of possession and their treatment correspond to different psychic states. Possession by an unnamed jinn is probably representative of one psychic condition or dynamic process, and possession by a named-jinn is representative of another.

While the Ḥamadsha, as well as the Gnawa, Jilala, and adepts of similar confraternities are sometimes called to treat the victims of unnamed jnun, and while they are often successful in such cases, they are primarily concerned with the treatment of victims of named-jnun. They establish or reestablish a working relationship between the patient and his jinn. I do not mean to imply that the Ḥamadsha consciously decide to treat one man because he is known to be the victim of a named-jinn and not to treat another because he was attacked by an unnamed jinn. Rather, the Ḥamadsha are called on to treat a patient because it is believed that that patient was attacked by ʿAïsha Qandisha,

[20] The verb *saraʿ,* to overcome, to throw to the ground, means also to exorcise. Its basic meaning is indicative of the permanent expulsion of the jinn in exorcism.

Sidi Ḥammu, or some other jinn over whom the Ḥamadsha exercise control. Sometimes the Ḥamadsha are invited to perform when it is not certain who attacked the patient. Since a ḥadra is expensive, these trial and error cures are quite infrequent. When they do occur, there are invariably other causes for the invitation. Even in cases where the jinn is known to be ʿAïsha Qandisha or Sidi Ḥammu, other, cheaper cures such as a pilgrimage or attendance at a public ceremony are sometimes tried first and found to be successful. It is my impression that often such cures are not of long duration. The patient will have a relapse, and this ultimately necessitates an invitation to one of the brotherhoods.

The major difference between exorcistic and symbiotic cures is that exorcistic cures are one-shot affairs and symbiotic cures are continuous. The patient, in the case of a symbiotic cure, is incorporated into a cult, and, as a member of that cult he must go through "curing" periodically. The exorcistic cures are much simpler. They may involve nothing more than placing a little tar in the victim's nostrils and other body orifices, bathing him in water endowed with baraka, or burning incense over him. Often, a Koranic teacher or an exorcist will incant verses from the Koran over the victim until the jinn leaves him. Sometimes sacrifices are required. These sacrifices may be conceived either as a gift (*hadiyya*) to the jinn or as an *ʿar*—literally, shame; "an act which intrinsically implies the transference of a conditional curse for the purpose of compelling somebody to grant a request" (Westermarck 1926(I):518). Or they may involve the ritualized preparation of special food such as a chicken cooked without salt (*massus*), which is fed to the patient (that is, to the jinn within him). Both sacrifices and the eating of special foods (*dyafa*) are not restricted to exorcistic cures; they are often part of the symbiotic cures as well.

Symbiotic Cures

The first step in the symbiotic cure is to establish the identity of the jinn who has struck or possessed the patient. This may be accomplished informally, if there is some evidence that a particular jinn has struck the patient. The evidence is often circumstantial.

Q. was about 14 years old when he was first struck by a jinn [*madrub*]. His family had recently moved to Moulay Idriss to find work and were staying with his sister. Q. laughed at a group of Sidi ʿAli's followers who were performing in the street. He claims that he had never heard the

Ḥamadsha before. The moment he laughed, he was stricken with a paralysis of the lower limbs. His sister immediately understood that ʿAïsha Qandisha had struck him, and invited in the Ḥamadsha to perform the ḥadra for her brother. First a sacrifice—probably a goat—was made, and then the Ḥamadsha danced for Q. Q. too began to dance and to slash his head. He has been a follower of Sidi ʿAli ever since, and considers himself to be dependent [*muwali*] on ʿAïsha Qandisha.

Identification may also result from a dream at the time of the jinn's attack or shortly afterward.

M., who had been a member of the Miliana, a brotherhood whose members play with and eat fire, reported the following dream which converted him to the Ḥamadsha and was responsible for his becoming a follower of ʿAïsha Qandisha. "I was sleeping. Lalla ʿAïsha grabbed me by the neck and threw me to the ground. This happened three times. [M. had the dream on three consecutive nights.] When I changed over to the Ḥamadsha, I got better. ʿAïsha told me, 'Either you work for me, or I'll have your neck.' 'God is my witness,' I cried out with all my might. But there was nothing to be done. I was sick the next day. My whole body was sick. I could not walk. My wife brought me this black chemise and this red turban. [These are the colors of ʿAïsha Qandisha.] Then I felt better." M. danced the ḥadra on the third day and slashed his head. " ʿAïsha asked me to work for her [perform the ḥadra] for the rest of my life. I will always work for Lalla ʿAïsha."

Often the victim of a jinn travels to a saint's tomb and waits there for a dream which will reveal the cause of his illness.

If there is neither circumstantial evidence nor oneiric evidence for the identity of the jinn, the patient may be taken to the ceremonies of the Gnawa, the Ḥamadsha, the Jilala, or other popular brotherhoods—ceremonies held for other people—to see whether or not he responds to their music. This is one of the most common diagnostic methods in the shantytowns of Meknes, where there are ceremonies almost nightly. Attempts to identify the patient's jinn are often made during these ceremonies; his ear is pulled until the jinn speaks. Here, suggestions play an important role.

F., a girl of 7 or 8, was struck in the tongue by a jinn, so that every time she wanted to talk her tongue would roll back and she would remain speechless. It was thought that ʿAïsha Qandisha was perhaps responsible for this, and F. was taken to a Ḥamadsha ceremony given by a neighbor who had been blinded by ʿAïsha. F. was placed in a small room opening out onto the court where the Ḥamadsha were performing and was generally ignored. After the Ḥamadsha had performed for almost an hour, the muqaddim came in to see how she was doing. (He was excited but not in trance.) F. had not responded to any of the riḥs that had been played.

Following is an excerpt from my notes, taken at the time: F. looked at me curiously. Her eyes were wide-open, popping. Her focus seemed out of control; her pupils rolled from side to side. Her gestures, especially with her hands, were clumsy: she would reach out too far in front of her for an object. She seemed disoriented. Her body and eye movements were "sexy," in the way hysterics tend to be sexy. (I found this surprising in such a young girl.) F. would occasionally lean toward one of several other girls of about her own age who were seated near her, and rub cheeks with her; she would then kiss the girl, or slap her, or both—there was no way of predicting which. The little girl's mother, who was watching, would push F. away when she slapped her daughter, but would ignore F. otherwise.

The muqaddim came in unexpectedly. Suddenly he pulled F.'s ears very hard. She was pained and resisted a little. He cried out: "Leave her! Leave her! Leave her alone! Let her be free!" The muqaddim then banged his head against the terrified child, whose eyes were popping out. He had not banged her head very hard; it was more of a rubbing movement. He then spit into her mouth several times. He crossed her arms and squeezed her fingers tightly until it hurt her. He cried out again: "Leave! Leave, leave, leave her! Let her be free!" F. sat back terrified and wide-eyed. She looked at me and the others uncomprehendingly, her pupils rolling around. Occasionally her hands tightened spasmodically; I was told that from time to time her hands had become paralyzed before she was brought to the ceremony. The muqaddim returned to the dance floor as abruptly as he had appeared, and F. sat back, ignored, for a few minutes. Ten minutes after the muqaddim's two-minute treatment she got up and walked out into the court to watch the dancing. Then she disappeared and was not seen again. I imagine she had gone to sleep.

F. did not dance and had not shown any particular response to the music of the Ḥamadsha. A few days later I met her mother and was told that she was in much the same condition. Two months later I saw the mother again and was told that F. was better. She had received no further treatment in the interim. Even though she had not responded to any of the riḥs, ʿAïsha Qandisha was considered responsible for her illness, and it was not unreasonable to expect that F. would become a devotee of the Ḥamadsha and a follower of the camel-footed she-demon.

Sometimes the victim of a jinn is taken to the muqaddim of one of the local brotherhoods, who will try to discover the jinn's identity by reading or chanting words from the Koran over him. Incense may be burned. Often the muqaddim will yank at the patient's ears or, if he is a Ḥamdushi, will knock his head against the patient's head. Once slashed, the head of a Ḥamdushi is considered to be greatly endowed with baraka and to have powerful influence over the jnun. The muqaddim also may take the patient to the place where he was first attacked, and he may even sacrifice a chicken or some other sacrificial victim there. When the patient sees the blood of the sacrifice, he—or his jinn—becomes excited and begins to speak.

Since the ceremonies are expensive, shorter trial performances are sometimes given, especially if no regular ceremonies are scheduled in the neighborhood. In the countryside, where the ceremonies are less frequent, one of the musicians may visit the patient and play various riḥs on the ganbri to find the riḥ to which the patient responds.

H. was struck by a jinn. A musician who played the ganbri was invited to her house and played all of the riḥs he knew over her until he learned which one was to the liking of her jinn. This took nearly three days. When the appropriate riḥ was found, the Ḥamadsha were called in to perform the ḥadra.

One of the commoner ways of identifying an attacking jinn is to call in a *tallaᶜ*, or exorcist-seer, many of whom are women.[21] Although these seers appear to be most closely associated with the Gnawa and the Jilala—for example, a tallaᶜ must sponsor a ceremony for the Gnawa and another for the Jilala every year—the seers in Meknes are by now also associated with the Ḥamadsha, the most active of the brotherhoods. The tallaᶜ attempts to identify the jinn by either mechanical or oracular divinatory practices. The most popular of the mechanical methods employed in Meknes involves casting cowrie shells and "reading" from the pattern in which they fall. I do not know to what extent the rules for reading the shell-patterns are formulated and to what extent the reading is simply a theatrical device to add authority to the seer's words.

In the oracular divinations, the tallaᶜ burns incense and inhales the fumes. Then, in what would seem to be a state of partial dissociation, he begins to mumble often incomprehensible words and phrases. These utterances are usually highly interspersed with the names of jnun and saints. Finally the seer stops and informs the patient that he is possessed of such-and-such a jinn and must follow the jinn's commands. These may involve visiting a saint, burning special incense, or inviting the Gnawa,

[21] Although the tallaᶜ is sometimes referred to as a *shuwwaf*, he is usually distinguished from the run-of-the-mill seers who are not necessarily associated with one or more brotherhoods.

the Jilala—or, nowadays, the Ḥamadsha—to perform the ḥadra. Often the tallaᶜ will instruct the patient to wear certain colors. The remedies suggested by the tallaᶜ are stereotyped and not unfamiliar to the patient. It is significant that the seers usually ask no questions. They simply tell the patient what is wrong. Sometimes the patient will ask the tallaᶜ a few questions, in order to test him, before bringing up the matter at hand. What the patient seems to desire is an authoritative diagnosis and suggestion for treatment. Once again the element of suggestion is strong.

It is difficult to determine whether or not these seers believe completely in what they are doing. I personally had little contact with them and am only able to suggest that even the least sincere are, while performing a divination, convinced of its efficacy and its truth. They appear to put themselves into an extraordinary psychic state, perhaps one of partial dissociation, in which they give, not totally free reign to their associations, but limited reign. This procedure may be called *directed free association.* The extent to which a tallaᶜ in this partially dissociated state is more sensitive to the needs of his client remains an open question.

Perhaps, phenomenologically speaking, it is irrelevant to refer to an individual in this state in terms of bad faith. In fact, "suspended disbelief" may well be one of its essential characteristics. To what extent the seers are sincere and have faith in their powers when they are not dissociated is another question, and must be answered on individual bases. Certainly their close ties with a team of performers, their well-recognized greed, and their highly streotyped responses suggest an element of self-interest in their behavior. Most Moroccans consider them charlatans but will not hesitate to use them in a time of crisis. As constituent elements in the total therapeutic process—a process which is often highly successful—the seers cannot be dismissed as entirely ineffective.

Having established the identity of the attacking jinn, it is then necessary to discover what, in fact, the jinn wants from his victim. Often the jinn's demands follow directly from its identity; the jinn is asking the usual, well-known things it asks of all its followers. The victim must wear special colors, burn special incense, and dance to particular riḥs. Often he must make a sacrifice to the jinn and sponsor a ceremony of one of the popular brotherhoods. If the person is struck by ᶜAïsha Qandisha, a pilgrimage to Beni Rachid and Beni Ouarad, with a stop-off at ᶜAïsha's grotto with a red or black sacrificial chicken, may be necessary. Frequently the pilgrimage may be followed by a sponsored ḥadra, either in front of Sidi ʿAli's or Sidi Ahmed's mausoleum or, more commonly, at home.

In some instances, the demands of the jinn are not known. A seer or the muqaddim of a team who knows the jinn's riḥ will be consulted. The tallaʿ, who receives a kickback from the team he recommends, or the muqaddim who is anxious to have his team perform, will usually suggest that the jinn requires the ḥadra and a sacrifice.

A., a boy of 8 or 9 who lives with his mother and brother in Sidi Baba, was struck by a jinn. He fell into a mudhole in convulsions, and when he recovered, his right hand was partially paralyzed. The following day, while he was at work in the public ovens where he is an apprentice, he suddenly picked up some red-hot coals and, squeezing them in his hand, announced that it was necessary to call in the Ḥamadsha and that he should be taken to a nearby spring. He then released the coals, which were too hot for anyone else to touch; he had shown no signs of pain and suffered no burns. In the afternoon he was taken to the spring by the muqaddim of a local Ḥamadsha team. It was assumed that ʿAïsha Qandisha had struck him there. Although I was not present at the spring, I was told that the muqaddim was unsuccessful in learning the demands of the jinniyya. He evidently pulled the boy's ears, rubbed mud from the spring on him and his mother, and knocked his head against A. It was finally decided to give a trial performance of the ḥadra. Since A.'s mother was very poor and depended on her son, a short ḥadra was performed in one of Sidi Baba's squares. Donations from all the neighbors of the child's mother were made. These paid for the team, and some money was put away for the sacrifice, which was considered necessary. The ḥadra was performed, and the little boy entered a light trance and attempted to hit his head first with a knife which was taken away from him and then with his shoe. He danced off to the side and was generally ignored. After about five minutes the music stopped, and the boy fell to the ground.

Following is a description by my field assistant of what I was unable to see further back in the crowd (note the way he refers to the possessed boy by the name of the possessing jinniyya, ʿAïsha): ". . . The boy's mother watched the dancers. She herself did not dance. She was dressed in black. The sick boy danced hitting his head. I found this curious. Yesterday I saw his hand paralyzed, and today he is hitting his head with the very same hand. The hand is perfectly normal. . . . When the music stopped, the boy fell down. An old man took the boy by the hand and made an *ahd* [squeezed the right hand of the boy with his own in a solemn oath]. In making the ahd, he tried to talk to ʿAïsha. ʿAïsha did not want to speak. ʿAïsha made only gestures. It is the boy who makes the gestures, but it is in fact ʿAïsha who *makes* them. The old man asked ʿAïsha what she wanted. 'If you want a sacrifice,' he commanded, 'tell me what kind you want.' ʿAïsha beat her chest. 'Leave the little boy!' the old man commanded. 'Why do you attack him? Why don't you attack someone else?' ʿAïsha beat her chest again. The old man said, 'I ask you in the name of God and Sidi ʿAli to tell me what you want. Or leave forever.' ʿAïsha said no. She moved her hand across her chest. 'If you want a sacrifice,' the man continued, 'do not hesitate. We are ready to make it.' The boy said no. The Ḥamadsha burned more incense. They moved the [right] hand of the sick boy over the brasier. Then the man ordered the boy to be taken to the public oven. I do not think the jinniyya accepted the sacrifice."

Before the boy was taken to the oven, one of the team members, who claims to be a sharif, a descendant of the Prophet, spit into the boy's mouth several times, massaged his hands, and said a prayer (*fatḥa*) over him. I believe that there was more mention of a sacrifice than my field assistant reported. One of the men distinctly suggested a he-goat. The boy himself was in a dreamy, semi-conscious state. Occasionally he would beat his hand against his chest. Everyone seemed eager to accept this as an indication of ʿAïsha's will. (It should be noted that a few months earlier, A.'s brother was attacked by ʿAïsha and had a performance of the Ḥamadsha sponsored for him. A. is said to have been jealous of his brother.) Several days later, A.'s hand was still weak, although now he could move it. It was assumed that he would remain in this condition until a sacrifice had been made. No sacrifice was made, to my knowledge, because A.'s mother was too poor. A.'s condition improved slightly in the following months. He appeared at other Ḥamadsha performances and danced the ḥadra.[22]

It is significant here that everyone concerned with the patient was sure of ʿAïsha's demands. The problem was simply that of ʿAïsha's accepting the offering. And the question that remains is this: To what extent was ʿAïsha's "refusal" indicative of the boy's desire for prolonged attention and to what extent was it indicative of the boy's knowledge of his mother's inability to make the sacrifice and of his own inability to take no for an answer? I was never able to establish sufficient contact with A. or his mother to explore and clarify this. Nevertheless, his case again calls attention to the role of suggestion in the diagnostic process.

Once the identity of the attacking jinn and its demands are established, it is then necessary to satisfy these demands if the patient is to be cured of his symptoms. The manifest aim of the cure is the elimination of symptoms, and not the permanent expulsion of the jinn. The therapeutic process, however, is conceptualized, often confusedly, in terms of the jinn. The jinn must be placated, since the patient, wittingly or unwittingly, has incurred its wrath. This placation, then, is

[22] The question of sharing expenses for a ḥadra is discussed in Chapter Ten.

accomplished by complying with the jinn's commands. If the patient is possessed or partially possessed, the elimination of symptoms necessarily involves the expulsion of the jinn. If the patient has been struck, the cure usually involves the jinn's taking possession of the patient and then leaving him. In neither case is the break complete. Although the jinn leaves the patient, it does not abandon him. It remains with him, and so long as the patient obeys it, the jinn will do him no harm. If, however, the patient breaks any of the jinn's commands, then the jinn attacks him. It appears that cure is effected by the establishment of a relationship between the patient and his named-jinn. The patient becomes a follower of the jinn and remains always dependent on it. This relationship, as we have seen, is by no means a negative one. The jinn is a support for the patient.

The Explanation of the Cure

There are several divergent and often confusing theories as to how exactly the cures are brought about. Usually it is said that either Sidi ʿAli or Sidi Ahmed or both, as intermediaries to God, are ultimately responsible for the cures. If the patient was struck by ʿAïsha Qandisha, it is sometimes added that Sidi ʿAli commanded ʿAïsha to leave her victim alone. I have been told by the followers of Sidi ʿAli that their saint not only commands ʿAïsha Qandisha but also Sidi Ahmed, and that sometimes he will instruct Sidi Ahmed to order ʿAïsha to leave the patient. Sidi Ahmed's followers are not so anxious to relinquish ultimate control to Sidi ʿAli, and they talk of an agreement (*ʿar*) that Sidi Ahmed made with ʿAïsha Qandisha, wherein ʿAïsha agreed to keep out of Sidi Ahmed's way. Sidi Ahmed, thereby, is not without his own effect on the camel-footed she-demon.[23]

The most frequent explanation of the cures involves the notion of baraka. The baraka of Sidi ʿAli and Sidi Ahmed, which is lodged in the saints' paraphernalia, in their descendants, and in some of their followers at least some of the time, is considered to be the cause of the cures. In the case of the saintly paraphernalia—the tomb, the water of the ʿAyn Kabir, and objects sold by the saints' families—and the saints' descendants, the baraka is passed directly to the patient, and in the process of transference is transformed, as we have seen, from a highly con-

[23] On several occasions I have been told that the Ḥamadsha cure the possessed by allowing the possessing jinn to enter themselves. The curers, who are in a special relationship to the possessing jinn, are not bothered by it. This explanation, which resembles explanations of the Zar cures, is unusual among the Ḥamadsha (cf. Leiris 1958).

tagious potentializing force to a noncontagious potential or actual state of being. The baraka may be sufficient to eliminate the patient's symptoms, but it is rare in those cases where the patient has been attacked by a named-jinn. Usually, in such cases, the baraka seems to be transformed into a potential state of health which will be actualized only if the patient follows a regime. The regime is the command of the jinn or jinniyya.

With the Ḥamadsha themselves, explanation of the therapeutic process is more complex. In the first place, the baraka of the saints enables the adepts, the devotees, and the patients to perform the ḥadra, which is pleasing not only to the saints but to the jnun as well. It also enables the ghiyyata to play the various riḥs which draw the jinn into the patient and then expel it. Finally, it enables some of the performers not only to enter trance but also to slash their heads; the blood from these wounds is again pleasing to the jnun. The baraka of the saints is, then, a potentializing force enabling the adepts, the devotees, and patients to enter an extraordinary state (*ḥal*) in which they all—in varying degrees—have the ability to pass on the baraka of the saints. This baraka is the force behind the cure.

While it is sometimes said that the follower of a saint—an adept—possesses baraka which he is able to transfer, just as the descendant of a saint can pass on baraka, it is usually claimed that to do this the adept must be in an extraordinary state. I have heard this contradicted in theoretical discussions, but I have known of only two or three instances in which baraka was said to have been transferred to a patient for curative purposes by a saint's follower who was not in trance. (In these few instances, it was the muqaddim of one of the urban zawiyas—a disinterested party in the transfer of wealth—who passed his baraka to the patient.) The entranced state, then, appears to be a key to the cure. In this state, the adept may pass on his saint's baraka by massaging the patient, by hitting his head against the patient's head, by smearing blood from his own wounds onto the patient, and by other similar acts which are discussed in the next chapter. Often the mere presence of an adept in trance is sufficient for the transfer of baraka. Then, too, the patient and other devotees who are also in entranced states are said to possess the baraka of the saint and may themselves have a curative effect. Often they, as well as the adepts, will recite prayers and invocations for participants during pauses in the dance. These invocations are frequently recited in an entranced state, and they are considered especially effective.

To summarize, baraka may be transferred either directly or indirectly to the patient. In either case, if the patient is the victim of a named-jinn or jinniyya, this baraka is not usually sufficient to effect a cure, but rather puts the patient in a state of potential cure. The cure is then effected by the patient's following a regime pleasing to the jinn or jinniyya. One important element in this regime is the ḥadra, which permits patient and curers alike to enter trance. Again, the saint's baraka is considered the potentializing force behind the ḥadra. This process is illustrated in Figure 9.

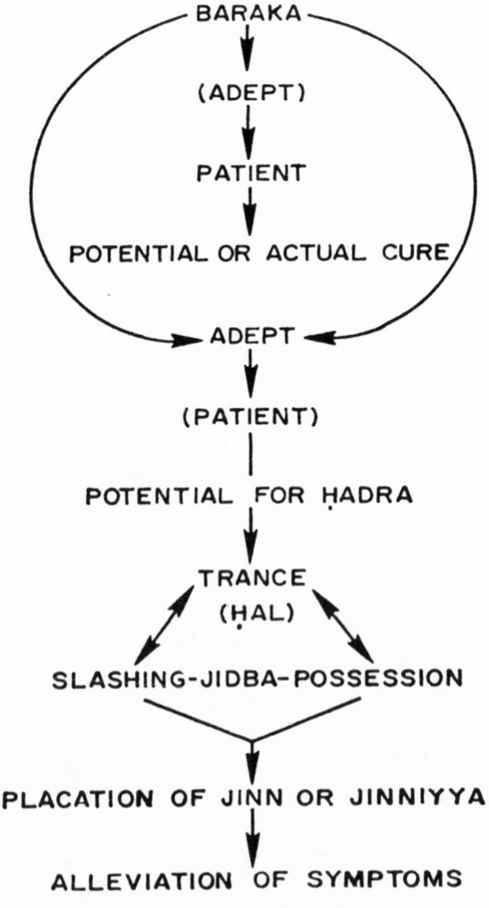

FIGURE 9.

9

The Pilgrimage

There are two principal Ḥamadsha rituals that are designed, among other things, to cure the sick. The first of these, the pilgrimage to the tombs of Sidi ʿAli ben Ḥamdush and Sidi Ahmed Dghughi, is of more general scope and appeal than the second, the performance of the ḥadra. Although it has certain distinctive features, particularly with respect to ʿAïsha Qandisha, it is not dissimilar to pilgrimages to most of the other marabouts in Morocco and elsewhere in the Maghreb. It is by no means restricted to adepts or devotees of the ḥadra, nor is its efficacy limited to those suffering from attacks of the jnun. The Ḥamadsha ḥadra, too, resembles the performances of other popular brotherhoods in Morocco; but it, too, differs from them all in certain outstanding respects. Although its efficacy, theoretically, is not restricted to cases involving the jnun, its principal therapeutic aim is the cure of the jinn-struck and the jinn-possessed.

The pilgrimage to a saint's tomb is referred to in Moroccan Arabic as a *ziyara*,[1] a visit, and must not be confused with the *ḥajj*, or pilgrimage to Mecca, which is required of all good Muslims. Although the ziyara and the ḥajj have certain features in common, neither the Ḥamadsha nor other Moroccans of their background seem willing to draw any comparison between the two. For the Muslim, there is an absolute distinction between a visit to a local sanctuary, no matter how powerful the saint involved, and a pilgrimage to Mecca, the seat of Islam. To the non-Muslim scholar, however, the structural parallels are of some significance.

[1] *Ziyara* is also used to refer to the offerings one leaves at a saint's tomb.

In the most general terms, the purpose of a pilgrimage to a saint's tomb is to obtain the baraka of the saint. Often the pilgrim hopes to have a dream in which the saint appears and gives instruction as to how to deal with his complaints. While visits to saints' tombs, especially local ones, are sometimes made only to receive a saint's blessing, they are usually made with a more explicit purpose. The pilgrim goes to the saint's tomb to ask the saint to intercede with God for him. He is anxious to obtain *something:* a child, a spouse, business success, a favorable verdict at court, poetic inspiration, the cure of an illness, the alleviation of the symptoms of an attack by a jinn, or simply a change in fortune. The saint, who can do no wrong, will intercede for him; the success or failure of the mission is dependent upon the not-to-be-questioned will of God. Some saints, however, are particularly effective for specific things (cf. Voinot 1948). In and around Meknes, for example, Sidi Saïd is considered especially helpful for coughs and chest diseases; Moulay Ahmed Shibli for fevers; Sidi Abdullah l-Gazzar, the butcher, for female alopecia; Sidi Sliman Mula l-Kifan, the master of the cave, for rheumatism and other arthritic pains; and Sidi Abdullah ben Ahmed for the insane (*ḥmeq*). Not all saints are specialists, though, and even among those who are, there is considerable variation in their reputations. It is impossible, strictly speaking, to claim that one saint has more baraka than another; but, nonetheless, the saints *do* appear to fall into a hierarchy with respect to their importance and efficacy (Dermenghem 1954:21). Since the exact relationship between the saint's intercessionary power with God and his own baraka is not clear, no one can say that the one or the other is responsible for the success of a pilgrimage. But while this distinction may be of some theoretical significance to the non-Muslim, it is of little concern to the Muslim, since all things ultimately derive from God. The pilgrimage to Sidi ʿAli's and Sidi Ahmed's tombs are still more complicated, because they actually involve a stop at ʿAïsha Qandisha's grotto. Similar cults are found at other mausoleums as well (cf. Brunel 1955:325 et seq.).

Although a pilgrimage to the mausoleums of Sidi ʿAli and Sidi Ahmed and to the grotto of ʿAïsha Qandisha is considered particularly therapeutic for barrenness, children's diseases, and illnesses caused by ʿAïsha, its value is by no means restricted. The pilgrimage is said to be one of the most powerful in Morocco, and it is not unusual for visitors, both Arab and Berber, to come from as far as Tetouan, Marrakech, or even Agadir to obtain some of the saints' blessing. The majority of pilgrims, however, come from the nearby countryside and from Meknes. Although pilgrims from Fez are not unusual, Fez seems to fall just outside the area of greatest devotion to the Ḥamadsha saints.

Pilgrimage Activities

The pilgrimage to the Ḥamadsha saints has a number of possible stop-offs: the mausoleum of Sidi ʿAli and Sidi Ahmed, the ʿAyn Kabir at Beni Rachid, the grotto to ʿAïsha Qandisha, and the mausoleums of the lesser village saints. It is not incumbent on a pilgrim to make all of these stops: he is free to visit any one of the shrines without stopping at the others. Once he has made a stop, however, he must follow certain rules of behavior, which can best be understood as marks of respect to the saints and to ʿAïsha Qandisha. He is also free to initiate certain activities at these stops—activities which, once initiated, are also subject to certain rules. The structure of the pilgrimage is not dissimilar to the hagiographic legends: there are a number of component themes which the narrator is free to recount or not to recount, but once he has initiated a theme he must follow it through to the best of his knowledge. The thematic components of the legends do not usually serve a straightforward etiological function. They are not usually explanations for ritual activities, but they do reflect their relative importance and their possible interrelationships. The components of the pilgrimage are summarized in Table 4.

While it is theoretically possible to make only one or two stops, most pilgrims, who are anxious to obtain the maximum benefit from their trip, visit both mausoleums, the two shrines to ʿAïsha Qandisha, and the ʿAyn Kabir. They rarely visit the tombs of the other village saints. The pilgrims may spend a few hours or a few days in the two villages. They sleep in the courtyard or the tomb room, and bring their own food. A trip that lasts a single day is the most common, and one that lasts a day and a night is considered ideal. Prolonged visits for weeks and even months are very rare at Beni Rachid and Ben Ouarad; they are not uncommon at some sanctuaries, such as Sidi Raḥal and Moulay Brahim near Marrakech. The Ḥamadsha shrines are not havens for beggars, wandering mendicants, prostitutes, and other social outcasts. No provision is made for them.

Decisions to perform optional ritual activities are based on individual considerations. The nature of the pilgrim's complaint plays a role. Henna, for example, is commonly smeared on pilgrims suffering from aching bones. The most important consideration is economic. Most of

TABLE 4

THE RITUAL COMPONENTS OF THE PILGRIMAGE

Required Conduct	*Optional Conduct*
	Mausoleum (Sidi ʿAli, Sidi Ahmed, Sidi l-Ḥafyan, other saints)
Purification	Placing head under catafalque
Removal of shoes	Sleeping (and dreaming) in tomb room
Kissing portals	Lighting candle
Circumambulation of tomb and kissing four sides of tomb	Taking earth
Sitting near tomb	Receiving blessing from muqaddim of mausoleum or another descendant of the saint
Recitation of fatiḥa or other Koranic verses	Sacrifice (as ʿar or gift)
	Sponsoring ḥadra
	Performing ḥadra
	ʿAyn Kabir
Purification	Drinking water
Alms (or payment)	Bathing
	Bottling water
	Receiving blessing from muqaddim of spring
	Sacrifice (as ʿar or gift)
	Sponsoring ḥadra
	Performing ḥadra
	Receiving blessing from holy fool (*majdud*)
	Shrines to ʿAisha Qandisha
Purification	Sitting (and pressing head against root system) in grotto at Beni Rachid
Removal of shoes	Tying rag or remnant of clothes to roots at grotto
Alms	Leaving amulets
	Taking earth
	Smearing earth on body
	Smearing henna on body
	Burning incense
	Receiving blessing from muqaddim
	Sacrifice (as ʿar or gift)
	Sponsoring ḥadra
	Performing ḥadra

the pilgrims are poor, and most of the optional activities are expensive. A blessing from the muqaddim of a shrine or a saint's descendant costs about a dirham; a package of candles 60 francs; a chicken for sacrifice from 5 to 10 dirhams; a she-goat about 60 dirhams; a he-goat from 45 to 75 dirhams; a ewe over 60 dirhams; a ram over 75 dirhams; a cow from 150 dirhams; and a bull well over 200 dirhams. The sponsoring of the ḥadra varies from 15 to more than 50 dirhams, depending on the instruments used, the amount of time spent, and the performer's perception of the wealth of the sponsor. (It has to be remembered that the average pilgrim spends at least 3 or 4 dirhams for alms, and must also pay for his transportation to the Jebel Zerhoun.)

The decision to perform one of these optional activities is dependent, then, on the financial situation of the pilgrim and on the nature and gravity of his condition. A father whose son is suffering from a paralyzed limb will more readily make a sacrifice than a husband whose wife complains of rheumatoid pains in her joints. Often, however, the decision is not made by the individual pilgrim but by a seer (*talla*ʾ) whom he has consulted and whose advice he follows. Then again, the performance of one of the options may not be conceived as a matter of choice at all, but as a command either by the saint or ʿAïsha Qandisha. The command may have been revealed in a dream, or the pilgrim may simply have the subjective conviction that it is what the saint or ʿAïsha desires.

Before making the pilgrimage to the Ḥamadsha saints—or to any saint, for that matter—the pilgrim must purify himself. He is not allowed into the sacred confines (*ḥorm*) of the tomb in a polluted condition. He must bathe carefully after having sexual intercourse. A menstruating woman is not allowed to enter the mausoleum. Usually, pilgrims will go to the baths the day before their trip and will refrain from sexual intercourse that night.

The Pilgrimage Sequence

The average pilgrim usually arrives at either Beni Rachid or Beni Ouarad with several members of his family. If he plans to give a sacrifice, he will often bring the animal or animals with him. The pilgrim tries to arrive early in the morning in order to spend the entire day at the sanctuaries. Although most pilgrims go to Sidi ʿAli's mausoleum first, both because he is considered the more powerful of the two saints and because taxis, which are the pilgrims' most common means of transportation, usually stop at Beni Rachid, those pilgrims who are msannad to Sidi Ahmed go directly to Beni Ouarad. It is sometimes said that if one makes the pilgrimage because of a sick child, one should visit Sidi Ahmed first. The average pilgrim brings provisions, and leaves them in the courtyard of whichever saint he is visiting. If he has brought a sacrificial victim, he gives it to the muqaddim of the sanctuary, who may sacrifice it for him during the course of the visit. The muqaddims, who are anxious to keep the victim alive to sell, will usually try to persuade the pilgrim that giving the animal is sufficient and that there is no need to slaughter it immediately.

The pilgrim removes his shoes before entering the mausoleum. He kisses the door jambs, first the right and then the left one, and he may drop a few coins into the alms box standing just inside the tomb room. Sometimes he waits to give alms until he is about to leave. Women turn to the left and walk clockwise around the tomb; men turn to the right and make a counterclockwise circumambulation. Both men and women kiss the four sides of the catafalque. Once the single circumambulation is completed, the pilgrim sits down—women to the left of the entrance, men to the right—and mumbles a fatḥa or a few verses from the Koran that he happens to know. At this time the pilgrim is said to experience the fear of God (*khushuᶜ*). Occasionally he will experience a trance-like state which he calls the *ḥal*, a term which is also employed for one level of trance in the ḥadra.

Often, especially if he is sick, the pilgrim will place his head under the coverings of the catafalque and press it against the tomb in order to have closer contact with the saint and to glean more of his baraka. Pilgrims often try to sleep in the mausoleum, hoping to have dreams in which the saint appears and gives them instruction. (It is sometimes said that the saint is not dead but alive within the sanctuary.) The dreams—or, better, the saint's appearance—are loosely interpreted.[2] All males in these dreams, especially when wearing white, are said to be saints. Women are often interpreted as ᶜAïsha Qandisha. If the dream is puzzling, the pilgrim may ask the muqaddim of the sanctuary what it means.

The pilgrim may spend only a few minutes in the tomb, or several hours. Before leaving, he may light a candle or two, and when he leaves he usually takes a little earth with him. This earth, which is called

[2] The extent to which these dreams are stereotyped "divine" dreams (*chrematismoi* of ancient Greece), and not simply interpreted in a prescribed manner, is impossible to determine. The element of secondary elaboration cannot be accounted for; Dodds (1966:107 et seq.) does not take the latter into due consideration in his work on the Greeks.

tuba,[3] has been placed in the sanctuary by the muqaddim and is said to contain much baraka. Pilgrims often put it under their pillows to prevent bad dreams or rub it on aching parts of their bodies. Taking the earth at Sidi Ahmed's tomb is said to commemorate Sidi Ahmed's throwing tar and then sand in the eyes of the Sudanese guards who pursued him after he had taken ʿAïsha Qandisha and the musical instruments from the palace of the King of the Sudan. No legend explains why one takes a little earth from the tomb of Sidi ʿAli. The practice is not restricted to the Ḥamadsha saints and, in fact, is widespread among both Berbers and Arabs.

The average pilgrim will usually settle down in the courtyard of the mausoleum after visiting the tomb. He drinks tea, eats a little food, and often gossips with other pilgrims. He may ask the muqaddim for a blessing or to arrange for the ḥadra. The latter is rare, both because the ḥadra is expensive and because most pilgrims prefer to sponsor ḥadras in their own homes, where they can invite friends and fellow devotees and thus assure themselves of reciprocal invitations. When he has finished his meal and is through gossiping, the pilgrim may enter the tomb again before moving on to the mausoleum of the other saint. If he is at Sidi Ahmed's tomb, he will usually leave something for ʿAïsha Qandisha. He may smear a little of her earth or henna on aching parts of his body, or even sacrifice a chicken to her. The pilgrim follows the winding path through Qelaa to the second saint's tomb and follows the same procedure there as at the first.[4]

Usually, before leaving,[5] a pilgrim will visit the ʿAyn Kabir. There he washes his face and hands in the holy water and drinks a little of it. Some pilgrims will take a bottle of water home with them. Women especially are apt to pay the muqaddim of the spring a half dirham in order to use the baths. Often the pilgrims receive blessings from a holy fool (*majdub*) who has been living in a cave nearby for at least ten years.[6] On very rare occasions, a pilgrim will arrange for a sacrifice or for the performance of the ḥadra in front of the ʿAyn Kabir.

The last stop on the pilgrimage is the grotto of ʿAïsha Qandisha in

[3] Literally, a clod. This word, which begins with an emphatic "ṭ," should not be confused with *tuba*, confession or repentance.

[4] Although there are no legends connected with this route, it is generally accepted as the appropriate path to take. Informants state simply that it is the shortest distance between the two mausoleums. They always stress the fact that they have taken it.

[5] If he spends the night, he sleeps in the mausoleum of the saint he considers the most powerful.

[6] It is not unusual to find such fools at saints' tombs; this one is not related to the descendants of Sidi ʿAli and is not from the village of Beni Rachid.

Beni Rachid. This grotto is visited most frequently by women. Men, too, visit it, although many of them consider it a place for women and seem embarrassed by their own visits. The male pilgrim will remove his shoes, enter the grotto, give something to the muqaddim, and leave. Women will spend more time there. They press their heads against the exposed roots of the giant fig tree, rub a little earth or henna on their bodies, and fumigate themselves with incense (black *jawi*). The henna and incense are brought by pilgrims and prepared by the muqaddim. Often the women will tie rags to one of the fig roots as a vow (*ʿar*) to give a sacrifice if their pilgrimage is successful. They may also leave amulets prepared by Koranic teachers there. Sacrifices, especially chickens, are not unusual, but the performance of the ḥadra in the grotto is rare. When it is performed, the dancers will often imitate pigs and grovel in the mud.

The pilgrim does not necessarily repeat this cycle of visits if he stays at Beni Rachid or Beni Ouarad for several days. Usually he will spend most of his remaining time at the tomb of the saint he considers most powerful. Often the pilgrim will refrain from sexual intercourse for several days after his trip to the Ḥamadsha saints. He may bring back candles, amulets prepared by the saint's descendants, and bread that is also prepared by them. Sometimes he will have to rub himself with or drink special herbal brews for several days after the pilgrimage.

Ḥadra and Sacrifices

Both the villages of Beni Rachid and Beni Ouarad, as we have seen, have teams of Ḥamadsha which perform whenever they are asked by pilgrims and villagers. Villagers will usually invite a team to their own houses, and the performance follows the general lines of the urban ceremony. It is held out of doors more often than in the city, especially when the ceremony is given not to cure an illness but to commemorate an event such as the naming of a child. Ceremonies sponsored by pilgrims usually take place in the courtyard of the mausoleum. On rare occasions they are held in ʿAïsha Qandisha's grotto or in front of the ʿAyn Kabir. I have never witnessed a ḥadra sponsored by a pilgrim, and can only report what I have heard from informants who participated in them. Village informants complained that the teams no longer performed as well as they did in the past; the team members are at odds with one another and their performances reflect this. Urban and shantytown informants who were aware of intra-village factionalism also complained about the ceremonies. They did not find the musicians as gifted as those of the city; the ceremonies were sloppy and not particularly satisfying. All that the team members wanted, they said, was money. Although I am unable to comment on these criticisms, I believe that the pilgrims missed the intimacy of their own ceremonies, in which their friends and neighbors participated, and musicians whom they knew well performed. To what extent they missed the authority and competence of their own muqaddim and ghiyyata remains an open question.[7]

Sacrifices are much more common than the sponsoring of ḥadras. Red, black, or multi-colored ("seven-colored") chickens are often sacrificed to ʿAïsha Qandisha in her grotto. Chickens, as well as goats and sheep, both male and female, are also sacrificed to the saints. A ram is considered the "best" sacrifice. Ideally, the muqaddim slits the throat of the animal in front of the saint's tomb or in ʿAïsha's grotto, following the procedure employed in the slaughtering of all animals. The meat and skin are then divided among the descendants of the saint, and a little of the meat may be given to the pilgrims. In fact, the muqaddim usually tries to dissuade the pilgrim from having his animal killed. Often, if the muqaddim succeeds, the animal is then sold to pilgrims who want to give a sacrifice but have not brought one to the village with them. Through a continued process of resale, the children of the saint are able to maximize their profits.[8]

Such a sacrifice is referred to as a *debiḥa*, or as an *ʿar*, and must not be confused with the *dḥiya*, the sacrifice of a sheep on the ʿAyd l-Kabir (The Feast of the Sheep), which commemorates the Abraham and Ismaïl story. The dḥiya, a yearly duty of all good Muslims, was recognized by all my informants as qualitatively different from sacrifices to the saints and to ʿAïsha Qandisha. The element of commemoration is not present in the latter: they are conceived, as Westermarck (1926(I): 188 et seq.) points out, as either an *ʿar* or a gift (*hadiyya*). A debiḥa is considered an ʿar when the pilgrim has come with a request, and as a gift when he comes to thank the saint or ʿAïsha Qandisha for granting a request made earlier. The gift-sacrifice, in fact, generally results from a vow (*ʿar*) to give an animal if a request is granted. This vow may be stated in public, or it may simply be a promise to oneself to give the sacrifice. The pilgrim may symbolically affirm his vow by tying a cloth to the roots of the giant fig tree in ʿAïsha's grotto or to the branches of the fig tree in the urban lodges. Sometimes a first sacrifice is offered, with the promise of another when the request has been fulfilled.

[7] A detailed description of the ḥadra will be given in Chapter Ten.
[8] A similar procedure is followed at Moulay Idriss, even at the musem.

M., who had been struck paralyzed by ʿAïsha Qandisha, came to Sidi ʿAli's mausoleum with a ram and had it slaughtered in front of the saint's tomb. He referred to this sacrifice as an ʿar to the saint. He explained that he had placed himself under the protection of the saint and had asked the saint to intervene with God and ʿAïsha Qandisha on his part. He vowed that if he were cured, he would make another sacrifice of a ram to the saint. Several days later—he was still at Sidi ʿAli's tomb—his condition improved after dreaming that the saint released him (ordered him to leave). He bought a ram from one of the saint's descendants—this ram had been brought by another pilgrim as a sacrifice, but had never been killed—and had it sacrificed in front of the tomb as he had promised. This time, he referred to the sacrifice not as an ʿar but as a debiḥa, and explained that it had been made in fulfillment of his first ʿar. He added that were he not to make it, he would incur the anger of the saint and ʿAïsha Qandisha and would fall sick again.

While it is possible to distinguish analytically between the sacrifice as an ʿar and as a hadiyya, it is my impression that in the minds of most pilgrims who offer a sacrifice this distinction is not so neat. The ʿar is also considered a hadiyya.

Fatima's Pilgrimage

What follows is a verbatim account of a pilgrimage to the Ḥamadsha saints. Fatima's mother, Fatna, told the story. Fatna, who lives in Sidi Baba with a son and four daughters, is by bidonville standards a comparatively wealthy woman. Her husband spends most of the year in France as a worker for a construction company. She is not a Ḥamdushiyya, but she considers herself to be supported (msannad) by Sidi ʿAli and has had several of her other children's hair cut in the mausoleum of the saint. She attends the annual pilgrimage at Sidi ʿAli whenever she can and often watches the Ḥamadsha's public performances in front of Sheikh al-Kamal in Meknes. Although she does not consider herself to be dependent (*muwala*) on ʿAïsha Qandisha, she is afraid of the she-demon and is worried about becoming ʿAïsha's victim. Nevertheless, she is emphatic about not being a devotee of the Ḥamadsha, and she does not want her children to become muhibbin.[9]

I will tell you about the time I took Fatima to Sidi ʿAli. Fatima was 3 years old then. [Further calculation revealed that Fatima was actually not quite 2.] It was at harvest time. My husband was back from France. The first sign

[9] The account was told to my wife.

of Fatima's illness was her falling down on the spot. She was feverish. She nearly fainted. Her eyes and her mouth were wide open. She cried and cried. She kept crying. I was pregnant with Najiya—not the Najiya you know [one of Fatna's daughters], but with the Najiya who died. I was about six months pregnant. [It was established that Fatna had not nursed Fatima for three months when the girl fell sick. Moroccan women stop nursing an infant the moment they know they are pregnant again. They believe the milk of a pregnant mother is poisonous. It is said that it is rendered poisonous by the embryo, who is jealous.] Fatima was sick at night. I touched her, and she was burning. She was sleeping next to me [along with Fatna's husband and two other children]. The moment she cried, I took her on my knee and then on my back and then again on my knee. She continued to cry a lot. I gave her milk, but she refused it. I gave her something to eat, but she refused that too. Then I knew that Fatima must be very sick. . . .

In the morning I decided to go to the fqiḥ [the Koranic teacher]. My husband said, "No, it is necessary to go to the hospital." I answered, "No, it is not an illness for the hospital. It is an illness for the fqiḥ." Then my husband let me go. [Fatna's husband's family lived next door and encouraged her to go to the fqiḥ and then, if the fqiḥ was unable to help, to go to a saint.] I, too, knew that it was the illness for the fqiḥ and the saint. When an infant falls sick and has the fever and breathes with difficulty, it is an illness which is for the fqiḥ. But when a child eats and vomits, when he is sick in the intestines, then it is an illness for the hospital. Also if he coughs [chokes] when he vomits, it is an illness for the hospital. I learned to tell them apart from the neighbors. . . .

So, that morning, I went to the fqiḥ. It costs 100 francs. I had not visited that fqiḥ before. One of my neighbors, a woman, had told me to go to that fqiḥ because he is especially good for children. I went to the house of the fqiḥ with the neighbor who recommended him. I said to him, "My daughter is sick. Can you write an amulet for her?" The fqiḥ looked at Fatima who was feverish, but he did not examine her. [The latter observation was in response to questions previously asked Fatna about fqiḥs.] "It is all right. She will not die." Then he wrote a verse from the Koran. He told me to put the verse along with some herbs—rue [*fijil*], harmal [*ḥormal*], and a type of absinthe [*shiba*]—in a red cloth and hang it from Fatima's neck. He also gave me another verse of the Koran and told me to put it in a bowl with some water, olive oil, and garlic. I was to rub the mixture all over Fatima. All over her, except the soles of her feet and the palms of her hands. I was to do this every morning and every night, twice a day, for three days. I was also to give Fatima a little of it to drink with each application. [Did the fqiḥ ask you anything?] The fqiḥ said absolutely nothing else. You go to him, really, only to know if the child will live or die. Three days later, Fatima was still sick.

My mother-in-law said, "Now you must try mint. You pound the mint into a powder and moisten it with water. You put it in a rag and squeeze out drops into the ears, mouth, and nostrils of the child." I did this to Fatima. During the three days I followed the fqiḥ's instructions, my husband kept telling me to go to the hospital. My mother-in-law said that we must try mint. After we had tried it, Fatima was a little better. She was still sick, though.

Now before having Fatima, a neighbor—she was a midwife—dreamed that I had washed a sheepskin rug in the fountain. The hair of the sheepskin had been shaved, and it was smooth. After she had the dream, the midwife came to my house and said, "When you have your child—be it a boy or a girl—you must take it to Sidi ʿAli to have its head shaved by one of the children of the saint." I was pregnant then with Fatima, and after she was born, when she was forty days old, I took her to Sidi ʿAli, and the muqaddim [of the mausoleum] shaved her head for 300 francs. Afterward, I said to him, "If all goes well with my child, I will return in a week's time with a chicken for you." [10] Then I went home.

After a week I saw that Fatima was well, and I thought that it was not worth going back to Sidi ʿAli, not worth spending a lot of money for a chicken. So I never went to him with the chicken. Now when my child took sick, I had this point—not having given the chicken—between my eyes. The muqaddim had shaved Fatima's head in the saint's mausoleum, right next to the tomb, and I had not returned with the chicken I had promised him. When Fatima fell sick, my husband said to me—and all the neighbors said to me—that it was because of the chicken. Two days after I tried the mint, I went to Sidi ʿAli.

There is one more thing. On the day I gave Fatima mint, I went to Moulay Abdullah ben Ahmed [a saint who is buried a mile from Fatna's house]. I left the verse of the Koran the fqiḥ had given me there. Moulay Abdullah ben Ahmed is where one takes people who are crazy. I was walking by with Fatima on my back. I was on my way to the madina to shop when I passed the mausoleum and decided to leave the verses there. When a fqih writes verses of the Koran, and they do not work, we leave them in a saint's tomb. If the verses work, you must always keep them. But when they do not work, you leave them in a saint's mausoleum because you cannot just throw them anywhere. Perhaps someone will walk on them and dirty them. There is always a shelf made of earth in a saint's tomb where you leave them. They are said to be thrown away and will not work again, not even from the saint's tomb.

Now then, everybody was saying, "It is because of the chicken that Fatima is sick." This was always between my eyes. Everybody said, "Go back to Sidi ʿAli so that God can help you." The woman who had taken me to the fqiḥ said, "Go to Sidi ʿAli." And although Fatima was a little better, my mother-in-law said, "I know that unless you give a chicken to the saint,

[10] Fatna does not mention that her child was sick at this time.

Fatima's sickness will last forever." The day after I used mint, I said to my husband that I was going. I did not do anything for Fatima that day. My husband bought three chickens. He agreed to my going, but he said, "You must find a neighbor woman to go with you. I will pay for her trip." [Fatna's husband, having worked in France, seems to have considered himself too modern to go with Fatna.] I tried my neighbors, but they were all busy. So my husband had to come. He bought the chickens the day before the trip. He ordered a taxi. For Sidi Ahmed, he bought a black and white chicken; for Sidi ʿAli, a red and white chicken; and for ʿAïsha, a chicken that was all red. Also, on the day before the trip, my husband went to the baths. I could not go because Fatima was very sick. I did not want to leave her. I washed very well and heated water for it at home. I washed well because it is not good to go to a saint when you are dirty. My husband bought a box of candles. There were 24 in the box. We also took something with which we could cut off a piece of Fatima's clothing to hang on ʿAïsha's tree. You say that on that piece of clothing, you have left the illness. [Did you wear any special clothes?] We put on our best clothing. We all had on our newest clothing except for our jallabas. I put new clothes on Fatima too. You should wear good clothes to the saint. They should be the best clothes, because it is possible you will meet people you know at the saint. From the point of view of the saint, you can wear new or old clothes. The saint can't see you. You must be clean. . . . I put on my new clothes for the trip. [Do you have to wear special colors?] It is not necessary to wear any special colors when you visit a saint. If a child is sick, you must not wear any perfume. You can wear other make-up. You bring whatever verses of the Koran the fqiḥ has written for the child, and you leave them in ʿAïsha's grotto. [Fatna explained that they were attached to the roots of the fig tree.] Whatever words of the Koran you are wearing when you make a trip to Sidi ʿAli, you leave with ʿAïsha—even those which work. [This practice is by no means universal.] So, when we went to Sidi ʿAli, my husband wore European clothes. It makes no difference for men, European or Moroccan clothes. Women should wear Moroccan clothes. It is more respectful. My husband had ordered the taxi for 8 in the morning. We were not planning to stay the night, because we wanted to keep the same taxi and return by noon, in time for lunch. The taxi driver had arranged to make the trip for us for 2,000 francs.

The taxi went directly to Sidi Ahmed. The moment we got into the taxi Fatima was better. At Sidi Ahmed, I put Fatima under the covers [of the catafalque]. My husband came in with me but left immediately because he was bored and there were too many people there. Before leaving, he gave the chicken to the muqaddim and left eight candles there on the alms box. He did not leave any money. When you enter a mausoleum, you kiss both sides of the door and the tomb. Fatima was too young to do that. But at Sidi Ahmed's and then at Sidi ʿAli's I rubbed her head and her face against the tomb. I left Fatima under the covers for about 30 minutes. She did not cry. She had been getting better since we got into the taxi. After 30 minutes, I took Fatima into the courtyard to Lalla ʿAïsha's hole. I sat down by the hole and took some earth [*tuba*] and rubbed it on Fatima's chest, forehead, and arms. It was Friday, if I remember. You visit the saints on Friday or Thursday. It is best then.

Then we went quickly to Sidi ʿAli, because the taxi was waiting. We followed the footpath, but the taxi went by the road. At Sidi ʿAli's we entered the tomb, kissed the jambs and the tomb. I rubbed Fatima's hands and face on the tomb and put her under the covers. I kept her there for 45 minutes. My husband stayed in the tomb room. He gave the chicken to the muqaddim and left eight candles. Fatima was not crying and was no longer feverish. I talked with my husband. He said, "You see, had you taken her here on the first day, she would have been better. It is all your fault because of the chicken." I had put Fatima under the cover, because one says that in that way you make an ʿar with Sidi ʿAli in order for the child to get better. The child is given to the saint for his protection. The child is like a sheep given to a saint [for sacrifice]. After you have made an ʿar with Sidi ʿAli, the child belongs to Sidi ʿAli. If the child gets better, he will get better right away. If he does not get better, he will die immediately after the visit. Sometimes the child will die right under the covers. So, like the sheep, you say, "This child, O Sidi ʿAli, belongs to you." We left no money at Sidi ʿAli, but we left the chicken and the candles.

Then we went to ʿAïsha's grotto. We gave the chicken to the muqaddim, as well as the last eight candles. Then we cut a piece of Fatima's clothing and hung it on the tree. I had a verse of the Koran hanging from my neck. I left that, too, at Lalla ʿAïsha's. My husband came with me to the grotto. I took some henna and put it on my forehead and on my chest and also on Fatima's forehead and chest. You find this henna in ʿAïsha's grotto. We left right away. There was no place to sit. We were the only people there. It was frightening, with the spring, with the tree. It is always dark there, even during the day. [Do you kiss anything there?] You do not kiss anything there.

Fatima was completely cured by the time we got home at noon. We did nothing for Fatima afterward. We left her in the clothes she had worn for three days without washing her. We kept her in the same pants too. We took them off when we knew she had to poopoo. Then we would put them on again. When she made peepee, we took them off to dry, but we did not wash them. This we did for three days. I changed my clothes immediately. So did my husband. My sister-in-law made us lunch, and Fatima ate for the first time since she had fallen sick. She had eaten nothing for five days—just a little water. We say that hunger does not kill until after 40 days. After lunch we slept. We slept and slept until 4 o'clock. Then we had a simple dinner of rice and milk. Before dinner, at 5 o'clock, all the friends and neighbors came over to congratulate us. They stayed until dinner. They drank tea with us. After dinner, we, the family, all talked until 10:30.[11]

Ah, there was one thing I forgot. After we returned, there were two things to do: one for Sidi Ahmed and one for Sidi ʿAli. For Sidi ʿAli, you take a little mint and squeeze it into the ears, nostrils, and mouth of the child. We say that then there will always be flowers in these places. For Sidi Ahmed, you take a little of the earth from the hole in the courtyard—the muqaddim gives it to you—and you put it in a rag and hang it from the child's neck. I did this for Fatima. I also prepared the mint for her. It is important not to forget the mint and the earth after a visit to Sidi ʿAli and Sidi Ahmed. Also, after a visit to Sidi Ahmed, the mother of a sick child must not eat butter for seven days. She must not put henna or perfume on herself. So I did not eat butter for seven days, or put on henna, or perfume myself. That is all I did.

I have presented Fatna's account of her pilgrimage in detail because it illustrates what one does on a pilgrimage and, more important here, how one makes the decision to pay a visit to the saints.[12] Such decisions are clearly not made on the basis of the objective condition of the patient alone. Although the patient's condition does delimit the range of choice, it does not specifically determine a particular cure. Factors not directly involving the patient play an important role. In this case, Fatna's decision to go to Sidi ʿAli—even when Fatima's condition was beginning to improve—seems to have been based on a conviction that she was responsible for her daughter's illness. She had neglected to give the chicken, as she had promised, to the muqaddim of the mausoleum. She either was encouraged in this belief by her neighbors or projected her own conviction onto them.

The Westerner would argue that Fatna had a guilty conscience and was determined to expiate her sin of omission by means of a pilgrimage and the sacrifice. Moroccans of Fatna's background, do not, however, organize their experiences in terms of guilt, sin, and expiation. They organize experience in a more externalized way, and would argue that Fatna's failure to give the chicken to the muqaddim angered either Sidi ʿAli or ʿAïsha Qandisha and thus resulted in her daughter's illness. Fatna does not specify who was angry, but we may assume that, since saints do no harm, it must have been ʿAïsha who was responsible for Fatima's

[11] The information in the above paragraph was in response to a number of questions put to Fatna. Her story of the pilgrimage ended with the family's return to Sidi Baba at noon. The final paragraph of her narration was again her own.

[12] Cf. Crapanzano and Kramer 1969 for an account of another pilgrimage.

condition. This, at any rate, is how similar cases were explained to me. The pilgrimage and the sacrifice of the chickens—they were not actually slaughtered—were means of appeasing the saints and ʿAïsha Qandisha. Fatna placed Fatima under the protection of Sidi ʿAli (and Sidi Ahmed)—"The child, O Sidi ʿAli, belongs to you"—and, in so doing, abrogated her own responsibility. The child's fate depended then upon the saint. "If the child gets better, she will get better right away. If she does not get better, she will die immediately after the visit." She does not specify whether the child was also placed under ʿAïsha Qandisha's protection.

The role of ʿAïsha Qandisha in these matters is very ambiguous. Although sacrifices to ʿAïsha are often referred to as ʿars, it is my impression that they are generally conceived of as gifts to placate the she-demon. ʿAïsha is said to like red or black chickens or to like blood. One does not give a child to her. It must be remembered that while it is possible for a human being to have a child msannad by a saint, it is not possible for a human being to make a child a follower of a jinn. It is the jinn who decides. Since both saints—especially Sidi ʿAli—have some influence over ʿAïsha Qandisha, one places the child in their hands and hopes, Allah willing, that they will exercise that influence and that ʿAïsha will accept it. The sacrifice to ʿAïsha is all that the pilgrim himself can do to placate her.

It has to be remembered that while the child's illness is the *raison d'etre* for the pilgrimage, the pilgrimage serves primarily to remedy a situation which affected the child, but for which the child was not at all responsible. Just as Thebes suffered the plague because of Oedipus' conduct, so Fatima suffers because of Fatna's negligence. Therapy is not patient-centered but situation-centered.

10

The Ḥadra

A ceremony at which the ḥadra is performed is most commonly called a *lila*, or night, because it usually is held at night. When it is held in the morning or the afternoon, it is called a *taqyil;* and in the late afternoon and early evening an *ʿashwiyya.* Whenever the ceremonies do not involve the recitation of litanies, they may be referred to simply as ḥadras. *Fraja*, which refers to a secular spectacle, is very occasionally used to refer to the public performances of the ḥadra. It is never used for private ceremonies.

One very common name for the Ḥamadsha ceremonies—and for those of other brotherhoods, especially when they are terminated by a communal meal—is *sadaqa.* "Sadaqa" means charity, gift, or alms, and is frequently used for the alms left by a pilgrim at a saint's tomb. It is also used to refer to money given the Ḥamadsha by spectators and devotees, and the money and gifts that the adepts of the urban lodges divide among themselves. In this sense, baraka may be substituted for sadaqa. One of its derivatives, *sdaq*, refers to the bride-price that a husband must pay to his wife's family. Mercier (1951:191) suggests that "sadaqa" may also mean the expiation of sins, but one has to be extremely cautious in dealing with the implications of such a definition. The adjectival form *sadiq* means honest, loyal, truthful, or sincere. A man who is sadiq is a man who lives up to the highest standards of the Islamic community. Its verbal form, *sadaq*, means to tell the truth or to act with sincerity, and the Ḥamadsha emphasize that their ceremonies must be performed with sincerity by men who are *sadiqin.* If a man is not sincere, not only will he not receive the blessings, the baraka, of the Ḥamadsha saints, but he will suffer the dire consequences of ʿAïsha Qandisha's wrath.

The ceremonies of the urban lodges are much more complicated than those of the bidonville teams. They usually involve the chanting of litanies as well as the performance of the ḥadra, whereas a team ceremony consists only of the ḥadra. Occasionally a few lines of a litany (*dikr*) will be chanted at a team ceremony, if the members happen to know any, but chanting is not central to the ceremony and it is generally ignored by the devotees, who are anxious to get on with the ḥadra and dance. The adepts of the urban lodges are called in to chant their litanies alone; these invitations are made on festive occasions, such as name-days or moving days, and they are said to bring much baraka to the sponsor and his family. The zawiya members never perform in public as their confreres in the bidonvilles do. I have seen them in attendance at public ceremonies, but never actively participating. Their ceremonies are less violent, less spectacular, than those of the shantytown Ḥamadsha.

The adepts claim to work—to perform their ceremonies—out of love for the saint they follow. They are much more explicit in their devotion to the Ḥamadsha saints than are the shantytown Ḥamadsha, who are more concerned with ʿAïsha Qandisha and the other jnun. The adepts conceive of their performances as a means of obtaining their saint's baraka—baraka which keeps them in good health and fortune, and which they can pass on to others during their ceremonies. It is by virtue of their saint's baraka that they are able to perform the ḥadra and fall into trance (*ḥal*). Both the urban and shantytown Ḥamadsha would consider any suggestion that their ḥal is a mystical union or communion with God, or their saint, as blasphemous. The ḥal is an end in itself, a revitalizing process. I have been told that awakening from the trance is like being reborn. The Ḥamadsha perform the ḥadra because their saints did so before them. The saints' performances were pleasing to God, who gave them their baraka, and now they, the Ḥamadsha, their followers, obtain their own baraka from them.

Since the bidonville Ḥamadsha are more concerned with the jnun than with the saints, they perform the ḥadra to please ʿAïsha Qandisha and the other demons. It is the saints who have given them the power to perform the ḥadra, but it is ʿAïsha Qandisha who enables them to trance and forces them to slash their heads. Sidi ʿAli ordered Sidi Ahmed to fetch the ḥal, and this he did by bringing ʿAïsha Qandisha from the Sudan. The zawiya members, too, acknowledge the importance of ʿAïsha Qandisha, but they are more reticent in talking about her and usually prefer to emphasize the role of Sidi ʿAli and Sidi Ahmed.

Both the madina and shantytown Ḥamadsha recognize the efficacy of their performances in the cure of illnesses, particularly those illnesses caused by ʿAïsha Qandisha and other jnun. The madina adepts perhaps lay less stress on the therapeutic effect of their saints' baraka than do the team members from the shantytowns. They conceive of their ceremonies as a means of passing baraka to everybody, both the sick and the healthy. The team members see their ceremonies as pleasing to the jnun—"ʿAïsha likes a particular riḥ," "ʿAïsha likes the sight of blood"—and thereby therapeutically effective. Their ceremonies are directed to the sick primarily.

The distinction between the two groups is difficult to communicate. It is one of tone and emphasis and not of belief. Belief itself is ambiguous and subject to many interpretations.[1] The adepts of the zawiyas are treated by both the Ḥamadsha and other Moroccans with great respect; they are the poor, the foqra, the sadiqin, who strive to live up to the ideals of the Islamic community as they themselves understand them. They are men possessed of baraka, and their ceremonies must be respected regardless of whether they are viewed with approval or disapproval. The team members of the bidonvilles are not treated with this same respect; they are often referred to as charlatans, money-grubbers, and whoremongers. Their ceremonies are accepted as necessary; they may be viewed with wonder and with awe, but never with respect. This difference is reflected in my own reactions and the reactions of my informants to the ceremonies of the two groups. I have been told that at the zawiya ceremonies one has the fear of God; at the bidonville ceremonies, the fear of ʿAïsha. Both my wife and I recognized a harsh and often histrionic quality in the bidonville ceremonies—a violent theatricality and an ambience of threat and even terror—which we never felt at ceremonies of the madina. Our reactions were confirmed by several of our non-Ḥamadsha friends.

The Madina Ceremony: Preparations

Once the decision to sponsor a ceremony has been made, the sponsor tells the muqaddim of the zawiya he prefers.[2] Date and time are set—most ceremonies begin between 7 and 8 in the evening—the fees for

[1] The ideology of the ʿAllaliyyin, under the leadership of their new muqaddim, appears to be changing in the direction of that of the more active bidonville teams. The Dghughiyyin have maintained a more conservative position.

[2] In what follows I assume for clarity's sake that the sponsor or host is not the patient, but a relative. Usually he is the father or elder brother of the patient, or the husband in the case of a married female patient.

the ghiyyata are discussed, and a deposit of 5 or 10 dirhams is left. The deposit, or at least 5 dirhams of the deposit, is given to the khalifa of the zawiya, who must let all the adepts know of the performance and bring the ritual paraphernalia to the sponsor's house on the appointed day. The paraphernalia consists of the zawiya's flag, a basket for collecting alms, and a few spare drums (*gwalat*). The muqaddim may arrange to invite a few of the zawiya's devotees, especially ones who are in need of a ceremony, but most of the guests are invited by the sponsor and his wife. They include members of the family, friends and neighbors, and any devotees the sponsor happens to know. Theoretically, anyone else who hears about the ceremony is welcome to attend. In fact, only acquaintances of the host and devotees who are driven to enter by the sound of their particular musical phrase attend the ceremony uninvited. Usually between 45 and 80 people will come. Some will stay for the full performance, others for just a few minutes. Only invited guests will remain for the meal with which the ceremony concludes.

The host, his family, and the patient will usually go to the public bath on the day of the ceremony. Others will bathe carefully at home before attending the ḥadra, if they do not go to the baths themselves. While technically no one should perform the ḥadra in an unclean condition, the fact that participation is not altogether voluntary means that great emphasis cannot be placed on ritual cleanliness. A man, clean or unclean, who hears his riḥ cannot resist dancing without incurring ʿAïsha's wrath or the displeasure of his own particular jinn. This, of course, has dire consequences.

If there is going to be a sacrifice, it is usually performed by the host the morning before the ceremony in the presence of his family, the patient, and perhaps a few friends. The muqaddim or the khalifa of the zawiya may sometimes help him.[3] A ram is the ideal sacrifice, but often a male or female goat, which is cheaper, is slaughtered. Although the sacrifice is not usually central to a madina ceremony, it is of considerable importance to the host, since it is his major expense. Goats may cost as little as 45 dirhams, and rams as much as 200 dirhams or more. The meat of the animal is used to make the couscous and stew

[3] Sometimes the muqaddim will force the patient to collect the blood of the sacrificial animal in his cupped hands and swallow it. He may smear a little blood from the knife on the patient's forehead and neck. This practice is very rare among the madina Ḥamadsha but, despite Koranic interdiction (Sura II, 1, 73), it is not infrequent among the bidonville and rural Ḥamadsha. When it is followed, the sacrifice takes place at the beginning of the formal ceremony after the guests have arrived.

(*tajin*) that are served at the ceremony to the adepts and the guests. The skin is given to the zawiya. Goatskins are used for drumheads; sheepskins may either be given to the saint's descendants or sold and the proceeds given. If no sacrifice is made, meat is bought from the local butcher. After making the sacrifice, the host will spend the rest of the day waiting for guests and entertaining early arrivals. Sometimes, these early arrivals are members of his family who have come from far away to attend the ceremony. The host's wife, usually aided by neighbors and girls and women in the family, spends the day preparing the ceremonial meal.

That evening, the adepts and ghiyyata parade in front of the host's house to attract attention. The host usually stands at his door and greets them. They play a few of the popular riḥs and dance a little. There is seldom any trancing at this stage. They will be surrounded by excited men, women, and children, who often follow them into the sponsor's house. Once inside, the muqaddim repeats a fatḥa[4] for the host and his family. A special prayer is usually said for the patient. The muqaddim or a sharif may massage or spit on the ailing part of the patient's body. Then all of the adepts sit down in a corner of the courtyard, and the host tends to them and the other guests. Men remain in the courtyard when the weather permits it; women stay in a separate room or on the roof. Both the men and women sit or stand pressed close together, as they do on all ceremonial occasions. While the guests wait for the host to serve them milk and dates—a sign of welcome and early return—and mint tea, the indispensable ingredient of

[4] *Fatḥa* is the dialect form of *fatiḥa,* which refers to the opening verses of the Koran. *Fatḥa* is used by the Ḥamadsha and other Moroccans of their background for an invocation which does not necessarily contain the Koranic verses. A typical fatḥa at a Ḥamadsha ceremony is:

> O my brothers, pray for me.
> I shall be cured, thanks to your invocation.
> Shelter me under your wings.
> O children of Mustafa, the chosen, the elected.
> There is no God but Allah.
> O Prophet, cure me.

All of the lines but the last are repeated three times. Sometimes the fatḥa is much shorter. The following one was repeated at a curing ceremony in a bidonville.

> Thanks to Allah and Sidi ʿAli.
> Allah will give you bread that is not
> prepared by the hands of men but by angels.

This fatḥa, repeated by a sharif, was considered to be particularly good. One of the listeners described his reaction to it in the following words: "I felt my heart to be very hot at this time and then I heard the fatḥa and then it was as though a pail of cold water—cold wind—made my heart go cold."

Moroccan hospitality, the adepts gossip among themselves. The drummers may tighten the membranes of their drums over a brasier at this time.

Litanies

When all of the guests are served, the muqaddim leads the adepts in a responsive recitation of the *ḥizb:* a long, laudatory invocation to Allah, whose forgiveness is sought.

A. In the name of Allah, the compassionate and the merciful
B. May eternal happiness rest with our lord Muhammad, His family, and His companions
A. Let us praise Allah the benevolent
B. Him, the adored Allah
A. May He hear my wishes
B. May He pardon me and grant me His mercy
A. I am a sinful slave
B. And I implore my lord
A. Because it is my duty
B. To ask Him to guide me
A. O, the compassionate one, the merciful one
B. Protect us from hell
A. You are the only one, the unique
B. You are the unique and the omnipotent one

etc. etc.

This is a section of the ḥizb recited by the Dghughiyyin of Meknes. The ʿAllaliyyin zawiya has a different ḥizb. There is in fact no standard ḥizb for either Ḥamadsha brotherhood, and differing texts are used throughout the country. It is claimed that the ḥizb of the ʿAllaliyyin of Meknes was composed by al-Shadhili, but this seems unlikely, since al-Shadhili left no writings (Rahman 1968:197). The Dghughiyyin do not know the origin of their ḥizb, but I have been told by a Fasi in-law of one of Sidi ʿAli's descendants—a man whose wisdom is generally respected—that it was composed by Sidi Heddi, the founder of the mendicant brotherhood known as the Heddawa. The language of the ḥizb and of the other litanies is written in what the Ḥamadsha refer to as classical Arabic but which is, in fact, a mixture of classical and dialectical Arabic. Most of the adepts do not understand it very well and are content reciting it.

The muqaddim takes no special place when he leads the recitation. He remains seated with the adepts, who are pressed together and who may sway slightly from side to side. The adepts do not engage in any of the gymnastics reported for other brotherhoods; they often close their eyes during the recitation of the ḥizb. From time to time, one adept or another will replace the muqaddim as leader of the recitation. The men in the audience center their attention on the adepts, but they may occasionally gossip or finish drinking their tea. The women seem less interested in the recitation of the ḥizb and other litanies. The patient—or patients—is generally ignored.

Sometimes, in place of the ḥizb, short moralistic tales and prayers called *wanasa* are recited. The most popular of these songs are said to have been composed by al-Maghrawi, a bard in the court of the Saadian sultan al-Mansur ad-Dhabi (1578–1602) who was considered one of the greatest of the composers of dialectical lyrics (*malḥun*) (Chottin 1938:104). A pilgrim, for example—I am not sure whether this poem is by al-Maghrawi—makes no provisions for his journey to Mecca, but he is aided by another "pilgrim" and has a successful journey.

> I made a pilgrimage with faith and conviction.
> I came back happy and with changed name.
> All listeners called me ḥajj.
> My heart was filled with joy.
> Allah satisfied my wishes.
> I came back surrounded by friends and brothers. . . .

When the ḥizb or the wanasa is completed—it lasts anywhere from about five minutes to over an hour—there may be a pause for tea before the recitation of the *dikr* begins. The dikr, resembling the ḥizb in content, consists of shorter phrases which are said more rapidly. The adepts may accompany the recitation with hand-clapping and a gentle tapping of drums. The ganbri may be played.

> A., B. In the name of Allah, the compassionate and the merciful
> A. I begin with the name of Allah
> B. To him I dedicate the following words
> A. Muhammad, O Perfect Creature
> B. You are as soft as beeswax
> A. You, who have brought the light
> B. You, who have come as an envoy
> A. You are the enlightened man
> B. You are the savior at the last judgment
>
> etc., etc.
> (Section of dikr used
> by Dghughiyyin)

Although the adepts are still seated, they do sway back and forth more rapidly as they recite the short dikr phrases, and they also start to hyperventilate. I have been told that they have the fear of God at this time. As the dikr is repeated faster and faster and louder and louder, both the adepts and the spectators become excited. A wave of heat passes through the courtyard. The women, in their separate room or up on the roof, begin to ululate their excitement and their impatience to begin the ḥadra. I have seen women become so excited during the recitation of the dikr that they begin to dance as if the ḥadra had already begun. The men disapprove of such behavior, and they shove the women roughly out of the court. "The ḥizb and the dikr are for men," they often say. In fact there appears to be considerable tension between the men and women at this stage of the performance, a tension which, of course, is dramatically symbolized by the separation of the sexes. Children, too, become more excited and belligerent and are treated equally roughly by the adults and the curious teenage boys who inevitably show up at these Ḥamadsha ceremonies. The patient, who does not actively participate in the recitation of the litanies, is nevertheless moved by the excitement of the group. Finally, when the excitement is at a peak—anywhere from 5 to 45 minutes or more from the beginning of the dikr—the adepts stand, hiss out the name of God or the last syllable of His name, "llah," as rapidly as possible, and start to dance the ḥadra, while the ghiyyata blare out their whining tunes and the drummers beat out their monotonous rhythms.

The Hot Part of the Ḥadra

The ḥadra is divided into three principal parts: the hot part (*es-skhun*), in which the ghita is played along with the *tabil* and the gwal; the cold part (*al-barid*), in which the ghita is replaced by the nira or sometimes the ganbri; and the *ḥadra gnawiyya*, which uses the instruments of the cold part but is derived from the ceremonies of the Gnawa.

The hot part of the ḥadra comes first and is the loudest, fastest, and most violent part of the performance. The two ghiyyata, a snare drummer or two, and three or four gwal players stand at one end of the dance area; the other adepts, and any male guest who wants to, line up shoulder to shoulder, opposite the musicians and forming an outer boundary to the dance area. This line is called the *siffa* (literally, configuration) and resembles the dance position of the Berber *ahidus*. The number of men in a line will vary during the performance of the hot part, but it seldom exceeds 25. Occasionally, a woman will join the line "to cool down."

The men pound up and down on their heels, "knocking the breath out," raise and lower their shoulders, and hiss out their breath as they seek the ḥal. They are encouraged by the muqaddim, who dances in front of them. He leaps, turns in mid air, lands on his knees, leaps again, and stabs at his chest with his fists as he lands. His stabbing motions are reminiscent of those of the followers of the Barong who stab themselves with krisses in the Balinese dramatic portrayal of the struggle of the forces of good (Barong) and evil (Rangda) (Belo 1960:96–124). A few women are usually drawn by the music of the ghita out of their separate quarters and into the dance area, where they bob up and down, in trance, or pitch from side to side in front of the ghiyyata. Their feet remain in place; their pitching movement is faster than anything possible in a fully conscious state. Often they swing their heads so low as to graze the floor with their hair, but I have never seen them hit it. They are generally ignored at this stage of the ḥadra, but if they become too excited they are made to join the line of men. The patient, especially if he is a man or boy, is encouraged to participate in this part of the ḥadra. He is sometimes forced to join the line, or he is placed in the center of the dance area and made to dance by the muqaddim.

The audience shuffles about when the ḥadra begins. Spectators appear to take the positions that are most satisfying to them. Some prefer to huddle near the ghita players, others to stand behind the line of men, and still others to remain as far back from the dance as possible. The basic dance pattern is illustrated in Figure 10.

From time to time, the men in the line will chant short phrases or simply the name of God. The most common of the phrases is "Allah! Allah! Allah the Eternal! Allah the Adored!" which Sidi ʿAli is said to have chanted whenever he performed the ḥadra. Other popular phrases are: "By the grace of Mohammed"; "Allah, our master, it is the door, it is the door to my refuge in Allah the eternal"; "O Allah, our master, it is the dearest door of communion since the commemoration of the celebration of the birth of the Prophet"; "O Sidi ʿAli, help the tardy. O ben Ḥamdush, be generous with your satisfaction with me"; "You are the possessor of safety. Help me, O son of Lalla ʿAïsha, help me"; "O you who have abandoned me, denuded of spirit, whose love has embraced my heart"; "I seek your help, O Moulay Abdelqa-

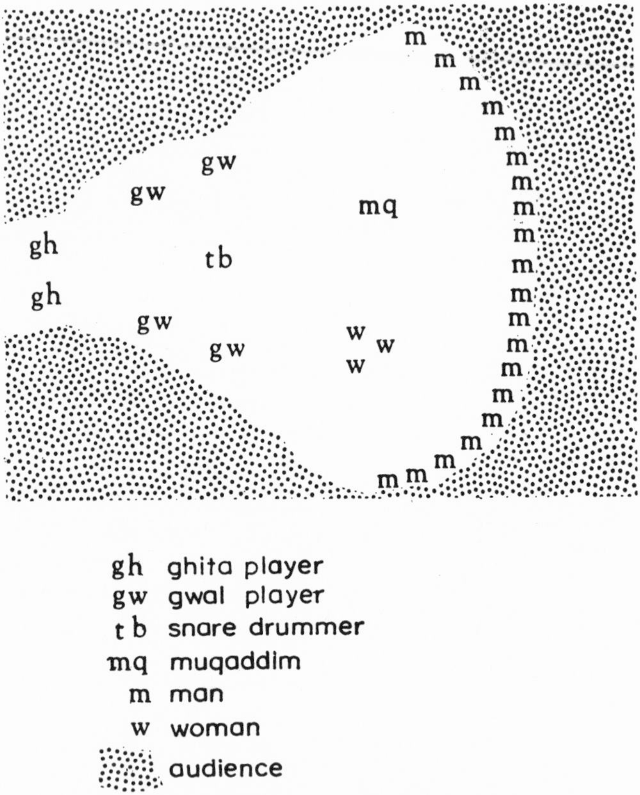

Figure 10. The basic pattern of the hot part of the ḥadra.

der Jilali, my protection. Come to my aid. I shall carry myself to Tadla to make a pious visit to you, O Buʿabid, the nobility of my eyes"; "O Prophet of God, nothing can save us from the fires of hell"; "Moulay Idriss, the house of safety"; "O saints, whose role is to bring aid and assistance"; "Door of doors. The house here below is the life of error and waywardness. Do not build palaces, because you shall move and abandon them"; and "There is no God but God, my helper. I pray to God the generous. He, my eternal master." There is no order to these phrases, and their meaning often remains obscure. I have been told that they are the phrases the ghita speaks. "You hear them just as you see things in those pictures you showed me," one of my informants explained, referring to my Rorschach cards.

Trance and Dance Patterns

The ḥadra is designed to lead the performers, including the patient, into an altered state of consciousness, or trance.[5] The Ḥamadsha recognize two such states: *ḥal* and *jidba*. *Ḥal*, which means temperature, condition, or state, and is in general use in Moroccan Arabic, has, as I have noted, a specific meaning in the Sufi lexicon. It refers to one of the psycho-gnostic states (*aḥawal*), such as nearness to God or divine intimacy, over which the mystic has no control. These states are descended from God. In at least the popular brotherhoods of Morocco, *ḥal* refers to the entranced state which in the Sufi lexicon is known as *wajd*, or ecstasy. Insofar as the Moroccan trancer has no control over his ḥal—it is descended from a saint or a jinn and ultimately from God—the ḥal resembles the aḥwal of the Sufis.[6]

For the Ḥamadsha, *ḥal* is both a generic and a specific term. Generically, it refers to any trance which occurs during the ḥadra; specifically, it refers to a nonviolent trance, which corresponds roughly to what is known in the literature on hypnosis as a somnambulistic state.[7] It is usually attributed to the saint, and may be preliminary to the more violent jidba. Its semantic field probably varies slightly with reference to men and women, for it seems to encompass a deeper trance and more frenetic behavior when used for women. This may result from the fact that women fall into trance with much more ease than men, and their initial dance steps are more violent.

Jidba, which is a more frenetic trance, is derived from the Arabic

[5] Trance shall be loosely defined as a complete or partial dissociation, characterized by changes in such functions as identity, memory, the sensory modalities, and thought. It may involve the loss of voluntary control over movement, and may be accompanied by hallucinations and visions which are often forgotten.

[6] It is curious, however, that in Morocco a person in trance is said to be "out of his conditions" (*kharij al-aḥwal*); a lunatic is also said to be "without his ḥal" (*bila ḥal*). To enter ḥal may be rendered *tlaᶜ fih l-ḥal* (the ḥal mounts in him) or *jah l-bal* (the ḥal arrives in him). The second expression may also mean to ejaculate (Mercier 1951). The connection between ḥal and the mental state at the moment of ejaculation is not made, however. *Tḥayyar*—which is related to words meaning bewildered, confused, or dumbfounded (*ḥayr*) and anxious, angry, and confused, *mḥayyar*—is also used with reference to entering trance.

[7] During the somnambulistic state, quite complex behavior can be carried out—"behavior which is 'unconscious' but nonetheless subject to control, which clearly bears the imprint of the culture to which the individual belongs, and which is modified according to the makeup of the individual personality, the positive impulses which fit in with the trance role he is playing, and the negative or inhibiting restraints which the remainder of his normal personality, although in abeyance, is able to exert" (Belo 1960:212–213).

for attraction. It is used by the Sufis for the mystical attraction to God. Although the transition from ḥal to jidba is always abrupt and dramatic, jidba does not altogether correspond to such "strong seizures" as are described for trance in Bali (Belo 1960:213). It is, as we will see, a structured experience in which the performer carries out relatively complex behavior, but does not appear to have the same control as he does in ḥal. It is comparable to a state of extreme rage (cf. Belo 1960:223). Except in its most extreme manifestations, it does not exhibit the universal features which come "from too deep a level to be influenced by custom or by idiosyncratic trends in the personality" (Belo 1960:212).[8] Jidba is usually attributed to ʿAïsha Qandisha or another jinn, and not to the saint. It may occur in any of the three parts of the ḥadra.

Men and women differ significantly in their trance and dance patterns.[9] Women, who fall into trance much more readily than men do, remain in the audience until "they are driven by the music of the ghita into hal." They may either work their way through the audience to the dance floor and begin to dance in front of the ghiyyata or fall to the ground, unconscious and paralyzed, and remain in this cataleptic state for a few minutes before they rise and start to dance.[10] The audience, whether in the intimate private ceremonies or in the more impersonal public ones, is always ready to allow women (or men) to move through it to the center dance area. Women who are driven to the center can easily be recognized by the ease and even grace with which they manipulate their way through the crowd; they appear to float. Their movements are slow, their eyes are glazed and transfixed, and they seem oblivious to all but a "goal" in front of them, in the dance center. They are in a light trance. The moment they reach the dance floor, they move as close to the ghiyyata as they can—as though seeking stimulation—and begin bobbing up and down and swaying from side to side in their stylized way. They may continue to wear the veil while

[8] Belo (1960:212) argues that while the affective interpretation or coloring of trance experience determines the "mood" in which the somnambulistic trance activity takes place, the "cataclysmic discharge of nervous tension" of the strong seizure is not affected by such interpretation. Its features remain constant, despite the emotional background, be it of anger, fear, or sexuality.

[9] I have observed on several occasions male transvestite dancers shift back and forth from male to female steps, apparently unable to decide on the appropriate style.

[10] I did not see enough performances with the same female performers to note whether these two preliminary trance patterns varied with the same trancer or with their hearing different musical phrases.

dancing, or they may remove it. This is one of the few occasions on which the veil can be removed in public.

Although women who fall to the ground before dancing give the impression that they do so immediately and abruptly, I have found that they are often in trance before their collapse. This is not unusual, since many members of the audience, especially people closest to the ghiyyata, fall in and out of trance throughout the performance. I, too, have felt myself momentarily lose contact with what was going on around me. It is possible that the women who do collapse either have resisted dancing, as may be the case with certain teen-age girls who attend school and consider the ḥadra backward, or are not yet fully aware of the prodromata of their trance dancing, as may be the case with young and inexperienced trancers. My general impression is that the majority of women who collapse before dancing are younger and less experienced trancers than those who make their way through the audience. The first trance experience of every woman—and every man, for that matter—that I have heard about or seen has been sudden and abrupt and has involved a collapse.

Before falling to the ground, the female dancer appears semi-conscious—sleepy, one might say—and disoriented. Her eyes are glazed and unfocused, and she seems to be oblivious to her surroundings. She may nod her head slightly to the rhythm of the music. If someone speaks to her, she acts as though she were suddenly awakened from a deep reverie and appears to be slightly irritated by the interruption. Her collapse is always sudden and involves a loud thud, which attracts a good deal of attention. She remains on the ground for several minutes, in a cataleptic state which may have been preceded by convulsive movements. Sometimes, during the paralyzed phase, she exhibits a slight tremor of the hands or feet. Her breath is shallow, her hands clammy, and her body cold. If she is left alone, she will gradually start responding to the music and will either rest on her knees or stand and dance. Often she will begin to dance before her whole body has recovered from paralysis. It is not unusual to see a woman dancing with her left forearm and hand still stiff. The woman who collapses is, however, rarely left alone. Rather, as soon as she shows any sign of life, she is helped to her feet by a woman in the audience or by one of the female caretakers from the zawiya, who may dance with her for a while until she is able to go on alone.

The dancer continues to dance in the stylized manner until the music ends or she herself is exhausted—"until her jinn has had enough."

She follows the rhythm of the music and is capable of loosening her clothes or removing her veil. Sometimes a woman in the audience will tie a kerchief around her chest to keep her breasts from flopping. Often her hair will loosen and fall in front of her face or swing around it in long snake-like curls. Loosened hair always makes an impression on the men in the audience. Often, too, the hood of her jallaba will fall down over her face. No effort is ever made to remove it. In this state of ḥal, the woman will usually exhibit a slight exophthalmos. Her breath will be rapid, her face flushed, and her movements, again, much more rapid than would be possible in a normal state of consciousness.

Sometimes a woman will suddenly fall out of rhythm—this is said to happen when her special riḥ is played—and enter a frenetic trance that is called *jidba*. She may charge around the dance floor, screaming; she may act as though she is seeing things in front of her; she may fall into a convulsive state; she may suffer temporary paralysis of a limb or severe contraction of the face; and she may scratch at her head, or even demand a knife and slash at it, with more abandon than the men. Sometimes she will use the knife to cut her forearm—usually the left one.[11] These acts of self-mutilation are rare among female dancers, and especially rare at the ceremonies of the zawiya members. During the jidba, the woman's eyes will also exhibit marked exophthalmos. She will appear transfixed. Her breath will be very rapid, almost rasping, her face flushed, and her movements abrupt and disorganized.

Certain women in jidba are compelled to imitate pigs. They begin to squeal and grunt and grovel on the ground, and can only be appeased when a little water is sprinkled around them. Such a woman is looked on with a certain disgust by both male and female members of the audience. She is often said to be *marja* (lit., bog or swamp), to have a wet vagina, possibly from leucorrhea.[12] It has to be remembered

[11] I have on at least one occasion seen a woman try to cut off her breast. Female worshippers of Cybele cut off their breasts just as her male devotees castrated themselves (Weigert-Vowinkel 1938, quoting Henri Graillot, *Le Cult de Cybèle, Mère des Dieux, à Rome et dans l'Empire romain*, Paris: Fontemoing, 1912).

[12] A woman with a moist vagina is regarded with disgust. It is impossible to determine whether the moisture referred to is the normal moisture of the vagina during intercourse or a pathological condition. Given the fact that most of my male informants preferred to ejaculate as rapidly as possible after penetration and did not stimulate their women first, it is possible that they were referring to the vaginal secretions of an aroused woman. It is said that a woman becomes a marja if her husband ejaculates when he deflowers her (and, sometimes, for three days afterward).

that pigs are considered lowly animals and their meat is taboo to the Muslim (cf. Belo 1960:223).

Most women will stop dancing before the music ends. Some will continue to the very end of the music and stop then without any difficulty. They may appear disoriented for a few minutes, but that will be the only visible aftermath of their trance. Others, however, will not have had enough when the music stops, and these women will fall to the ground in a state of paralysis or remain in a cataleptic, often grotesque, standing posture until the music has begun again. This state is called *yabis*, and is associated with dryness, as of a plant. It is said that the jinn of such a woman has not had enough. She exhibits the symptoms of someone who has fallen before beginning to trance. If the musicians do not begin to play again immediately, she is usually covered with a blanket by the other women. She will remain paralyzed, sometimes for hours, until the musicians play her riḥ. It is said that if her riḥ is not played, she will remain paralyzed or at least suffer a general malaise that is often described as "pinching bones." If she is never given the opportunity to dance again, it is believed that she will die and that the musicians and her family will suffer dire consequences.

Although some of the young male dancers, particularly at their first trancing, enter ḥal in the same way the women do, most male trancers work themselves into the trance slowly. They join the line of dancers voluntarily, and then, by means of the breathing and the dance techniques, work themselves into the ḥal. In ḥal, they are able to follow the rhythm and dance steps of the ḥadra; their movements may be simplified and appear graceful and even dreamy. Their eyes are fixed and often exhibit slight exophthalmos. Their limbs may quiver slightly or become stiff. Their speech is slurred, and they seem disoriented. They are able to fall out of trance with ease, especially if the situation demands their conscious attention—as, for example, attending to guests if one should happen to be host. Subjectively, informants report a loss of temporal and spatial orientation and of body consciousness, except in the head, which feels swollen and warm and may itch slightly. They hear nothing but the music of the ghita, and they see shadows (singular form, *khayal*) before their eyes. Often they remember nothing of the experience.

My body tightens. It becomes more and more tight. Then I throw myself to the ground. I feel hot. I see only ʿAïsha during the ḥadra. She is in front of me. She too dances the ḥadra. My head itches. My eyeballs do not move.

I am not conscious of my body. I sweat a lot. I do not know where I am or what time it is. I remain this way for about two minutes and then I begin jidba.[13]

From time to time, one or two of the male dancers will leave the line and begin to dance in the center in a more frenetic fashion. Or he will fall to the ground in a cataleptic state, followed occasionally by convulsive movements and violent tremors of the limbs. Then it is said that the dancer has heard his special riḥ and has fallen into jidba. Gradually, as the musicians continue to play a particular tune to which he is responsive, the dancer's body will relax, and he will stand and charge wildly around the dance area, screaming and scaring the women and children in the audience.[14] At this point he is unable to follow the dance rhythms, although he may become obsessed with the ghita and push at it or beckon it seductively. Sometimes he will stimulate his genitals with his hands or by rubbing himself against another dancer of the same sex.[15] He may scratch his head, and occasionally he will ask for a pocket knife and slash at his head with it until his face and shoulders are drenched in blood. The knife is held so that the blow is softened by the dancer's thumb. These wounds are usually of a superficial nature and do not reach the cranium, although most slashers report having mutilated themselves at least once in the course of a lifetime with more abandon than usual.[16]

[13] Reported by an experienced Ḥamdushi in his middle thirties.

[14] Those dancers who charge around most violently, simulating attack, usually end up slashing their heads. Aggression is first turned outward but controlled and then turned toward self with less control. This pattern is also found among the Balinese kriss dancers. Belo (1960:3) has called attention to parallels with the amok psychosis. This pattern of aggression turned inward is not infrequently seen in the sudden transition from rage to depression found among at least those Moroccans of the Ḥamadsha's milieu. A man who, for whatever reason, is enraged and exhibits all the overt symptoms of his anger, suddenly retires to a corner of his house and sits there silent and immobile for hours if not days. Such a man is described generally as *mqallesh* and, significantly, by the Ḥamadsha as *mqandesh*. "Mqandesh," they say, is derived from "Qandisha." Several of my head-slashing informants were prone to such depressions.

[15] None of my male informants have ever reported having had an ejaculation during trance. The Ḥamadsha ignore sexual behavior during trance, and they make no comparison between trance and the sexual act. Indeed, they are shocked by the very suggestion. Some women have remarked, however, that "the feeling after a 'good' trance is like the feeling you have when you have made love, and no one has interrupted you."

[16] It is possible that the wounds then reach to the cranium. I have seen several Ḥamadsha with large cup-like indentations in their skulls which resulted from a blow with a club. Ḥamadsha who have hit themselves on several occasions with such abandon often seem punch-drunk. It is said that some Ḥamadsha have killed

Traditionally—and today during the musem—the Ḥamadsha slashed their heads with a single-bladed iron axe (*shaqur*) or a double-bladed one (*shaqria*) that resembles the medieval halbard and is not dissimilar to the axes found at Cnossos. They also hit their heads with an iron ball (*kura*) often weighing as much as twenty pounds, with a club (*zarwata*) covered with nails and also weighing as much as twenty pounds, and with bundles of sticks. The Ḥamadsha are proud of these instruments of mutilation and handle them with great care.[17]

Some male dancers in jidba imitate camels; they walk stiffly together in pairs, and then move apart and battle each other as camels often do. They make deep, rasping sounds which are likened to the grunts of camels.[18] A few men imitate pigs.

Subjectively, the dancer in jidba reports the same symptoms as in ḥal, but more extreme. He hears nothing but the sound of the ghita and the blood throbbing in his head, which feels ready to explode and itches intensely. This itching sensation has been described as "like a wasp under the skin." [19] When it occurs, the dancer may see ʿAïsha Qandisha before him, slashing at her own head with a piece of iron and compelling the dancer to do the same. Most of my informants who had experienced jidba could recall nothing of the experience.

I fall to the ground then. If I am made to get up right away then I can tell you what I have seen exactly. If I am not forced to get up, but get up on my own, then I do not remember what I have seen. I am hot and breathe heavily. I feel myself throbbing. There is much itching. I am not conscious of my body. I do not know where I am. Nor do I know what time it is. My body feels like boiling water. It is frightening. I see only ʿAïsha. [How do you feel during the head hitting?] It is ʿAïsha who makes me hit my head. I see her in front of me. She has a piece of iron. She is hitting her head. I begin to hit my head also. I am not aware of the fact that I am hitting my head. There is itching and sweating, and my whole body is hot. When ʿAïsha stops hitting her head, so do I. Then I continue to dance. My body and head continue to throb. I am not aware of my wounds. I am still hot. I am sweating a lot, and my breath is very fast.[20]

It is said that it is the itching that makes the dancers slash, and the flow of blood that calms ʿAïsha. The Ḥamadsha often smear blood

---

themselves by hitting their heads with a jug that cracked; a shard penetrated to the brain.

[17] The instruments may be seen in the Musée de l'Homme in Paris.

[18] Camels are often castrated to make them more tractable.

[19] ʿAïsha Qandisha is sometimes said to take the form of a wasp.

[20] Cf. fn. 13.

from their head wounds on ailing parts of a patient's body. Westermarck (1926(I):203) reports that they dipped cubes of sugar into the blood and gave it to the sick to eat. I have heard that they also dipped bread in their wounds and fed it to the ailing. In those instances in which ʿAïsha is not "seen" dancing in front of the head slasher, she is considered actually to have entered his body and lodged herself in his head. She is responsible for the itching. There is no consciousness of pain during jidba, immediately afterward, when the dancer has "cooled down" and is again in ḥal, or after the dance itself. Often dancers do not know that they have wounded themselves until they discover bloodstains on their clothes. They do nothing to help the wounds heal.

Hot Part of the Ḥadra Falls

The hot part of the ḥadra may last from five or ten minutes to over an hour, depending on the mood of the musicians and the condition of the dancers. Usually it ends unexpectedly with several long blasts of the ghita. The ḥadra is said to have fallen. Most of the dancers will return to their places in the audience. These dancers appear to come to their senses with considerable ease, although they may be disoriented for a few minutes. Some dancers do not return to a normal state of consciousness, but remain in a sort of daze until the cold part of the ḥadra begins. There are usually a few dancers who do not recover from the trance at all and will stay paralyzed on the floor or in a standing position. By playing their riḥs, the musicians will make them recover their senses during the cold part of the ḥadra. The Ḥamdushi whose experiences I have been quoting describes his sensations at the end of the hot part of the ḥadra this way:

> The moment the ḥadra stops, my body begins to tremble. Sometimes I fall. I am still not conscious of having hit my head. There is no itching. I have cooled them [the jnun] down with the axe. I am not conscious of my body. I still do not know where I am or what time it is. I can repeat the fatḥa, but I do not know what I am saying. It is the body orifices that speak—the children of ʿAïsha. They are in my body when I make the ḥadra, and ʿAïsha is in front of me. There is one of them on each of my shoulders. I am not aware of the words I am saying. I do not remember them afterwards. My body is still hot.

This description is somewhat confused. My informant seems to have identified the "children of ʿAïsha" inside him with the two angels who are said to keep count of the good and bad deeds a man commits each day.

The musicians on one side of the courtyard and the men in line on the other form the boundaries of the area in which the action of the ḥadra takes place. They set off the dance area from the audience and transform it into a stage. On stage there is a tension, in dramatic terms, between the two groups. Women dance individually in a less controlled fashion next to the ghiyyata; men, until jidba, dance together in a more controlled manner. The ghita and the drums excite the dancers and lead them into trance. "The ghita talks to me" and "The ghita speaks to my jinn" are common descriptions of the ghita's effect. The line, the most distant point on "stage" from the ghiyyata, is said to cool down those who entered jidba.

The ghita draws men from the line, as well as members of the audience, into the center of the stage. Here they dance individually, often fall into jidba, and sometimes slash their heads. Occasionally the musicians—especially the drummers—are drawn into the center too. The muqaddim, whose principal function at this stage of the ḥadra is to encourage trance, may also fall into jidba and lose control of his dancing. The patient is encouraged to fall into jidba, and exhibits the symptoms described above for other dancers. It is not necessary for him to slash his head in order to be cured, although the experience of jidba is usually necessary. Sometimes the muqaddim or a sharif, if a sharif should happen to be present, will walk on the patient's back or spit on him. ʿAïsha Qandisha is said to be under the ground at the center of the stage, and it is from there that she will emerge to possess an individual dancer or to dance in front of everybody when her particular riḥ is played. (ʿAïsha's riḥ is played later, during the cold part of the ḥadra.) It is ʿAïsha's presence that accounts for the fact that the Ḥamadsha must dance barefoot and that they become enraged and tear at anyone who wears new slippers and walks in them across the stage.[21] Her presence also explains why some dancers fall to the ground and kiss the dance floor.

[21] I have never seen or heard of a case where the Ḥamadsha have attacked a person in slippers. Members of the audience are careful not to wear new slippers in front of the Ḥamadsha. In fact, one of the most important jobs of the female caretakers is to take the guests' shoes and put them away. It should be noted that the ʿIsawa in trance attack and tear apart any one wearing black. This occurs frequently at the musem. Women frequently wear black at this time, despite their knowledge of its possible consequences.

Music of the Ḥadra

The music of the hot part of the ḥadra is sometimes called the music of the father, and it is said to have the color white. The ghita is the hot part's most important instrument. Drums play the constant, monotonous background music, but the ghita—and in other sections of the ḥadra the nira and the ganbri—carries the highly ornamented melodic phrases which drive the participants into trance. The riḥs of the hot part of the ḥadra are classified into at least four groups, each of them named for a tribe: Zerhuni, Ḥasnawi, Gharbawi, and Bukhari. The Zerhuni group is sometimes divided into an ʿAllaliyyi and a Dghughiyyi subgroup; the Gharbawi has one major subgroup, the Khalifi, named after a saintly lineage of the Gharb called the Wulad Khalifa. The phrases are also divided according to old and new riḥs, but this division appears to be purely personal and refers to the power of the riḥ. The older the riḥ, the more powerful it is said to be.

Individuals are said to respond specifically to certain riḥs. One riḥ may leave a man unaffected, a second may drive him into trance, and a third may cause him to be possessed by a jinn he follows. I know of one man who claims to follow four different jnun—he is a member of one of the bidonville teams—and who responds to at least four different riḥs in four different ways. His dance style and his trance behavior vary with the phrase played. One riḥ makes him dance in much the same way the muqaddims do; a second sends him into a sort of dreamy trance in which his movements slow down considerably; a third drives him into a frenzy during which he dashes around madly, eyes protruding, until he spots a glass, chews it to pieces, and swallows it; the fourth riḥ causes him to slash his head. Once a man's riḥ is played and he falls into a trance, the musicians must continue to play variations on that riḥ until the man has had enough—"until his jinn has been satisfied." If the riḥ changes before he has had enough, he will usually end up in a cataleptic state, as we have noted, until his riḥ is resumed. Then he will dance "until his jinn is satisfied."

The phrases of the hot part of the ḥadra do not, however, have specific and generally accepted associations with specific named-jnun. They are all vaguely associated with ʿAïsha Qandisha, but they have no color and incense associations. Some Ḥamadsha relate one or more of them to specific jnun they follow, but these tend to be personal associations. They are perhaps modeled on the elaborate jinn-riḥ associations of the ḥadra gnawiyya. In this section of the ḥadra, individual riḥs within the named groupings do not have names. They are indicated by either humming or by singing them with the word *ba* (father). Sometimes they are referred to by the words that are chanted when they are played, but this sort of reference tends to be very personal, since the phrases are not necessarily associated with any particular chants.

There does not seem to be a fixed order to the musical phrases. The adepts of one zawiya usually begin with one order and those of the second with another, but the order soon changes and will vary from performance to performance. The choice is made by the ghiyyata while they play. There are no pauses during the hot part of the ḥadra, and the ghiyyata move from riḥ to riḥ and elaborate on them all, in much the same way that a group of jazz musicians will improvise at a jam session. The decisions are not fully conscious and seem to depend both on the mood and whims of the ghiyyata, the condition of the audience, the needs of individual dancers—including the patient, if he should happen to be dancing—and perhaps on certain structural necessities within the music.[22] The ghiyyata manage to maintain a high emotional pitch throughout the performance. I have found in my notes, for example, that whenever I remark that I—or the audience—am getting bored, a notation almost invariably follows indicating a change of tune and consequently the appearance of a new trancer who is driven to perform some dramatic feat such as slashing his head or sitting on hot coals. It is impossible to determine to what extent the ghiyyata, who are familiar with the trance patterns and musical phrases of many of the performers, choose to play the phrase, and to what extent the performer himself responds to the boredom and distraction of the audience by seeking attention.

The musicians take the major responsibility for leading dancers into trance, but they are *not* Svengalian puppeteers who control the emotions, the trancing, and the behavior of the dancers with only an eye to the dramatic quality of their performances. They are concerned about the individual dancers, and will refrain from playing a person's riḥ if they feel he ought not to dance that night because he has, say, been sick with dysentery or the flu. They also respect the wishes of a person's friends and relatives who may ask them not to play his riḥ for one reason or another. Finally, they never stop before a trancer has had enough.

The first section of the hot part is called *trish l-ḥadra*, or the slap

[22] The music has not yet been analyzed.

of the ḥadra.[23] It has been described to me, not in the musical terms I expected, but in terms of its effect upon a participant.

It is the beginning of the ḥal. The body of the dancer feels caressed. His body is swollen and itches. Slowly he becomes absent from his conditions [*kharij l-aḥawal*]. There are "degrees" which climb slowly to the head. When they reach the head, the dancer no longer feels his body. It is like being drunk. You no longer know your father from your mother or brother. Your eyes appear normal. You no longer see anything but darkness. You breathe a little faster. The person looks as though he is fainting. He does not swear. He does not see the jnun; he can still distinguish people. You can tell the notes apart. You are aware of where you are and what time it is. The head is dizzy. He is not yet in jidba. There is no head hitting at this stage. [I had asked a few questions toward the end of this report.][24]

The Ḥamdushi who gave this description was referring to a man who danced in line.

The second section of the hot part of the ḥadra is called *wast l-ḥadra.* My informant described this stage of the ḥadra as follows:

There is still the ḥal, but now he is in jidba. He no longer sees anything but the musicians. The ghiyyata are also in jidba. You can tell because they begin to sway back and forth. The head throbs. The eyes are open but cannot see anything. The breath is fast. You sweat. You are no longer conscious of your body even if you hit your head with an axe. Your muscles are swollen. There can be head-hitting. You see ʿAïsha, who dances the ḥadra in front of you. Her hair is falling all over.

The ʿAllaliyyin of Meknes call the third section the *khammari.* I have been told that this describes a rhythmic group like the Bukhari and the Gharbawi. Non-Ḥamadsha suggest that the word is derived from *khamr,* or wine.

The dancers are deeper in jidba. There is even more head-hitting. Six axes at a time! The head is stiff and itches. It palpitates. The person's eyes are wide open. You do not know where you are. You only know that ʿAïsha is in front of you, and that if you do not dance she will scratch out at you. She has nails like human fingernails. She is just like a person, except her feet are like a camel.

[23] "Trish" is related to the verb *tarsh,* to slap or make deaf. "Matrush" is also derived from *tarsh,* and the expression *tarshuh ej-jnun,* to be slapped by the jnun, is used to refer to someone who is slightly crazy, touched.

[24] For this description and the following three, see Fn. 13.

The khammari may be followed by ʿAïsha's ḥadra, but usually it is not played until the cold part of the ḥadra.

You care only for ʿAïsha. You are not afraid. Those who are in ḥal are never afraid. The ḥal is the same at this time as during the khammari. ʿAïsha does not let people sit at this time.

It is clear from these descriptions of the hot part of the ḥadra that what is important to the dancer is the subjective experience. My informant's comments on the objective condition of the dancer were probably a response to my own questioning. The ḥadra is seen as a single experience that reaches a climax with the appearance of ʿAïsha Qandisha. Dr. Theodora Abel, who has examined the Rorschach responses of some of my Ḥamadsha informants, was struck by the way they responded to the test emotionally as a whole, as a total experience. Dr. Abel suggested that this response may have been analogous to the total emotional response of the trance experience. To the individual Ḥamdushi, whether a dancer or a musician, the experience can be divided only artificially, and these divisions have more to do with the subjective experiences of the body than with the musical sections of the ḥadra.

The hot part of the ḥadra ends abruptly. The muqaddim or one of the dancers who is still in trance begins to recite the fatḥa. A fatḥa is said for anyone who wishes to obtain a blessing (*baraka*). Women often ask for children or the cure of menstrual pains; men, too, ask to be cured of various pains and illnesses. Whenever a fatḥa is said, the person who requested it must give some money. These donations vary from a few francs to 10 or more dirhams. They are the brotherhood's major source of income. Although the host is not necessarily obliged to give at this time, he usually offers the muqaddim a comparatively large donation (5 to 15 dirhams) for the fatḥa that is said over the patient. Sometimes the muqaddim or a sharif will massage the patient or spit on him while a fatḥa is recited. Fatḥas are said until every spectator and devotee who wants to receive a blessing is satisfied.

The Cold Part of the Ḥadra

When the recitation of the fatḥas is over, the cold part of the ḥadra begins. This part is quieter, and it is danced individually rather than in line. There are usually a few women who will dance through the cold part in front of the musicians, but most of the performers only have to dance for a few minutes before they—or rather, their jnun—are satisfied. When an individual hears his riḥ, he dances in front of the musicians. It is at this time that some of the more extreme acts of self-mutilation occur. These include slashing the head, drinking boiling water, sitting on hot coals, eating glass, and similar practices. They are intensely dramatic because the performer, usually one of several dancers, is the center of attention.

The cold part of the ḥadra seems specifically designed to satisfy individual needs. If the patient has not danced during the hot part of the ḥadra, or if his jinn has not been satisfied, he will be encouraged to dance and to enter jidba during this part of the ceremony. Different riḥs will be tried until the one that sends him into jidba is found, and it will be played until his jinn has been placated. If he should happen to be suffering from a paralysis, his limb will loosen up while his riḥ is played and will remain so if he has been satisfied. Usually he experiences some sort of collapse before his jinn has had enough. If the riḥ is stopped too soon, not only will his limb again tighten but he will usually fall into a cataleptic state. There is seldom a dramatic ending to his dance. He will usually walk off to the side and sit down in a slightly disoriented condition that lasts for ten or fifteen minutes. Very little attention is paid to him.

Some of the musical phrases that are played on the nira and the ganbri, the instruments of this part of the ceremony, are associated with named-jnun. All of them appear to affect only certain individuals and do not have the wide appeal of the riḥs of the hot part. It is said that the individual dancer "cools down" during this part of the performance.

> During the cold part of the ḥadra, I do the rest of the jidba. It is the small surroundings. It is the small ḥal. I begin to remember myself. My head returns to the place where it was. My body relaxes. I know where I am and when it is. If I have hit my head, I still do not know it. There is still a slight throbbing. My body begins to cool down. When ʿAïsha stops the ḥadra, so do I.[25]

The dramatic excitement of the cold part of the ḥadra usually culminates in the performance of ʿAïsha's riḥ: "O ʿAïsha. Rise and place yourself in the service of the cause of Allah and the Prophet. . . ." Often this takes place just after a dancer has abandoned himself to one

[25] I have never witnessed or heard anyone in trance talking in tongues in either the madina or shantytown ceremonies. Once I heard a man who was said to be possessed by an unknown jinn, and whom the Ḥamadsha claimed they could not cure, talk in an imitation French, a language he did not know. He often talked in this language when not in trance.

of the more extreme acts of self-mutilation. The lights are suddenly extinguished, and the riḥ is played and chanted for a few minutes. ʿAïsha is said to rise out of the ground and dance in front of her devotees, many of whom claim to see her at this time. ʿAïsha's riḥ is frequently accompanied by screams of terror, and when the music stops and the lights go on there are often several children on the floor, whimpering and in a state of semi-consciousness.

The Ḥadra Gnawiyya

The cold of the ḥadra—it may be interrupted from time to time for the recitation of fatḥas—flows directly into the *ḥadra gnawiyya,* which is "played for the women." Usually, in the course of the cold part, certain phrases are played which throw women in particular into trance but which do not seem to satisfy them. A special repertory of riḥs is then played, until the phrase that will satisfy each particular woman is found. These are the riḥs associated with specific jinniyyas, like Lalla Mira and Lalla Mimuna, and consequently with special colors, incenses, and perfumes. Rags or scarves of the color pleasing to a particular woman's jinn are tied to her if she has not come to the night wearing that color, and the correct incense is burned. Some women—they, too, are often called pigs, although they do not actually imitate pigs themselves—will begin to dance just as the ceremony seems to be ending and the audience is exhausted. They will continue for hours before being satisfied. In organization, the ḥadra gnawiyya resembles not only the dance of the Gnawa but also the last part of the ceremonies of a number of other popular brotherhoods: the ʿIsawiyya, the Jilaliyya, and the Raḥaliyya.

The End of the Ceremony

When all of the participants are satisfied, the ḥadra ends, more fatḥas are recited, and dinner is served. The ceremony seldom lasts less than four hours, and I have heard of ceremonies that began at 7 in the evening and ended at 7 the following morning. Dinner includes couscous and a stew made from the animal sacrificed before the ceremony. The men and the women eat separately. Musicians and honored guests are given special portions. The dancers eat with voracious appetites. The atmosphere is relaxed, if "the ḥadra has been a good one"—satisfying both individually and generally. After everyone has eaten, the musicians say a last fatḥa for the host and for the patients who, if he has danced during the ḥadra, is usually cured of his paralysis or his possession. His behavior during the ḥadra will have been no different from that of other dancers, and he is the center of attention only when a fatḥa is said over him. The musicians leave and, after a little something has been given to the "poor" adepts, the money is tallied and set aside. If a particularly large sum has been collected and the host is known to be poor, the musicians may give him a bit to help pay for the performance.

Male dancers who have slashed their heads do nothing for their wounds. If the ḥadra has been good, the dancers will sleep well and awake revitalized the following morning. If they have been suffering from paresthetic pains, they will experience at least some relief. In most cases of jinn attack, the patient will seem to have recovered if he has danced. He may still show some signs of stiffness, depression, and general malaise, but these will soon wear off. If the ḥadra has not been good, the dancer will spend a restless night, hearing the music of the ḥadra over and over again, and will wake up tired and depressed. It is said that he will fall sick if he does not perform the ḥadra soon again. In fact, he usually does perform the ḥadra again as soon as possible. As for the patient, he will probably suffer a relapse if his ḥadra was not a good one. Whether their ḥadras have been good or bad, most men report an inability to have sexual intercourse for at least one night after dancing. Although they justify this by their desire to remain pure, after receiving the saint's baraka, it is a source of considerable anxiety to them.

The Bidonville Ceremony

The ceremonies of the bidonvilles are much simpler in organization than those of the madina lodges. The sponsor follows the same procedure as his confrere in the old quarter of the city; however, the muqaddim and the team members play a much more active role in inviting guests. They are anxious to earn as much as possible from the ceremony, and tend to invite all the devotees whom they know will give generously. It is my impression that many more uninvited guests attend the bidonville ceremonies. This seems to follow from the more open life-style in the bidonville, the more public character of its ceremonies, and the higher percentage of devotees in the overall shantytown population. Financial arrangements between sponsor and team are the same as in the madina, and the cost of a ceremony is on the average also the same. The sponsor's deposit is divided among the team members, as are all of the other proceeds from the ceremony. The ghiyyata receive more than any of the other players.

The average bidonville ceremony takes place at night, although afternoon ceremonies, which tend to be shorter and less expensive, are more frequent there than in the madina. Often the hot part of the ḥadra is played out of doors, either in front of the house or in the nearest square. The music consists most frequently of the riḥs of the Gharb. There is usually trancing and head-slashing. If possible, the patient is made to dance and is much more in evidence than he would be in a madina ceremony at this stage of the ḥadra. Trancing patterns and dance steps are the same here and throughout the ḥadra as in the old quarter. Frenzies, however, tend to be more frequent and extreme.

The hot part of the ḥadra may be continued indoors, but often it is stopped "because the ghita are too loud." The guests enter the house as soon as the last, long blasts of the ghita are heard. Fatḥas are said for the host, the patient, and any guest who is willing to pay for one. The men and some of the women sit down in the courtyard. (Although women in the bidonville ceremonies tend to remain separate from the men, this division is never as extreme as in the madina. In fact, bidonville women play a much more active role throughout the entire ceremony.) The guests wait for tea, and they may also be given dates and milk, a fried saltless bread said to please the jnun, and black olives, which are reputed to drive the jnun away. The break between the hot part of the ḥadra and the subsequent parts is much greater here than in the old quarter.

Once all of the guests are served, the musicians who are sitting together in a corner of the courtyard begin to play. Sometimes they will chant a few words of a dikr to warm themselves up. Their dikr, accompanied by the ganbri, seldom lasts for more than four or five minutes. The rest of the evening closely resembles a madina ceremony, but here the cold part of the ḥadra becomes a major part of the ceremony and is much more frequently interrupted for the recitation of the fatḥas. The muqaddim and other team members do their very best to extract as much money as they can from the audience. They often earn as much as 60 or 70 dirhams in a night. Their fatḥas are more dramatic and often involve massaging, spitting, treading on, or knocking the head of the person over whom the prayer is said. Occasionally, a fatḥa-sayer, who is in trance, will predict the future. The ḥadra gnawiyya follows the cold part without any interruption. The riḥs played are chosen on the basis of the needs of the women dancers. When all of the dancers have been satisfied, the meal with which the ceremony ends is served.

11

The Explanation of Therapy

Therapy consists of a structured set of procedures for moving an individual from one state, most generally the state of illness, to another state, the state of health or proximate health. Concerned as it is with the individual as a total being, therapy necessarily involves changes in *all* significant levels of human existence—the physiological, the psychological, and the socio-cultural. Different therapies appear concerned primarily with one or another of these levels, often at the expense of the others. Although the nature of the illness itself frequently forces the emphasis onto one such level, cultural factors are often equally important determinants.

Ḥamadsha therapy, too, consists of procedures that move an individual from a state of illness to a state of health. "Illness," "health," and the therapeutic procedures themselves are grounded in the social and cultural life of at least a certain segment of Moroccan Arab society, and probably reflect tensions inherent in that life. Although I have not thought it appropriate to the level of analysis of this study to consider the origin and nature of such tensions, I have found it necessary to call attention to some of the more salient tensions as they are reflected in the Ḥamadsha complex itself. I have referred, for example, to tensions between city and country, when considering the relationship between the Ḥamadsha of the old quarter of Meknes and those of the shantytowns; and to stresses and strains in the male role, concomitant with the segregation of the sexes and the extreme patrilineality and patripotestality of the Arab world, when analyzing the hagiographic legends.

The following pages will recall the Moroccan's belief in the inferiority, treacherous nature, and insatiable sexual desire of women. This belief probably reflects an unarticulated if not altogether unconscious fear of women—a fear which finds expression in the segregation of the sexes in Morocco and elsewhere in the Arab world, and is probably compensated for by the Arabs' extreme emphasis on male virility. "Male" and "female" are, however, more than labels of sexual identity; they refer to a whole complex of behavioral traits and symbolize feelings that are experienced at some level of consciousness by both men and women and are not, it is suggested, insignificant in the aetiology and conceptualization of illnesses treated by the Ḥamadsha.

Ḥamadsha therapeutic procedures are provided with both a "mythic charter"—the hagiographic legends that integrate the therapeutic with the "religious"—and a theoretical explanation. Both the "mythic charter" and the theory of therapy can be conceived of as legitimating apparatus which, as such, give authority to the therapeutic system and are thereby themselves therapeutically significant. It has been suggested that the hagiographic legends reflect tensions inherent in the individual Ḥamdushi and in his social and cultural situation, tensions which may in fact be responsible for his illness or for the form it takes. That the elements of the theory—saints, jnun, and baraka—are more than logical constructs for the explanation of Ḥamadsha therapy has been implicit in my analysis of it. They are *images*, in Godfrey Lienhardt's (1967: 148 et seq.) sense of the word, grounded in the social and cultural reality of the Ḥamadsha, of what the Westerner would call psychic reality.[1] They are elements in which I would call the participational mode of explanation of illness and therapy. They may be considered *signs* of psychic states and *symbols* of socio-cultural processes. The dual ground of these "images" serves to strengthen the legitimations of therapy. ʿAïsha Qandisha and the Ḥamadsha saints are more than char-

[1] Lienhardt (1967:147 et seq.) speaks of some Dinka spirits, or Powers, as "images evoked by certain configurations of experience contingent upon the Dinka's reaction to their particular physical and social environment." These "images," he suggests, are "the active counterpart of the passive element in human experience."

> It is perhaps significant that in ordinary English usage we have no word to indicate an opposite of 'actions' in relation to the human self. If the word 'passions,' *passiones*, were still normally current as the opposite of 'actions,' it would be possible to say that the Dinka Powers were the images of human *passiones* seen as the active source of these *passiones*.

Reference to a Power then, Lienhardt remarks, is *not merely a description of the experience but an interpretation.* In other words, the experience, say, of guilt is immediately articulated, if not instantiated, in an interpretive idiom external to the individual.

acters in a story. They are rooted in both individual and social life. Moreover, the individual's conflicts are immediately and necessarily expressed in terms congruent with social reality. They are recast in universal terms. This in itself is of considerable therapeutic import. Therapy involves the articulation and manipulation of these images. Theory and practice are inseparable within the Ḥamadsha context, as they probably are within the contexts of other pre-scientific therapies.

Ḥamadsha therapy is pragmatic and subject to considerable variation. It treats patients in various conditions of life and health, and it should be stressed that there was considerable variation among patients whom the Ḥamadsha successfully cured.[2] In some cases, a crisis situation triggered a reaction that did not impress me as being deeply rooted in the patient's psyche; rather, the patient seemed to be following one of several cultural models appropriate to his situation.[3] Other patients, however, seemed to be suffering from hysterical, depressive, or even schizophrenic reactions. It is possible that a number of chronic cases were kept ambulatory by their intense involvement with the Ḥamadsha and their frequent performances of the ḥadra.

What follows is an examination of the elements of Ḥamadsha therapy which are recognized in Western theories of psychotherapy as therapeutically effective. The suggestions which I make about these therapeutically significant factors must be considered hypotheses based on a detailed consideration of the Ḥamadsha complex; they point ahead to a sequel to this study in which they will be tested against family and individual case histories. I have given particular emphasis to the social and psychological dimensions of Ḥamadsha therapy, not simply because I believe them to be the most significant therapeutically but because of the limitations of my own training and research opportunities. Primary attention has been placed on ceremonies involving the ḥadra; the pilgrimage is considered as a complement to them.

[2] Ortigues (1966) also stresses the varying personality types who become possessed by spirits in Senegal.

[3] The response to such crises may be considered an acute anxiety reaction of short duration, whose symptomatology may include incoherence of thought and delusional and hallucinatory activity. It has been claimed that such reactions are more common in primitive than in advanced societies. They may result from the failure to perform customary rites (Wittkower 1971). It must be remembered that alleged failure to perform ritual obligations may itself—as I believe is often the case for the Ḥamadsha—be symbolic of some breach in the individual's personal morality (cf. Crapanzano 1972).

Group Support

Group support, one of the most frequently cited therapeutic factors in "primitive" as well as "modern" psychotherapy, plays an important role in the Ḥamadsha cures. The ailing individual is not isolated and ignored, but becomes a patient who is the concern of the whole group. The group, which consists of family, friends, and neighbors as well as the Ḥamadsha, not only offers the patient sympathy, encouragement, and the hope of cure, but also mobilizes itself to cure the patient of his troubles. This mobilization serves to alter the relations between the patient and the members of the group themselves. Men and women, for example, are in closer, more intimate contact during the preparation for a ceremony. It is possible that such a rearticulation of social relations may help to reduce socially generated tensions that are in part responsible for the patient's condition. Mobilization of the group, moreover, involves sacrifices of time and money that serve the patient as an assurance of the group's care and concern. A responsibility not to let the group down is placed upon him.

The group also provides the patient with an interpretation of his illness, or reinforces his own or the diviner's interpretation, and this acts to reduce the anxiety that accompanies ignorance of the illness' cause and cure. Fatna, for example, was convinced by friends and neighbors that her child Fatima was sick because she had failed to carry out her promise to sacrifice a chicken to Sidi ʿAli. Members of the group often advocate such interpretations out of a vested interest in them. They, too, have often suffered, or are liable to suffer, from illnesses of similar origin. In supporting a supernatural explanation of the illness, the group affirms that the patient is not necessarily responsible for his own condition. Feelings of shame, remorse, and "guilt" are deflected. The patient no longer broods over himself. This technique may be of particular significance in depressive reactions. Moreover, since the patient is not held responsible for his condition, he is able to act on socially unacceptable impulses both before and during curing ceremonies without incurring public censure. These include the refusal to carry out tasks normally expected of him, excesses of self-mutilation, homosexual advances to other dancers, or acts of autoeroticism.

During ceremonies the group—the audience—becomes more than a backdrop for the patient's cure. The group actively participates in the cure. Its members not only tend to the patient's needs, but also often dance and trance themselves. They serve as models for the patient. They too must placate the jnun they follow. Ailing individuals who are unable to sponsor their own ceremonies attend in the hope of a cure, and it is not unusual for the patient to tend to their needs. The recitation of the fatḥa intensifies group sentiment. The patient is made to understand in dramatic terms that he is not alone in his condition, and that many others who have suffered in the past as he is now suffering have recovered. This "sharing of illness" also occurs at the pilgrimage centers, where the patient encounters many other ailing men and women and hears stories of extraordinary cures.

The ceremonies not only permit Ḥamadsha within the group to dance and trance and work through their own personal conflicts, but also serve a cathartic function for other members of the audience. The audience, like the audiences of exorcistic seances in Burma, does not consist "as might be the case in certain theatrical contexts, of jaded spectators, seeking entertainment to shake them from their boredom or to permit them to escape their routine concerns" (Spiro 1967:196). The audience lives through the conflicts that are symbolically played out before them and that undoubtedly have deep roots within their cultural tradition. This catharsis, too, may serve to reduce social tensions that are in part responsible for the patient's condition. Other tensions, such as tensions between men and women, are expressed in less obvious ways. Women in the madina ceremonies, for example, must wait to participate until the men have completed their chanting; at the end of the ceremony, however, a single woman whose jinn has not had enough can keep the musicians playing and the men waiting for hours.

Patient Participation

The patient plays a role in his own cure. Often he must help with the preparations for a ceremony or a pilgrimage. He must dance and trance during the night and, if possible, repeat the fatḥa for others. Should he happen to be host, he must tend to the needs of his guests. On pilgrimages, he must carry out various ritual activities such as circumambulating the tombs of the Ḥamadsha saints, bathing in the ʿAyn Kabir, or smearing himself with henna from ʿAïsha's grotto. After the pilgrimage or night, he is often required to follow certain rules. These may be stereotyped and appear arbitrary; still, apart from whatever symbolic role they play, they give the patient the feeling that he is doing something for himself. He is keeping his jinn or jinniyya at bay.

The importance of patient participation in the Ḥamadsha cures should not, however, be exaggerated. The patient's role is not as active as in psychoanalysis or psychodrama. He is passive before the exorcist-seers, who uncover the source of his troubles and suggest a cure; he is passive before the saints, the jnun, and even the music of the ghita. This passivity can be considered as indicative of the patient's basic existential stance toward his world or as a period of socially sanctioned regression to a stage of dependency which may be of therapeutic value. During the cures, and especially during the pilgrimage, the patient is removed from his normal position in society with its concomitant demands and pressures; he is given a respite.

The patient is not necessarily the center of attention during ceremonies, although he is the manifest cause for the ceremony. Indeed, he is often almost completely ignored. I remember, on several occasions, leaving a night only to discover that I had not made a single notation about the patient. This lack of attention during the formal curing may be of significance in the cures of certain hysterical individuals whose dramatic symptoms and life histories suggest that feelings of neglect and the desire to be the center of attention are important etiological factors for their condition. The group sometimes appears to treat them with the same *belle indifférence* with which they treat themselves.

Patient-Curer Relationship

Although the importance of the patient-curer relationship has been stressed in explanations of the effectiveness of psychoanalysis, hypnosis, shamanistic cures, and other therapeutic techniques, I have not found this relationship to be particularly significant in the Ḥamadsha cures. I do not mean to imply that the role of the curers—the exorcist-seer, the saint's descendant, or the muqaddim of a team—is unimportant. It *is* important, especially when the curer has a strong, charismatic personality. I am suggesting, rather, that neither a deep transference relationship with archaic features nor an important personal bond is established between patient and curer. Whatever transference is established is immediately deflected to supernatural agents—the saints and the jnun. Even the power of the curer is conceived in supernatural terms, in terms of baraka. This, in my opinion, is not simply an instance of defensive projection. The saints and jnun are a given in the patient's world, providing him with a symbolic schema for the interpretation of his experiences. It is on this level that relationships are manipulated. The patient's relationship with ʿAïsha Qandisha, for example, is fundamentally changed.

The passive role of the patient is reflected in his relationship with the curer. Even when the curer plays an important, *personal* role in the treatment of the patient, he does not attempt to elicit confessions from the patient or to review his life. He tries to suggest to or persuade the patient that he has in fact been attacked by a jinn, that the jinn requires a sacrifice or a night, and that the patient, if he follows the commands of the jinn, will be cured. The curer's suggestions are not patient-specific. He reiterates what the group and the patient know already or at least suspect.

Insight and Suggestion

No attempt is made either by the curer or by members of the patient's group to give him insight into the nature of his problems. There is no psychic probing in the Ḥamadsha cures. Since the patient is not responsible for his condition, any self-examination would be inappropriate. Instead, the patient is provided with an interpretation and dynamic explanation of his condition. He is urged by the group and by individual curers to accept this explanation. Techniques designed to increase his suggestibility play an important role in Ḥamadsha cures. Often dreams, especially at the saints' tombs, will be interpreted in terms of the explanations proffered and considered authoritative.

Cult Membership

The patient who has been treated by the Ḥamadsha is not the "same" person that he was before his illness. Most Ḥamadsha cures do not end with the pilgrimage or ceremony. In the case of the pilgrimage, the patient forms at the very least a strong dependency on the saint and perhaps on ʿAïsha Qandisha. Although he does not necessarily become a devotee of the Ḥamadsha, his subsequent experiences will usually be interpreted in terms of the saint and ʿAïsha. In the case of the ceremonies, the patient often recovers but is required to follow certain rules to please his jinn. Usually he will have to perform the ḥadra from time to time and sponsor an annual ceremony to commemorate his cure. If he fails to perform or to sponsor a ceremony, there is a strong likelihood that he will again fall ill. In other words, the patient becomes a member of the Ḥamadsha cult.

Cult membership provides the patient with a new social status. He is now a Ḥamdushi or a devotee of the Ḥamadsha. His social relations are now articulated with respect to this new status. Others must take cognizance of it. A husband whose wife becomes a Ḥamdushiyya must, for example, sponsor an annual ceremony for her and permit her to attend the ceremonies of other devotees. Membership in the cult enlarges the patients' social network and, at least in the case of the bidonville Ḥamadsha, gives them the opportunity to develop multiplex relations in a new and alien environment. Should the patient happen to become a member of a team or zawiya, he is entitled to the benefits of this association.

With a change in social status, there is a change in social identity and in self-image. The patient is treated as a Ḥamdushi or a devotee of the Ḥamadsha. Within the cult, especially if his behavior during the ḥadra is dramatic or if he should happen to know many litanies, the patient is considered to have a great deal of prestige—prestige which he might not have had before. Outside the cult, he is treated with a mixture of awe and respect by other Moroccans of his background. He has, after all, been in contact with the jnun and, as a trancer, he is not without his share of baraka. However, he is looked down upon by other, better educated Moroccans as a poor wretch and a victim of barbarous superstition.[4] The patient is well aware of this characterization. Within the group he has prestige and outside it humiliation. This humiliation should not be ignored. It may well reflect—and support—the patient's self-image, and be of some secondary gain.

Membership in the cult also reinforces the patient's faith in the Ḥamadsha and in their world-view. Again and again, at private and public ceremonies, he is given the opportunity to witness their success. Attendance at the annual musem renews his faith in the Ḥamadsha saints and their descendants. Finally, and most importantly, he is given the opportunity to perform the ḥadra and as we shall see, to work out —in a structured, albeit symbolic, fashion—conflicts which are responsible for his condition.

Trance, Abreaction, and Catharsis[5]

The Ḥamadsha consider the trance to be of paramount importance for their cures. They say that their patient must dance until his jinn is "satisfied." Usually, to satisfy his jinn, the patient must enter jidba, a deep frenetic trance that in many cultures is interpreted as a state of possession. The Ḥamadsha themselves do not *necessarily* explain jidba as possession; it is simply that the patient must enter jidba before his jinn is said to have had enough.

[4] The Ḥamadsha are referred to by many of them as "black"—a possible indication of lower status.

[5] See the Appendix for factors that appear to induce trance for the Ḥamadsha.

I would like to suggest that trance is in fact an important element in Ḥamadsha therapy, and affects the individual both physiologically and psychologically. The physiological effects of trance and possession, like those of shock therapy, have not been worked out. William Sargant (1964), who has considered the problem from the perspective of Pavlovian neurophysiology, compares trancing and possession to narcotherapy, psychoanalysis, shock treatment, leucotomy, techniques of religious conversion, and brainwashing. He suggests that all of these techniques produce a state of emotional exhaustion and collapse in the subject. This collapse involves the erasure of former conditioned patterns and beliefs and a heightened state of suggestibility.[6]

The role of collapse in Ḥamadsha therapy presents a problem. Some trancers fall into a state of collapse before they begin to dance and enter jidba; others collapse in the middle of the dance; and still others do not collapse at all. No ceremony is terminated with a dancer in a state of collapse. It is not altogether clear, however, what Sargant means by "collapse." He suggests that the terminal sleep of the possessed is the period of complete inhibitory collapse, but this does not appear to be a satisfactory solution. Most trancers recover from a possession state well before retiring. They usually show signs of renewed vitality, well-being, and recovery from the symptoms of an attack by a jinn.[7]

Suggestion does appear to play an important role in any case. This applies to dancers and members of the audience as well.

[6] Sargant's work has been criticized for assuming a neurophysiological basis for the kind of "collapse state" produced, say, by the fiery preaching of John Westley (Prince 1968:132). Nevertheless, his observations concerning the erasure of former conditioned patterns and beliefs, including a tendency in the so-called "ultraparadoxical phase" for such patterns to turn from positive to negative and from negative to positive, and the heightened suggestibility of the subject during periods of emotional exhaustion, are of considerable significance.

[7] Prince (1968:131) suggests that Sargant confuses the initial collapse with the final sleep of exhaustion. Sargant himself recognizes that the threshold for collapse probably varies with the temperament of the trancer. One might well add that it also varies with his life circumstances, including such factors as stress, and his experience of the trance.

> Some persons can produce a state of trance and dissociation in themselves, or in others, with a decreasing need for strong and repeated emotional stresses, until it may become so much a conditioned pattern of brain activity that it occurs with only minor stresses and difficulties; for example, in the primitive religious context, at the renewed beat of a drum, or the screaming roar of the rhombos (Sargant 1964:103).

Experienced trancers among the Ḥamadsha enter trance with greater ease than inexperienced ones. The first notes of their particular riḥ will often send them into a deep trance or into a state of collapse.

States of possession or trance have also been used by numerous religions to try to help the spectator, as well as the possessed person, to accept the relevant doctrine as true. If the trance is accompanied by a state of mental dissociation, the person experiencing it can be profoundly influenced in his subsequent thinking and behavior. Even if the spectators remain unmoved and devoid of any emotional excitement, it may still help to persuade them of the truth of the belief professed, especially if they have been led to think that a trance means that the person concerned is possessed by, or in communication with, a certain god. (Sargant 1964:103)

As we have seen, members of the Ḥamadsha audience are often on the brink of dissociation, oscillating between normal and dissociated states, or in a state of dissociation.

The period following collapse, whether initial, medial, or terminal, is of extreme importance. Not only is the trancer in a state of extreme suggestibility but, if Sargant is correct, he undergoes an erasure, or partial erasure, of previously learned behavioral patterns and beliefs. New behavior patterns and beliefs may be instilled, or old ones, including "neurotic" ones, may be renewed and reinforced. Of paramount importance is the suggestion that the experience of such a state is of therapeutic value. The jinn has been satisfied!

The extreme suggestibility of the individual in either case calls attention to the "learning" aspect of therapeutic procedures like the Ḥamadsha's. Belief in the Ḥamadsha and in their lore is instilled, reconfirmed, and reinforced. The lore includes the Ḥamadsha's "psychology" and "pathology." Both of these have a profound effect upon the individual.

Psychologies pertain to a dimension of reality that is of the greatest and most continuous subjective relevance for all individuals. Therefore the dialectic between the theory and reality affects the individual in a palpably direct and intensive manner. (Berger and Luckmann 1967:176)

In other words the socially accepted interpretation of psychic reality—the psychology—"realizes itself forcefully in the phenomena it purports to interpret." This point is of extreme importance if, as I suggest, Ḥamadsha therapy involves the manipulation of "images" of psychic reality.

The erasure of behavioral patterns and beliefs that Sargant postulates may be related to the "regressive behavior" often observed in hypnotic and ceremonial trance. It has been found that a person who is deprived for a sufficiently long period of access to "the usual clues for maintaining a normal sense of reality" becomes oversensitive to both internal and external stimuli and appears vulnerable to both (Gill and Brenman 1966:5). This state of heightened sensitivity and vulnerability, corresponding roughly to what the Ḥamadsha call ḥal, is often followed by "outbursts from the *internal world* in one form or another" (Gill and Brenman 1966:6). This second stage may itself correspond to what the Ḥamadsha call jidba and interpret as possession by a jinn, or at least as the result of jinn activity. Such states are considered to be therapeutically significant.

Explanations of the curative value of such "outbursts" have emphasized either the positive value of these regressive states—"regression in the service of the ego"—or their "cathartic function." The patient is given a socially sanctioned opportunity for the "stormy discharge" of emotions rooted in traumatic experiences of the past or in psychic conflicts of the present, and he experiences a reduction of anxiety and a consequent alleviation or elimination of anxiety-produced symptoms. He "works through" or "acts out" his conflicts, or "relives" his traumatic experiences. Although the value of emotional discharge has been recognized at least since the publication of Breuer and Freud's *Studies in Hysteria* in 1895, it should be stressed that the mere outburst of emotion is not necessarily of therapeutic value (Gill and Brenman 1966:356). It may indeed have the contrary effect. I would suggest that all such outbursts must be structured if they are to be of positive therapeutic value, and that the structures must reflect the symptom-producing conflicts.

This point needs elaboration—and here I am indebted to Lévi-Strauss' article "The Efficacy of Symbols" (1963a). The cure involves a twofold process. First, a conflict originally existing on an emotional level or in the unconscious is made explicit. Second, an opportunity for the working out or resolution of conflicts thereby made explicit is offered. The making explicit of unconscious processses may involve—or claim to involve—the uncovering of actual, lived-through experiences, as in the case of psychoanalysis, or it may provide the patient "with a *language*, by means of which unexpressed and otherwise inexpressible psychic states can be immediately expressed," as in certain shamanistic cures[8] (Lévi-Strauss 1963a:198). In the case of psychoanalysis and similar therapies, the rendering of unconscious processes factually articulate provides a means for their "free development" and their resolution.

[8] This may be related to the degree of interiorization typically encouraged by a given culture.

This development and resolution may be subject to strict structural laws, but it always remains on a personal, particularistic level. The psychoanalytic patient "constructs an individual myth," as Lévi-Strauss puts it, "with elements drawn from his past" (1963:199). In the case of shamanistic cures—and Ḥamadsha cures as well—the symbolic expression of unconscious processes is followed by a highly structured—ritualized—resolution of symbolically expressed conflicts. Resolution here is impersonal and universalistic. The patient "receives from the outside a social myth which does not correspond to his former personal state" (Lévi-Strauss 1963a:199).

Whether or not the structural laws of both types of cures are the same, as Lévi-Strauss suggests, there is a manifest difference in the existential stance of the patient vis-à-vis the therapeutic system. In the case of psychoanalysis, the patient is active and the therapist is passive. In the case of the shamanistic cure, the patient is passive and the shaman is active.[9] The shaman is an authoritarian figure, often identified with a mythic figure, who "molds" the patient's unarticulated conflicts into a socially given schema. If the elements of the schema are *images* of psychic states, grounded in social and cultural reality (as I believe is true for the Ḥamadsha), then the shaman's symbolic manipulations are of considerable therapeutic importance. In any event, the special nature of the dialectical relationship between "psychology" and "psyche" probably permits the curer to modify, at least temporarily, the patient's psychic reality. Since suggestion plays a manifestly important role, techniques such as trancing, which increase the patient's suggestibility, are especially important in shamanistic cures.

The Ḥamadsha "pathology" and "theory of therapy" not only explain these "outbursts," but structure their very expression. Theory and practice cannot be separated here. In the simplest terms, ʿAïsha Qandisha or whatever jinn is held responsible for the patient's condition is said to take possession of the patient or, in the case of certain men, to force him to slash his head. When the jinn has been satisfied, it not only leaves the patient but is transformed into the patient's support. A symbolic transformation has taken place which may involve at least a temporary restructuring of "psychic reality"—and perhaps, as Lévi-Strauss (1963:201) would suggest, even a physiological transformation.[10]

[9] In Ḥamadsha cures, where the role of the curer is not as important as in certain shamanistic cures, the patient is still a passive actor and not an innovator.

[10] It is assumed in the following analysis that the patient is a man. The manner in which Ḥamadsha therapy functions for the female is not considered, because of the spottiness of my data concerning women. This has resulted from the strict

The illnesses for which ʿAïsha Qandisha is responsible and which the Ḥamadsha are able to cure include paralysis of the limbs, "pinching bones," sudden deafness, blindness, and mutism unaccompanied by organic lesions, children's diseases, menstrual difficulties, and barrenness. (ʿAïsha Qandisha is also able to limit a man's virility or render him impotent, but Ḥamadsha cures are not usually effective in these cases.) All of the illness caused by ʿAïsha Qandisha prevent the patient from actively performing his social roles and concomitant tasks. He is unable to meet the demands of a "male-dominated" society like Morocco, which is organized along the lines of extreme patrilineality and patripotestality. The symptomatology of many of the illnesses—paralysis of the limbs, pinching bones, impotence—suggests an inability to play the male role; barrenness and children's diseases prevent the continuation of the male line. Illness, especially for men, is conceived at some level of consciousness as an inability to live up to the ideal standards of male conduct. That is, illness is associated with being rendered a woman. Feelings of inadequacy, weakness, and impotence are symbolized by the female.

This conception of illness as feminization may indeed be rooted, as the analysis of the legendary cycle of Sidi ʿAli and Sidi Ahmed suggests, in the relationship between father and son. In order to obtain his father's baraka—to live up to the male ideal—the son must play the passive role before the father (and identify with the mother). If he refuses this solution, he finds himself incapable of meeting the ideal. It seems likely that many but by no means all of the illnesses for which the Ḥamadsha are called in have such an origin. Certainly—and here I am stepping out of the limits set by the level of analysis of this study—the often arbitrary, harsh, and inconsistent behavior of the Moroccan father toward his son would seem to preclude the possibility of the son's strong and positive identification with him. It provides the son with the ideal but demands behavior contrary to the ideal. The son must remain passive—unmanly—before the father. He must be as woman to the father.

Women are stereotyped not simply as weak and helpless, but as treacherous, whimsical, untrustworthy, unfaithful, and sexually insatiable.[11] They are the image of ʿAïsha Qandisha and must be pacified

segregation of the sexes in Morocco. It should be pointed out, however, that women rarely slash their heads. The jinniyyas appear to function as supporting doubles for them. They are capable, however, of turning on their female followers, and may serve as an externalized conscience.

[11] This aspect of the figure of the woman suggests to the psychoanalytically orthodox that the mother has in some manner betrayed the son to the father.

and controlled. ʿAïsha Qandisha and the other female jnun are, at least for the majority of Ḥamadsha, the cause of their illnesses; they must be placated and transformed. This—the cure—is accomplished by means of the saints' baraka.

The cure involves an attempted resolution of two opposing figures —ʿAïsha Qandisha and the Ḥamadsha saints. As they are described in legend and folklore, they represent a number of different elements within the Moroccan's experiential world and are commonly, though less consciously, associated with still other elements. These are summarized below; the less conscious associations, which have been derived from life-history material not examined in this work, appear in parentheses.

ʿAÏSHA QANDISHA		SIDI ʿALI AND SIDI AHMED
Jinn		Saint
Earth	Water	Sun
(low)	Green	(high)
Dark		Light
Black-red		White
(left)		(right)
(interior)		(exterior)
Female		Male
Blood (menstruation)		(semen)
Infertility		Fertility
Impotence		Virility
Disease		Health
Death		Life
Two-faced		Single-faced
Whimsical		Constant
Bad		Good
Demanding		Giving
Destructive		Constructive
(castrating)		(virilizing)
(mother)		(father)
(mother's family)		(father's family)
Possession		Mysticism
Jidba		Ḥal (ḥizb/dikr)
Dream (nightmare)		Dream
Bad luck		Good luck
Sacrifice		Sacrifice

To these the anthropologist, as an outsider, might well add to the list of ʿAïsha's associations "low tradition," Dionysian, and expressed, and, to the saintly associations, "high tradition," Apollonian, and repressed. It is clear that these two figures span several spheres of reality and are subject to a complex logic which must "fit" the demands of these difference spheres[12] (Berger and Luckmann 1967:40).

The figure of the saint, who is representative of the ideal social and moral order, is not altered in the attempted resolution of these polar opposites. He makes no special demands on the patient, although the patient may have promised him a sacrifice or some other gift.[13] Despite the saint's ability to master the everyday affairs of the masculine world, as the legends attest, the role is too specialized, too removed from the daily concerns of the average patient, to provide a model with which he can identify. (This may in fact be indicative of the child's image of the father.) Rather, the saint provides the patient with baraka, the symbolic equivalent of semen, virility, and the principle of patrilineality, and it is this baraka which is held responsible for the patient's cure. It revitalizes—"revirilizes" is perhaps more accurate—the patient and enables him to overcome his illness—which is, as we have seen, associated with femininity, his feelings of inadequacy and weakness, and his inability to live up to the standards of male behavior. It enables him to bring about the transformation of ʿAïsha Qandisha.

Resolution of the opposition between the figures of saint and jinniyya is attempted by transforming ʿAïsha Qandisha. Although she retains all of her chthonian-Dionysian associations, she ceases to be a socially disruptive force and, in fact, like the Eumenides, becomes a support of the moral and social order.[14] She no longer takes away the patient's health, virility, fertility, or good fortune. Rather, she preserves them. The transformation is not simply a change in her character. It demands a change in the patient's relationship—in *his* character—to her. The patient must first placate ʿAïsha and then follow her commands.

[12] As a given of the world in which the individual is born, they serve to organize his psychic reality; they become *images* of his experience which must be congruent with socio-cultural processes and perhaps even physiological ones.

[13] The adepts of the urban zawiyas are required to work for the saint. ʿAïsha Qandisha does not play as important a role for them. They must work for the saint in order to receive his baraka—to remain healthy, successful, and virile. They do not identify with the saint, but work for him as a son works for his father. Failure to work for the saint is conceived of as a loss of baraka and consequent vulnerability to attacks by ʿAïsha Qandisha and other jnun. The saint himself can do no harm.

[14] That such a change is possible is suggested by ʿAïsha's ability to appear as a beauty or a hag; however, she is usually considered to be more dangerous when she manifests herself as a beauty (Crapanzano 1971).

Placation involves ʿAïsha Qandisha's taking possession of the patient and often forcing him to symbolically enact his own castration—that is, to slash his head. In order to be cured, the man must become a woman. Thanks to the baraka of the saint, he is able to pass through this feminization and become a man again. From a psychological point of view, he is provided with a structured and socially sanctioned opportunity to regress and to act, at least symbolically, on the unarticulated desire to become a woman. "There are many ways," Bruno Bettelheim (1955: 107) has written, "in which man can deal with a socially unacceptable desire. One way is to dramatize it, act it out, and through intense but in the long run only token satisfaction, try to rid himself of it permanently." This "acting out" appears in the Ḥamadsha case to have at least some immediate therapeutic value.

Having once placated the jinniyya, the patient must obey her commands, or she will attack him and make him ill. These commands—wearing certain colors, burning special incense, making periodic sacrifices, and the like—seem arbitrary. I have found in the analysis of life histories that the breaking of a command is in fact, at one level symbolic of a breach in public or private morality and at another, symbolic of the feelings—the Westerner would call them "guilt"—which this breach has produced in the individual. The following example may help to clarify my point.

Driss became a Ḥamdushi, he explained, after he laughed at the Ḥamadsha who were performing in the center of his village. He fell to the ground and was raised up by the spectators and forced to dance. He became a follower of ʿAïsha Qandisha and followed her commands explicitly. Many years later —he was 14 at the time of the above incident—he again fell sick. "All my bones stung. My body was heavy. I could not move. My nose bled." He did not know why he had fallen sick again. He had forgotten to buy some black jawi, he remembered, and had not burned any incense in a little altar, which he had constructed for ʿAïsha, for several days before falling sick. He continued to reminisce. His sister had been struck at the time and had wanted him and his wife to accompany them on a pilgrimage (*ziyara*). He had refused. He was sure that his sister's husband had instructed her to ask him to go with her to Sidi ʿAli's. He wanted to split the cost. (Driss, I had learned on another occasion, did not get on well with his sister's husband, who somehow cheated him out of some money. Driss was not related to him by blood.)

Driss' case illustrates a dynamic that I have encountered in many Ḥamadsha life histories. The circumstances leading to the initial attack by the jinn were such that a Westerner, given the Moroccan Arab moral code, would describe them as having "caused a guilty conscience." (In this case they were perhaps stereotyped and masked still another cause of guilt.) The very stance of the individual vis-à-vis himself and others within his world—therapy itself—is here articulated not in what Marie-Cécile and Edmond Ortigues, in their study of the Oedipus complex in Senegal (1966:196–197), have called "the novelistic mode of individual adventure and inner guilt," but "in the tragic mode of persecution by the powers of destiny." [15] Having once defined their "feelings" in terms of the jinn, the Ḥamadsha will interpret every subsequent "guilt reaction" of similar magnitude with reference to the jinn. Extreme reactions are often somatized in the form of paralysis or other conversion reactions. They are said to result from a failure to obey the jinn's commands. These arbitrary commands become symbolic masks which may cover the actual moral fault (Crapanzano 1972).

ʿAïsha Qandisha is transformed from a force disruptive to the social and moral order into a force to preserve that order. So long as her follower obeys her commands, he receives her support. So long as he follows his society's moral code, she enables him to live up to the ideals of male dominance, superiority, and virility which are congruent with the extreme patrilineality and patripostestality of the Arab world. It is ʿAïsha Qandisha who keeps him a man, and not the saints. They provide only the baraka with which to transform her, and not a model with which to identify. Neither saint is represented as a strong, virile figure who has overcome the very ills his baraka is able to cure.[16] Sidi ʿAli rendered himself a woman by playing the passive role before Buʿabid Sharqi and the other saints; Sidi Ahmed rendered himself a woman by symbolically castrating himself.[17]

If the follower fails to obey her commands, she attacks him and

[15] To be sure, at least in the cities, the Ḥamadsha cures—the jnun they work with—are not articulated to the lineage structure as they are in Senegal. The individual Moroccan—and not his family or lineage—becomes dependent upon the jnun. No communal altar is established (Ortigues 1966:158).

[16] It is noteworthy that the saints are also not figured as economically successful.

[17] The fact that both saints retain their baraka despite their feminization is suggestive of the roots of the Arab male's attitude toward sex. Great emphasis is placed on the number of ejaculations, and not on foreplay or prolonged coitus. There are tales told, not without admiration, of men who ejaculated so many times in a night that their "vein," which transforms blood into semen, was unable to keep up with them. They ejaculated blood. Such men were said to have had 12 to 15 ejaculations in the night. The transformation of ʿAïsha by means of the baraka of the saint may mirror the man's conquest and "domestication" of the woman by the sexual act. The woman, who is often foreign to the patrilineage, or at least the household, just as ʿAïsha Qandisha is foreign, coming as she does from the Sudan, is dangerous and must be transformed—domesticated.

makes him sick. He becomes as woman. ʿAïsha seems to function as a sort of externalized superego.[18] Her transformation reflects the mastering of feelings of inadequacy, femininity, and remorse, resultant in part from the moral fault, and the conversion of these feelings into a socially and morally positive force. Mastery involves not a positive identification with a male figure but the individual's regression to a state in which he is able to act out these feelings and, at the same time, to chastise himself through acts of self-mutilation or simply through membership in a cult looked down upon by other members of his society.

The roots of these feelings of inadequacy and femininity must be sought in the lives of the Ḥamadsha. It is impossible here to determine whether they are rooted in a single trauma—such, for example, as circumcision—or in a more complex behavioral syndrome, such as an authoritarian father, too arbitrary and aloof for the child to form a positive identification with him. In any case, the ḥadra does provide the individual with an occasion to discharge tensions associated with these feelings in a socially acceptable manner. The cures may result from anxiety reduction following the reenactment of past traumata, or the acting out of repressed impulses; or they may result from an actual restructuring of psychic reality—a change in personality. It may be the case that these elaborate symbolic transformations are epiphenomenal and of little therapeutic consequence. The Ḥamadsha may indeed be compelled to relive the past's experiences and to renew their relationship with ʿAïsha Qandisha again and again in the hope of achieving permanent cure, and in fact obtain but temporary relief from the indelible scars of their past. That the majority of Ḥamadsha patients become devotees of the brotherhood and must periodically perform the ḥadra, enter jidba, and on occasion slash their heads suggests that there is no permanency to the cure, that there is no personality change of long standing, and that the Ḥamadsha are destined to reenact their suffering. It is, after all, written.

[18] Cansever in his study of the effects of circumcision on Turkish youth (1965) notes that the female is often perceived as the castrator. It should be pointed out that in the area from which the Ḥamadsha are recruited the mother leads her son to the house where he is to be circumcised. The father usually disappears for the occasion. The boy, who is usually under 5, is circumcised by a barber, usually a stranger to him, and held by an elder man of his village or family even. Immediately thereafter he is placed on his mother's back and wrapped up in blankets. Warmth is said to aid the healing. His mother, who had been waiting in front of the door to the house, surrounded by villagers and musicians, begins to dance. Often she has pulled down the back of her dress "so that her clothes will not get all bloody," the boy's penis being pressed against her naked, sweating back. Men who remember the event recall with horror the sting of the salty sweat on their bleeding penises.

Appendix

Studies of trance behavior throughout the world have called attention to a number of factors that induce trance. I will consider here those factors which may play a role in the induction of trance among the Ḥamadsha.

Sensory Deprivation and Sensory Overloading

It has been suggested that trance and possession states, like other altered states of consciousness, "may be produced in any setting by any agents or maneuvers which interfere with the normal inflow of sensory or proprioceptive stimuli, the normal outflow of motor impulses, the normal 'emotional tone,' or the normal flow and organization of recognitive processes" (Ludwig 1968:70). Levels of exteroceptive stimulation, either above or below "an optimal level," as well as an impoverishment of varied and diversified environmental stimulation, appear conducive to the production of altered states of consciousness (Ludwig 1968:70). Trance and possession states may be induced by either a reduction or an increase in exteroceptive stimulation. Sensory deprivation is more commonly employed in laboratory studies and in hypnosis (Gill and Brenman 1966:4–11; 123–126), and sensory overloading is more commonly used in trancing ceremonies (Lee 1968:49). It has been further suggested that the effects on the organism of both sensory deprivation and sensory overloading are similar (Alland 1961:212).

The Ḥamadsha employ primarily sensory overloading techniques to induce trance. Auditory overstimulation, which is produced by loud, monotonous drumming, the droning of the ghita, communal chanting, hand-clapping, and even the pounding of the male dancers in line, is the most important technique. Chanting is not as well developed among the Ḥamadsha as it is in other Islamic confraternities such as the Raḥmaniyya of Algeria (Haas 1943). With the exception of darkening the room during the performance of ʿAïsha Qandisha's riḥ, visual stimuli are not manipulated by the Ḥamadsha. Jallaba hoods and hair falling over the eyes, as well as the effects of rapid dancing, may, however, serve to reduce or alter the inflow of visual stimuli. The inhalation of incense can be considered as a means of producing olfactory over-stimulation. Alterations in gustatory and tactile stimuli—with the exception of the dancing itself—are not of central importance in the Ḥamadsha ceremonies. Sensory deprivation—quiet and darkness—may play a role in the induction of trances in the saints' tombs during a pilgrimage.

Changes in Motor Activity

Strict limitations of motor activity facilitate hypnotic trance[1] (Gill and Brenman 1966:6; 126–129), and may be of some significance in trances in the saints' tombs. The Ḥamadsha encourage heightened motor activity in their dancing; the monotonous and stereotyped character of these dances should not, however, be ignored.

Ideational Deprivation and Thought Confusion

Limitation in the range and variety of thought (Gill and Brenman 1966:6), as well as techniques productive of thought confusion (Erikson 1964), play an important role in hypnosis. Chanting, dancing, and music may also reduce "ideational stimuli." Dance leaders, like the muqaddim who tried to exorcise the jinn in the 7-year-old girl, often attempt to confuse the patient. In hypnosis, ideational deprivation is associated with an attempt to alter bodily awareness. The Ḥamadsha do not make any active suggestions with regard to bodily awareness, but the phenomenology of the ḥal and jidba is well-articulated; it is well-known to all dancers and devotees. The expectations of the Ḥamadsha may serve a function similar to that of the active suggestions of the hypnotist.

Rhythmic Stimulation

Attention has been called to the effect of drumming on ceremonial trance induction (Sargant 1964:92). Andrew Neher (1962:151–160) has noted the similarity between the effects of rhythmic flashing of light—photic drive—on laboratory subjects and the symptomatology of

[1] Although many authorities have attempted to equate hypnotic trance with ceremonial trance, I find this approach inadequate. It tends to lay emphasis on similarities and to blur what may be essential differences. This is not to say that induction techniques for both states may not be similar.

trancers. They include alterations in perception, especially visual, that are not present in the stimulus, kinaesthetic changes such as swaying, spinning, and vertigo, tingling and pricking sensations, fatigue, confusion, fear, disgust, anger, disturbances in time sense, hallucinations, "clinical psychopathic states," and epileptoid seizures. A number of "precipitators" are known to aid simply rhythmic stimulation in producing these effects: rhythms that accompany the main rhythm, rhythmic stimulation of more than one sensory mode, stress, hyperventilation, low blood glucose and adrenalin production resulting from fatigue and over-exertion. Neher suggests that drumming has an effect on the individual which is similar to that of photic driving.

Not only are the symptoms of photic driving similar to those reported by the Ḥamadsha, but many of the same "precipitators" are present. Several different drum rhythms are played at once; drumming is accompanied by dancing (kinaesthetic stimulation); many of the Ḥamadsha, especially the patients, are in stress; hypo- and hyperventilatory techniques are employed; prolonged dancing produces fatigue and in all probability a reduction in blood sugar and an increase in adrenalin production. The extent to which the riḥs of the Ḥamadsha correspond to different brain rhythms and induce trance in those dancers whose brain rhythm "corresponds" to the rhythm of the particular riḥ being played has yet to be explored.

Special Breathing Techniques

Breathing techniques which either over-oxygenate or under-oxygenate the blood are known to aid in the induction of trance (Haas 1943). Often they produce paresthetic sensations and visual changes that may be the result of an increase in carbon dioxide in the lungs and bloodstream (Alland 1961). Cerebral anoxia is a prominent and constant factor in precipitating convulsive seizures (Harrison et al. 1950:97). Although the Ḥamadsha have not developed their breathing techniques to the same extent as orders such as the Raḥmaniyya have, the dancers in line do hyperventilate. It is possible that members of the audience who do not join the line also hypo- and hyperventilate in time to the music or to the breathing of the dancers. The fact that one of the prodromal symptoms of trance is paresthesia would seem to suggest this.

Drugs

Critics of the Ḥamadsha and adepts of other brotherhoods sometimes claim that the Ḥamadsha's trances are produced by kif (marihuana) and hashish, but I found no evidence for this whatsoever. In fact, few of the Ḥamadsha smoked kif at all, and even fewer smoked hashish. Although one or two other hallucinogenic drugs are employed in Morocco—these include nutmeg—only two of my informants had taken them, and only on one or two occasions.

Dancing

Dancing can result in a state of fatigue and overexertion and a consequent reduction of blood sugar and increase in adrenalin. Hypoglycemia is known to produce convulsions, and a certain deteriorated form of adrenalin—androchrone—is thought to be hallucinogenic (Hoffer et al. 1954; Wallace 1956).

Dietary Conditions

The Ḥamadsha do not follow any dietary restrictions, such as preceremonial fasting, which might aid in trance induction. In fact, before beginning to dance they often drink large quantities of highly sweetened tea. This would tend to raise the level of blood sugar and prevent, or at least postpone, a hypoglycemic seizure. Nevertheless, some of the seizures resemble those of insulin shock. This is true also of Balinese trance seizures (Mead, Margaret, personal communication). It is possible that some of the patients suffer a loss of appetite, but this is not a typical symptom of the Ḥamadsha patients. Certainly, their diets merit a detailed examination. Consideration should be given to the relationship between a low protein diet and calcium metabolism, since hypocalcemia is known to produce convulsions (Wallace 1961).

Heat and Stuffiness

Although heat and stuffiness with a consequent increase in atmospheric carbon dioxide have been considered factors in the induction of trance (Alland 1961), neither factor appears to be of great significance in the case of the Ḥamadsha. Ceremonies are often held out of doors, and even those which take place inside are well ventilated.[2]

Ambiance

The ambiance of the ceremonies plays an important part in trance induction. The following factors appear to be significant: (1) Group excitement and overcrowding. (It should be noted that Ḥamadsha ceremonies are among the few occasions in which men and women are not strictly segregated.) (2) Heightened expectation. (3) Theatricality

[2] Women's quarters do tend to be stuffy, however.

and violence. (4) A permissive atmosphere. (5) Presence of strong models for trance and mutilation.

Leadership

One of the most significant factors in the induction of hypnotic trance is strong, authoritative leadership. Gill and Brenman (1966:xix–xx) have defined hypnosis as "a particular kind of regressive process which may be initiated by sensorimotor–ideational deprivation or by the stimulation of an archaic relationship to the hypnotist." They found that when one of these techniques was used, phenomena characteristic of the other began to appear. Investigators who have been anxious to equate the ecstatic experiences of the Sufi mystic with hypnotic trance have emphasized the role of the Sufi master and have considered his relationship to the adepts as analogous to the transference relationship between patient and psychotherapist (Shafii 1968). Although the role of the master is of paramount importance in many Islamic brotherhoods, the muqaddim of a Ḥamadsha team plays an unimportant role in the lives of the adepts and devotees during the ceremonies.

Individual Factors

There are probably a number of individual factors which also help to induce trance. These would include physiological ones such as sugar metabolism and psychological ones such as stress, anxiety, and emotional deprivation.

Glossary

ʿafarit: especially powerful and terrifying *jnun* (spirits).
aḥwal: see *ḥal.*
ʿar: lit., shame; a vow or promise.
aryaḥ: see *riḥ*.

baraka: holiness, blessing, good fortune; a spiritual or miraculous force that emanates from holy men and places. Bread is a recurrent symbol for baraka. Baraka can be either inherited or achieved.
bidonville: a shantytown. Such shantytowns have grown up around Meknes and other Moroccan cities since the arrival of the French.
burḥan: manifest evidence, proof; often used as a synonym for "miracle" (*karama*).

debiha: an animal sacrifice.
dirham: Moroccan money, worth about 20 cents in American money at the time of this study. There are 100 Moroccan francs to a dirham
dikr: a short, rapid invocation.

fatḥa: a short prayer
foqra (sing., *fqir*): members of a *zawiya;* adepts.
fqiḥ: a Koranic teacher.

ganbri: a three-stringed guitar, often made from a turtleshell.
ghita: an oboe, played by *ghiyyata* (sing., *ghiyyat*). Smaller ones are used in marriage and circumcision ceremonies; larger ones—*ghita gharbawiyya*—are used in the Ḥamadsha ḥadra.
ghwal (m. sing., *ghul;* f. sing., *ghula*): ogres, ghouls.
gwal: an hourglass-shaped pottery drum, played by *guwwala* (sing., *guwwal*).

hadiyya: gift.
ḥadra: the ecstatic dance of the Ḥamadsha and other religious brotherhoods.
ḥadra gnawiyya: the last part of the ḥadra, in which musical phrases allegedly from the Gnawa are played.
ḥal (pl., *aḥwal*): state, circumstance, time; an ecstatic trance.
Ḥamadsha (m. sing., *Ḥamdushi*; f. sing. *Ḥamdushiyya*): Members of the loosely and diversely organized religious brotherhood known as *at-tariqa al-ḥamdushiyya*. Followers of Sidi ʿAli ben Ḥamdush (*ʿAllaliyyin*) and Sidi Ahmed Dghughi (*Dghughiyyin*) are collectively referred to as Ḥamadsha.
ḥizb: a chant or litany, usually containing verses of the Koran.
ḥufra: grotto, cave, pit.
ḥorm: a sacred place.

jawi: incense; benzoin.
jidba: ecstasy; a frenetic trance state.
jnun (m. sing., *jinn*; f. sing., *jinniyya*): devils, imps; spirits; sprites.

khalifa: assistant; assistant to the leader (*muqaddim*) of a *zawiya*.

lila: lit., night; used to refer to a Ḥamadsha ceremony (*sadaqa*) which takes place in the evening and in which the ḥadra is performed.

madina: town, city; specifically, in the text, the old quarter of Meknes.
marabout: see *murabit*.
mizwar: the leader of a lineage group descended from a saint.
msannad: supported, sustained by; used in the Ḥamadsha context with reference to a special relationship one has with a saint.
muḥibbin (m. sing, *muḥibb*): devotees.
muqaddim: the caretaker of a saint's tomb (*qubba*); the leader of a Ḥamadsha lodge or team.
murabit: a man attached to God. The French word *maraboutisme*, a catchall word for activities associated with the worship of Muslim saints, is derived from it.
musem: an annual pilgrimage to a saint's tomb.
muttakil and *muwali*: both words mean leaning on, or near; used in the Ḥamadsha context with reference to a special relationship one has with ʿAïsha Qandisha and other jnun.

nira: a recorder, made from a reed.

qubba: a saint's tomb, usually a squat, white, cubical building with a domed roof.

riḥ (pl., *aryaḥ*): lit., air, wind; a musical phrase, played during a ḥadra, which is said to be the favorite of a particular jinn and sends a follower into trance.

sadaqa: charity, alms; also a Ḥamadsha ceremony in which the ḥadra is danced and a communal meal is served.

sharif (pl., *shurfa*): a descendant of the Prophet Muhammad.

shayatin: evil spirits, children of the devil (*Shitan*).

siyyid: a saint; the tomb of a saint.

tabbal: one who plays the snare drum (*tabil*).

tabiᶜ: the follower of a saint or jinn.

taïfa: a team; used specifically in the text to refer to a team of bidonville Ḥamadsha, although it may in fact also be used to refer to the members of a *zawiya.*

tallaᶜ: an exorcist-seer who identifies attacking jnun.

tariqa: lit., the way, path; a spiritual path, the teachings of a particular saint. Also used to refer to the religious brotherhoods.

wali: a saint.

wulad siyyid: lit., "the children of the saint"; the agnatic descendants of a saint.

zawiya: lit., a corner; the lodge or meeting place of a religious brotherhood. Used in the text to refer to both the meeting place and the members of an urban Ḥamadsha team.

ziyara: visit; pilgrimage to a saint's tomb. Also used to refer to offerings left by a pilgrim at a saint's tomb.

Bibliography

Abun-Nasr, Jamil M.
1965 The Tijaniyya: a sufi order in the modern world. London: Oxford University Press.

Alland, Alexander
1961 "Possession" in a revivalistic Negro church. Journal for the Scientific Study of Religion 1:204–213.

Andrews, J.B.
1903 Le culte des fontaines de Sebba Aioun à Alger. Alger: Jourdan.

Anonymous
1927? Les zaouias marocaines et le mekhzen (Manuscript 31 H 1). Aix-en-Provence: Dépot des Archives d'Outre-Mer.

Aubin, Eugene
1904 Le Maroc d'aujourd'hui. Paris: Armand Colin.

Barnes, J. A.
1968 Networks and political process. *In* Local-level politics: social and cultural perspectives, M. M. Swartz, ed., Chicago: Aldine Publishing Company, pp. 107–130.

Basset, Henri
1920 Le culte des grottes au Maroc. Alger: Ancienne Maison Bastide-Jourdan, Jules Carbonel.

Bastide, Roger
1958 Le condomblé de Bahia. Paris and The Hague: Mouton.

Belo, Jane
1960 Trance in Bali. New York: Columbia University Press.

Berger, Peter L., and Thomas Luckmann
1967 The social construction of reality: a treatise in the sociology of knowledge. Garden City, New York: Anchor Books.

Berque, Jacques
1958 Medinas, villeneuves, et bidonvilles. Les Cahiers de Tunisie 6:5–42.

Bettelheim, Bruno
1955 Symbolic wounds: puberty rites and the envious male. London: Thames and Hudson.

Boulanger, Robert
1966 Morocco. Paris: Hachette.
Bourgignon, Erika
1968 Divination, transe et possession en Afrique transsaharienne. *In* La divination, Vol. 2, Andre Caquot and Marcel Leibovici, eds., Paris: Presses Universitaires de France, pp. 331–358.
Brignon, Jean, A. Amine, B. Boutaleb, G. Martinet, and B. Rosenberger
1967 Histoire du Maroc. Paris: Hatier.
Brunel, René
1926 Essai sur la confrérie religieuse des ʿAissaoua au Maroc. Paris: Paul Geuthner.
1955 Le monarchisme errant dans l'Islam: Sidi Heddi et les Heddawa. Paris: Larose.

Canal, Joseph
1902 Géographie générale du Maroc. Paris: Augustin Challamel.
Cansever, Gocke
1965 Psychological effects of circumcision. British Journal of Medical Psychology 38:321–331.
Casablanca et les Chaouia
1915 *In* Villes et tribus du Maroc, Vol. 1, Paris: Leroux.
Cat, Edouard
1898 L'Islamisme et les confréries religieuses au Maroc. Revue des Deux Mondes 68:375–404.
Chelhod, Joseph
1964 Les structures du sacré chez les Arabes. Paris: Maisonneuve et Larose.
Chottin, Alexis
1938 Tableau de la musique marocaine. Paris: Geuthner.
Coon, Carleton S.
1964 Caravan: the story of the Middle East, rev. ed. New York: Holt, Rinehart, and Winston.
Crapanzano, Vincent
1971 The transformation of the Eumenides: a Maroccan example. Paper read at the annual meeting of the American Anthropological Association.
1972 The Hamadsha. *In* Saints, scholars and sufis, Nikki Keddie, ed., Berkeley: University of California Press.
Crapanzano, Vincent, and J. Kramer
1969 A world of saints and she-demons. The New York Times Magazine (June 22):14–38.

Delehaye, Hippolyte
1955 Les légendes hagiographiques. Bruxelles: Société des Bollandistes.
Depont, O., and J. Coppolani
1897 Les confréries religieuses musulmanes. Alger: Adolphe Jourdan.

Dermenghem, Emile
1954 Le culte des saints dans l'Islam maghrébin. Paris: Gallimard.
Dodds, E. R.
1966 The Greeks and the irrational. Berkeley: University of California Press.
Dundes, Alan, Jerry W. Leach, and Bora Özkök
1970 The strategy of Turkish boys' verbal dueling rhymes. Journal of American Folklore 83:325–349.
Draques, Georges
n.d. Esquisse d'histoire religieuse du Maroc: confréries et zaouias. Paris: Peyronnet.
Eliade, Mircea
1965 Le sacré et le profane. Paris: Gallimard.
Erikson, Milton
1964 The confusion technique in hypnosis. American Journal of Clinical Hypnosis 6:183–207.
Evans-Pritchard, E. E.
1949 The Senusi of Cyrenaica. Oxford: Clarendon Press.
Fenichel, Otto
1966 The psychoanalytic theory of neurosis. London: Routledge and Kegan Paul.
Festinger, L., H. W. Riecken, and S. Schachter
1956 When prophecy fails. New York: Harper and Row.
Figueras, Tomas Garcia
n.d. Hamadcha y Aisaua (manuscript). Madrid: Biblioteca nacional.
Fortes, Meyer
1953 The structure of unilineal descent groups. American Anthropologist 55:17–41.
Franchi, Jean
1959 Urbanisation d'un bidonville: Bordj Moulay Omar (Meknes). Bulletin Economique et Social du Maroc 23:255–291.
Frazer, James George
1961 Adonis, Attis, Osiris: studies in the history of Oriental religion. New Hyde Park, New York: University Books.
Freud, Sigmund
1941 Medusa's head. International Journal of Psychoanalysis 22:69.
1963 A neurosis of demonical possession. *In* Freud: studies in parapsychology, P. Rieff, ed., New York: Collier Books, pp. 91–123.
Garcia-Barriuso, P. P.
1941 La música hispano-musulmana en Marruecos. Larache: Artes-Graficas Bosca.
Gardet, L.
1960 Al-burhan. *In* Encyclopaedia of Islam, New Edition, Vol. 1, pp. 1326–1327.

Geertz, Clifford
1968 Islam observed: religious development in Morocco and Indonesia. New Haven: Yale University Press.
Gellner, Ernest
1963 Saints of the Atlas. *In* Mediterranean countrymen, J. Pitt-Rivers, ed., Paris: Mouton, pp. 145–157.
1969 Saints of the Atlas. London: Weidenfeld and Nicolson.
Gerth, H. H., and C. W. Mills
1958 From Max Weber: essays in sociology. New York: Oxford University Press.
Gibb, H. A. R.
1961 Mohammedanism: an historical survey, 2nd ed. London: Oxford University Press.
Gibb, H. A. R., and H. Bowen
1957 Islamic society and the west: a study of the impact of western civilization on Moslem culture in the Near East, Vol. 1, part 2. London: Oxford University Press.
Gill, M. M., and M. Brenman
1966 Hypnosis and related states: psychoanalytic studies in regression. New York: Science Editions.
Goldziher, Ignace
1880 Le culte des saints chez les Musulmans. Revue de l'Histoire des Religions 2:257–351.
Greenberg, Joseph
1946 The influence of Islam on a Sudanese religion. Monographs of the American Ethnological Society 10:vii–73.

Haas, William S.
1943 The zikr of the Raḥmaniya order: a psychophysiological analysis. The Moslem World 33:16–28.
Haimer, Mehdi
1968 Aicha Kandicha. Lamalif 28:52.
Harrison, R. R., H. H. Merritt, and D. Sciarra
1950 Coma, convulsions, and paralysis. *In* Principles of internal medicine, T. R. Harrison, ed., Philadelphia: Blackiston, pp. 91–109.
Herber, J.
1923 Les Hamadcha et les Dghoughiyyin. Hespéris 3:217–235.
Hoffer, A., H. Osmond, and J. Smythies
1954 Schizophrenia: a new approach, Part II: result of a year's research. Journal of Mental Science 100:29–45.
Howell, David
1970 Health rituals at a Lebanese shrine. Middle East Studies 6:179–188.

Jeanmaire, H.
1949 Le traitement et la mania dans les "mystères" de Dionysos et des Corybantes. Journal de Psychologie 42:64–82.
1951 Dionysos: histoire du culte de Bacchus. Paris: Payot.

Jones, E.
1951 The madonna's conception through the ear: a contribution to the relation between aesthetics and religion. *In* Essays in applied psychoanalysis, Vol. 2, London: Hogarth Press, pp. 266–357.

Julien, C. A.
1966 Histoire de l'Afrique du Nord, Vol. 2. Paris: Payot.

Lane, Edward
1963 The manners and customs of the modern Egyptians. London: Everyman's Library.

Lecoeur, C.
1969 Le rite et l'outil: essai sur le rationalisme social et la pluralité des civilisations, 2e ed. Paris: Presses Universitaires de France.

Lee, Richard
1968 The sociology of the !Kung Bushman trance performance. *In* Trance and possession states, R. Prince, ed., Montreal: R. M. Bucke Memorial Society, pp. 35–54.

Leiris, Michel
1958 La possession et ses aspects théatraux chez les Ethiopiens de Gondar. L'Homme 1.

LeTourneau, Roger
1949 Fez avant le protectorat: étude économique et sociale d'une ville de l'occident musulman. Casablanca: Publications de l'Institut des Hautes Etudes Marocaines 45: 1–668.
1958 La decadence Sa'adienne et l'anarchie marocaine au XVIIe siécle. Annales de la Faculté des Lettres d'Aix 33: 187–225.

Lévi-Strauss, Claude
1963a. The effectiveness of symbols. *In* Structural anthropology, New York: Basic Books, pp. 186–205.
1963b The structural study of myth. *In* Structural anthropology, New York: Basic Books, pp. 206–231.

Lewis, I. M.
1969 Spirit possession in northern Somaliland. *In* Spirit mediumship and society in Africa, John Beattie and John Middleton, eds., London: Routledge and Kegan Paul, pp. 188–219.

Lienhardt, Godfrey
1967 Divinity and experience: the religion of the Dinka. Oxford: Clarendon Press.

Ludwig, Arnold M.
1968 Altered states of consciousness. *In* Trance and possession states, R. Prince, ed., Montreal: R. M. Bucke Memorial Society, pp. 69–95.

Margoliouth, D. S.
1934 Shadhiliya. *In* Encyclopaedia of Islam, Vol. 4, pp. 247–249.

Massignon, Louis
1934 Tasawwuf. *In* Encyclopaedia of Islam, Vol. 4, pp. 681–685.

Mercier, Henry
1951 Dictionnaire Arabe-Français. Rabat: Editions La Porte.
Mercier, L.
1906 Les mosquées et la vie religieuse à Rabat. Archives marocaines 8:99–195.
Métraux, Alfred
1959 Voodoo in Haiti. New York: Oxford University Press.
Michaux-Bellaires, E.
1913 Le Gharb. Archives marocaines 20:1–477.
1921 Essai sur l'histoire des conféries marocaines. Hespéris 1:141–159.
1927 Conferences. Archives marocaines 27:1–334.
Michaux-Bellaires, E., and George Salmon
1906 Let tribus arabes de la vallée du Le Khous, 3ième partie. Archives marocaines 6:219–397.
Miner, Horace, and George DeVos
1960 Oasis and casbah: Algerian culture and personality in change. Ann Arbor: Anthropological Papers, Museum of Anthropology, University of Michigan, XV.
Mischel, Walter and Frances
1958 Psychological aspects of spirit possession. American Anthropologist 60:248–260.
Molé, Marijan
1963 La danse extatique en Islam. *In* Les danses sacrées, Paris: Editions du Seuil.
Montet, Edouard
1902 Les confréries religieuses de l'Islam marocain: leur role religieux, politique et social. Revue de l'Histoire des Religions 45:1–35.
Neher, Andrew
1962 A physiological explanation of unusual behavior in ceremonies involving drums. Human Biology 34:151–160.
Nicholson, Reynold A.
1963 The mystics of Islam. London: Routledge and Kegan Paul.
Ortigues, Marie-Cécile and Edmond
1966 Oedipe africain. Paris: Libraire Plon.
Pâques, Viviana
1964 L'arbre cosmique dans la pensée populaire et dans la vie quotidienne du nord-ouest africain. Paris: Travaux et memoires, Institut d'Ethnologie 70:i–702.
Paquignon, Paul
1911 Notes et documents. Revue du Monde Musulman 14:525–536.
Parsons, Talcott
1964 Social structure and personality. New York: The Free Press.
1966 Societies: evolutionary and comparative perspectives. Englewood Cliffs, N.J.: Prentice-Hall.

Peters, Emrys
1960 The proliferation of segments in the lineage of the Bedouin of Cyrenaica. Journal of the Royal Anthropological Institute 90:29–53.
Planhol, Xavier de
1959 The world of Islam. Ithaca, New York: Cornell University Press.
Prince, Raymond
1968 Can the EEG be used in the study of possession states? *In* Trance and possession states, R. Prince, ed., Montreal: J. M. Bucke Memorial Society, pp. 121–137.

Quedenfeldt, M.
1886 Aberglaube und halbreligiöse bruderschaften bei den Morokkanern. Zeitschrift für Ethnologie 28:671–692.

Radcliffe-Brown, A. R.
1962 Introduction. *In* African systems of kinship and marriage, A. R. Radcliffe-Brown and D. Forde, eds., London: Oxford University Press, pp. 1–85.
Rahman, Fazlur
1968 Islam. Garden City, New York: Anchor Books.
Rinn, Louis
1884 Marabouts et khouan: étude sur l'Islam en Algerie. Alger: Adolphe Jourdan.
Ritter, Helmut
1955 Das meer der seele: mensch, welt, und gott in den geschichten des Fariduddin ʿAttor. Leiden: Brill.

Salmon, G.
1904 Confréries et zaouyas de Tanger. Archives marocaines 2:100–114.
Sargant, William
1964 Battle for the mind. London: Pan Books.
Schoen, Captain
1937 Les confréries musulmans dans le sud marocain. Report 89 of the Centre des Hautes Etudes d'Administration Musulmane, Paris (unpublished).
Service d'Urbanisme
n.d. Meknes. Rabat: Ministère des trauvaux publics.
Shafii, Mohammed
1968 The pir (Sufi guide) and the western psychotherapist. Newsletter-Review of the R. M. Bucke Memorial Society 3:9–19.
Spiro, Melford
1967 Burmese supernaturalism: a study in the explanation and reduction of suffering. Englewood Cliffs, New Jersey: Prentice-Hall.

Talha, Abdelouahed ben
1965 Moulay Idriss du Zerhoun: quelques aspects de la vie sociale et familiale. Rabat: Editions Techniques Nord-Africaines.

Terasse, Henri
1930 Histoire du Maroc des origines a l'établissement du Protectorat français, 2 vols. Casablanca: Editions Atlantides.

Tremearne, Arthur J. N.
1914 The ban of the bori: demons and demon-dancing in West and North Africa. London: Health, Cranton and Ouseley.

Turner, Victor W.
1967 The forest of symbols: aspects of Ndembu ritual. Ithaca, New York: Cornell University Press.
1969 The ritual process: structure and anti-structure. Chicago: Aldine Publishing Company.

Van Grunebaum, G. E.
1954 Islamic studies and cultural research. *In* Studies in Islamic cultural history, G. E. Van Grunebaum, ed., Memoir of the American Anthropological Association 76:1–22.
1955 The structure of the Muslim town. *In* Islam: essays in the nature and growth of a cultural tradition, Memoir of the American Anthropological Association 81:141–158.

Voinot, L.
1948 Pèlerinages judéo-musulmans du Maroc. Paris: Larose.

Wallace, Anthony, F. C
1956 Mazeway resynthesis: a bio-cultural theory of religious inspiration. Transactions of the New York Academy of Sciences 18:626–638.
1959 Cultural determinants of response to hallucinatory experience. A.M.A. Archives of General Medicine 1:74–85.
1961 Mental illness, biology, and culture. *In* Psychological anthropology: approaches to culture and personality, Francis L. K. Hsu, ed., Homewood, Illinois: Dorsey Press, pp. 255–295.

Weigert-Vowinkel, Edith
1938 The cult and mythology of the Magna Mater from the standpoint of psychoanalysis. Psychiatry 1:347–378.

Westermarck, Edward
1926 Ritual and belief in Morocco, Vols. 1 and 2. London: Macmillan.

Windus, John
1725 A journey to Mequinez. London: Jacob Jonson.

Wittkower, E. D.
1971 Transcultural psychiatry. *In* Modern perspectives in world psychiatry, J. G. Howells, ed., New York: Brunner-Mazel, pp. 697–712.

Yalman, Nur
1964 The structure of Sinhalese healing rituals. *In* Religion in South Asia, Edward B. Harper, ed., Seattle: University of Washington Press, pp. 115–150.

Index

Morality, and commands of jinniyya, 227
Mosques, in madinas, 106
Moulay Brahim: pilgrimage to, 171
Moulay Idriss (saint): 37; in legend, 37, 43; location of tomb, 62, 177; in dreams, 84
Moulay Idriss (town), administration of, 63
Moulay Ismaïl, 18, 76, 32, 33, 34, 35, 36; conflict with Sidi ʿAli, 40; at tomb of Sidi ʿAli, 40; influence on Meknes, 78
Moulay Rachid, 35
Msannad, 83, 84–85, 173, 178
Muḥibbin: definition of, 89; and zawiyas, 89–91; characteristics of, 96–97; in shantytown teams, 124–125, 127; and ʿAïsha Qandisha, 125
Mulud, 115
Muqaddim (Ḥamadsha): definition of, xii; role in ceremonies, xii, 161–162, 187, 188, 190, 207, 235; qualifications for, 80; election of, 80–82; duties of, 82–83, 108; in taïfa, 108–109; and devotees, 111–125; at saintly villages, 173, 174
Muqaddim (municipal), 104
Musem, 45; in Zerhoun, 63, 115; property distribution at, 70; description of, 115–118; sacrifices at, 116; function of, 117–118; baraka at, 11; as faith renewal, 219
Mushar, 154
Mutism, 4
Muttakil, 157
Muwali, 157

Nadir, 68
Nafaʿ, 117
Name-day celebrations, 74, 98–99
Named-jnun: description of, 140, 141–149; origin of belief in, 141; relationship to human beings, 142; in cures, 156–157, 167. *See also* Jnun; Symbiotic cures
Naturalistic explanations, of illness, 134
Nira, 89

Oboe. *See* Ghita
Oboe players. *See* Ghiyyata
Oil, in legends, 40–41
Olive trees, 61, 62
Ortigues, Marie-Cécile and Edmond, 227

Pâques, Viviana, 141n
Paraesthesia, 5, 97, 199–200
Paralysis: cured by Ḥamadsha, 4; resulting from attack by jnun, 113; classification of, 152–157
Participational Mode of Responsibility: defined, 151; role of jnun in, 151–152; in explanation of therapy, 213
Patient: symptoms of, 4–5; participation in Ḥamadsha therapy, 216–217; passivity of, 217; relationship with curer, 217–218
Pathology: Ḥamadsha theory of, 134, 135–149. *See also* Jnun
Patrilineality, 7; and passage of baraka, 48, 52, 55, 56; and institutional baraka, 120–121; and wulad siyyid, 67–71; importance in Moroccan social organization, 224
Patripotestality, 224
Phylacteries, 140. *See also* Amulets
Pigs, imitation in trance, 198, 201
Pilgrimage (*ziyara*): activities during, 2, 171–173, 176–178; made by devotees, 96; and musem, 115–118; and cures, 134n, 159, 169; cost of, 159, 169; comparison with ḥajj, 169; sequence of, 173–176; Fatima's, 178–183. *See also* Hajj; Musem
Poisoning: in legends, 39; in therapeutic theory, 149–150
Pomegranate, 38
Possession: Ḥamadsha cures of, 4, 166, 231; classification of states of, 151–157; and trance, 152–153n, 220; and exorcism, 157–159; in ancient world, 158; and symbiotic cures, 159–166
Prickly pears, in legends, 39
Prostitutes, 62, 171